THE COMPLETE BOOK OF
CAKE DECORATING

THE COMPLETE BOOK OF
CAKE DECORATING

NEW
BURLINGTON
BOOKS

A QUINTET BOOK

Published by New Burlington Books
6 Blundell Street
London N7 9BH

ISBN 1-85348-158-0

Reprinted 1990, 1991

This book was designed and produced by
Quintet Publishing Limited
6 Blundell Street
London N7 9BH

Creative Director: Peter Bridgewater
Art Director: Ian Hunt
Designer: Nicki Simmonds
Project Editor: Bridget Jones
Editor: Belinda Giles

Typeset in Great Britain by
Central Southern Typesetters, Eastbourne
Manufactured in Hong Kong by
Regent Publishing Services Limited
Printed in Hong Kong by Leefung-Asco Printers Limited

The material in this publication previously
appeared in Creative Cake Decorating, Step-by-Step
Cake Decorating and The All-Colour Cake
Decorating Course.

CONTENTS

INTRODUCTION

The art of cake-making and cake-decoration is usually appreciated by everyone, whether they hold a particular interest in food and culinary skills or not. Even those who tend not to indulge in sweet specialities, always admire a beautiful cake, lovingly prepared.

Cake-decorating draws upon varying degrees of imagination and perfection, and covers a broad range of skills and techniques of differing standards. For example, those skilled in sugarcraft may attempt to create the most spectacular four-tier wedding cake, laden with intricate dressings. While, on a different scale, the enthusiastic, patient cook can create a stunning, irresistible gâteau or a clever novelty cake.

The message is that cake-decorating is for all, and this book shows how with enthusiasm, time and just a few basic skills even the beginner can produce beautiful cakes. Once you have mastered the basics, you may decide to be more adventurous with moulding icing, piped designs or chocolate work. The chapters that follow take you through techniques, step-by-step, encouraging experiment-ation and the use of imagination. The most important key to ensure success is to 'take time' — allow enough time to achieve the standard which you are aiming for. A three-tier wedding cake cannot be dec-orated in a week; a complicated novelty cake takes more than 30 minutes to pro-duce; a luscious gâteau takes longer to prepare than a simple Victoria Sandwich cake. Keep this in mind and you will both enjoy and have success with your creative cake-decorating work.

FOLLOWING THE RECIPES

Before you start to make or decorate any of the cakes, there are a few points to remember. Most of these are points of common-sense but they can so easily be overlooked in haste, often leading to disaster.

READING THROUGH FIRST

Before you rush into the kitchen to make any recipe, start by reading it through. Check that you have all the ingredients in the quantities in which they are needed. Make sure that you have the right utensils, including baking tins, or find suitable substitutes. Take careful note of the timing involved – does the cake need hours of baking? Does the decoration work involve many hours, or days, of drying? Lastly, is there any aspect of the recipe that you may feel too inexperienced to tackle; in which case, should you allow time for a practice run? These may all seem to be rather pedantic points but they are important if you want to ensure success.

WEIGHTS and MEASURES:
All-important Accuracy

Whenever you are weighing or measuring it is vital that you use reliable utensils – kitchen scales should be in good working order. Always use proper, British Standard measuring spoons for preparing the ingredients that are given in spoon measures. Do not use serving spoons and other table cutlery as they yield quite different proportions.

When measuring liquids always use a proper measuring jug and make sure that it is on a level surface. Cake mixtures are, on the whole, fairly delicate and it is important that the proportions given in the recipes are closely followed.

USING THE OVEN

For baking, it is most important that the oven controls are accurate and that the temperature is maintained at a constant level throughout the cooking period. You can buy thermometers that are specially manufactured to check the temperature in the oven with the setting selected. If you do have problems with your oven, then it is a good idea to have it professionally checked if you intend to do a lot of baking.

OVEN TEMPERATURES

110°C	225°F	Gas ¼
120°C	250°F	Gas ½
140°C	275°F	Gas 1
150°C	300°F	Gas 2
170°C	325°F	Gas 3
180°C	350°F	Gas 4
190°C	375°F	Gas 5
200°C	400°F	Gas 6
220°C	425°F	Gas 7
230°C	450°F	Gas 8
240°C	475°F	Gas 9

KITCHEN CLEANLINESS

Although it must be taken for granted that any area that is used for food preparation must be scrupulously clean, when icing cakes it is particularly important to avoid having particles of dust or tiny specks of dirt anywhere near the cake. Cakes that are set aside for icing to dry should be placed in a cool, dry place and as soon as the icing is set fairly firmly, a piece of greaseproof paper should be draped loosely over the cake to keep it clean.

CAKE-MAKING EQUIPMENT

A few basic rules apply to baking, which when observed remove many of the uncertainties and help avoid possible mistakes.

Clean and dry all the equipment required. Grease and line the baking tins. Use the right utensils for weighing, testing, sifting, grinding, grating and chopping.

Before baking, switch on the oven to pre-heat it to the correct temperature. The oven should be well insulated and draught-proof, as a discrepancy of a few degrees in the temperature can have a disastrous effect.

1 Copper egg white bowl
2 Gupelhupf mould
3 American measuring spoon
4 Plastic spatula or scaper
5 Nylon mesh sieve
6 Metal spatula
7 Large metal spoon for folding in
8 Large cake slice or spatula
9 Balloon whisk
10 Sugar thermometer
11 Guttered mould or Rehrücken tin
12 Wire cooling racks
13 Deep tartlet tins or bun tins
14 Swiss roll tin
15 Angel cake tin
16 Madeleine tins
17 Deep, loose-bottomed cake tin
18 Fluted flat tins with loose bases
19 Loaf tins
20 Spring-form tins
21 American measuring cups
22 Patterned ring or savarin mould
23 Unlined copper sugar boiler
24 Biscuit cutters
25 Plain rolling pin
26 Pastry brush

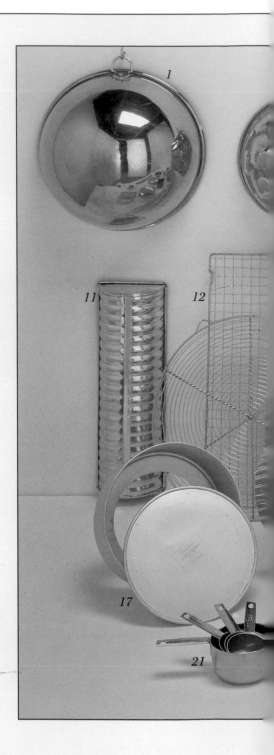

A comprehensive selection of baking equipment is illustrated here.

PREPARING CAKE TINS

To get the best results from decorating a fruit cake, whether you are planning to cover it with royal icing, fondant icing or glacé icing, it is essential to work on a cake with a good smooth finish. This is why correctly lining the cake tin, to give the cake a firm even shape, is of such vital importance.

LINING PAPER

You can use either greaseproof or brown paper to line the tin when cooking rich fruit cakes. If you use greaseproof paper, you need to pack the cake well in order to get a good finish. If possible use good quality brown paper. It is stiffer and will peel away from the cake more easily after cooking. It does not have to be greased – the fat from the cake will be enough to stop the cake and the paper sticking together.

Greaseproof paper should be used for light fruit cakes and sponge cakes; it should be evenly greased before the mixture is put in the tin.

Whatever shape cake tin you use, be it round, oval, heart-shaped, square, hexagonal or octagonal, you will need only two simple techniques for shaping the paper to line curves or angles.

CAKE HATS

In the days of cooking with solid fuel, when oven temperatures fluctuated according to the heat of the fire, extra precautions had to be taken to ensure that cakes would get the long slow cooking they needed and would not burn as more coal or wood was shovelled into the stove. A thick insulating layer of paper was wrapped around the tin and then tied up with string. Sometimes the cake tin was put in a baking tray on a layer of rock salt or in a wooden frame.

With modern ovens where temperatures can be regulated, there is no need to protect the cake in this way. But it is often a good idea to cut a 'hat' for the cake to prevent it drying on top. This is a double thickness of paper approximately 5 cm/ 2 in bigger than the cake tin. It should rest, not on the cake mix, but on the 2.5 cm/1 in of paper that rises above the sides of the tin. Put it on as soon as the cake goes in the oven. This is a pointless exercise if your oven is a fan or convection model, because it will be blown off.

LINING A ROUND TIN

1 To line a round tin with greaseproof paper, place the tin base down on the greaseproof and draw a circle around it. Cut the circle out about 5 mm/¼ in inside the line to allow for the thickness of the tin. Cut two pieces of paper for the base because you will need a double thickness for better insulation.

2 To line the sides of the tin, put the tin on its side on the paper. Make a pencil mark where the tin touches the paper, roll the tin along until you reach the same point and make another mark. Use the join in the tin as a starting point. Add on 5 cm/2 in for overlap. Cut a strip that is 5 cm/2 in wider than the depth of the tin, so that you have 2.5 cm/1 in to turn in at the base and the same amount overlapping the top of the tin. If you are using thin paper, such as greaseproof, you need a double thickness, so cut two linings for the sides.

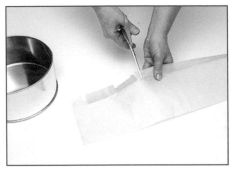

3 To make the side lining fit the base of the tin, fold it to a depth of 2.5 cm/1 in along its length. With any curved tin, snip the paper along its length, at intervals of 5 mm/¼ in, to the depth of the fold.

4 Now slip the lining into the tin. The nicks will overlap and the paper will fit the curve of the tin snugly. When you have lined the sides of the tin with two layers of greaseproof paper, drop in the two base liners. You should have a perfect fit. When you are using greaseproof paper brush it with oil or melted lard, clarified butter, vegetable shortening or margarine to coat it evenly.

LINING A SQUARE TIN OR CAKE FRAME

1 To line a square tin or cake frame with greaseproof or brown paper, first place the tin on the paper and mark out the base. With a cake frame, draw inside the base. With a tin, draw round and cut just inside the line.

2 Cut out the square, remembering to make it 5 mm/¼ in smaller than your outline if you have drawn around the outside of a cake tin, to allow for the thickness of the tin. Cut another square the same size. You will need a double thickness for the base.

3 To line the sides of the tin or frame, put it on its side on the paper. Make a pencil mark where the first corner of the tin touches the paper, 'roll' the tin along until you reach the same point and make another mark. Add on 5 cm/2 in for overlap. Then cut a strip 5 cm/2 in wider than the depth of the tin, so that you have 2.5 cm/1 in to turn in at the base and the same amount overlapping the top. If you are

using brown paper, you only need one thickness for the side lining.

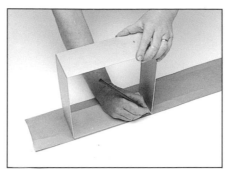

4 To make the side lining fit the base of the tin or frame, fold it to a depth of 2.5 cm/1 in along its length, starting about half way along one side of the tin so that the paper join does not end up in a corner. Use a distinguishing mark on the tin, such as a join, or mark the tin so that you know where you started. Now turn the tin along the paper again, and mark each angle with a pencil, remembering that you are lining the inside of the tin and not the outside and allowing for the width of the tin. It is much safer to mark the paper in this way, rather than dividing your paper into four for a square or eight for an octagon, because very often tins are not exactly true to shape.

5 When you have marked all the angles of the tin, fold the paper along the pencil marks. Make a good firm crease for each angle and check that you are keeping the base parallel, so that the creases run upwards from it an angle of 90°. Now snip along the creases at intervals from the

edge of the paper to the depth of your 2.5 cm/1in fold.

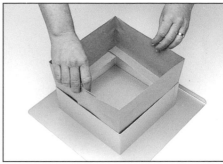

6 Fold out the paper to the shape of the tin, and you will see that you have very neatly mitred corners to fit its shape. With a straight-sided tin, be it square, hexagonal or octagonal, you only have to nick the folded edges at the corners, and not all the way along as with a curved edge, to get a good fit. Slide the side lining into the tin, or into the cake frame on a baking sheet, to fit it snugly. Put in the two layers of base lining. If you are using brown paper, there is no need to grease it.

The cooked cake comes out of the oven with beautifully squared corners.

Draw round the base of your tin and cut out the circle just inside the line, allowing for the thickness of the tin.

LINING A SWISS ROLL TIN

1 To line a Swiss roll tin, place the tin on greaseproof paper and draw around the base. Increase the rectangle by 2.5-5 cm/1-2 in at each side to allow for the depth of the tin plus overlap. Cut out the rectangle and nick each of the corners diagonally down to the size of the original rectangle, subtracting 5 mm/¼ in for the thickness of the tin.

2 Fold the rectangle to fit the base of the tin. As you put the paper into the tin, the nicked edges will overlap to form mitred corners. Secure the corners in position with staples or paperclips.

3 Brush the lining with melted lard or oil, clarified butter, vegetable shortening or margarine, and dust it with flour.

Baking Sponges

*T*here is no need to line the tin if you are baking a light cake, such as a Victoria sandwich or a Genoese or whisked sponge, though some people do like to put a layer of paper in the base of the tin. All you need to do is brush the tin with melted lard or oil, clarified butter, vegetable shortening or margarine, and then dust it with flour and sugar. Always use a brush rather than your fingers to oil the tin to ensure an even coat.

COOLING, STORING AND FREEZING CAKES

COOLING

When you turn your cake out of its tin, do not turn it onto a wire rack. The lattice pattern of the rack will be imprinted on it as the cake settles, especially if it is moist. To get a clean finish you would then have to fill in the imprints before putting on the marzipan.

1 Leave a fruit cake to cool in the tin for at least a couple of hours until it consolidates. You will then find that you can lift it out of the tin quite easily by pulling the brown paper jutting above the sides of the tin.

2 Instead of putting a sponge cake on a wire rack, turn it out onto a sheet of greaseproof paper dusted with caster sugar to stop it sticking. The sugar will give a good finish when you turn the cake over. If you do use a wire rack, stand the cake base down on it so that you do not spoil the flat top of the cake.

3 When you peel the brown paper from the cooled cake it will come away cleanly, leaving the cake with perfectly smooth sides. If you have used grease-proof paper to line the tin and it has stuck to the cake, brush it with cold water and it will peel away more easily.

STORING

Rich fruit cakes were originally made as a means of preserving summer fruit for the winter months and they would be stored for long periods. Today, though the fruits they are made with are available all year round, there is still good reason for keeping a cake for two or three months before you decorate it. The taste of the individual ingredients becomes less distinct as the cake matures and their flavours mingle into richness.

1 To store the cake before you marzipan it, leave it in the paper you baked it in to protect it against getting knocked and having its shape spoiled.

2 You may wish to keep the cake for two or three months before you marzipan it. Do not store it in a tin, or wrap it in clingfilm or aluminium foil. Unless you vacuum pack or hermetically seal a cake inside a tin, you will be sealing stale air in with the cake. If you wrap it in clingfilm, it will sweat. If you wrap it in foil, the natural acids in the fruit will eat through the aluminium, and when you come to decorate the cake you will find the foil full of little holes. The best way of keeping a cake is to wrap it first in one or two layers of greaseproof paper. Then wrap it in a tea towel, or in brown paper, or you can use aluminium foil at this stage.

3 While the cake is maturing, you can 'feed' it with brandy or rum, or any spirit of your choice. Do not attempt to do this before the cake has completely cooled, or the alcohol will merely evaporate. You can make holes in the cake with a skewer, then pour on a tablespoon of alcohol. Alternatively you can buy a syringe from a chemist and inject the cake to avoid it being full of large holes. Feeding a cake definitely improves its flavour. Be careful not to add too much alcohol, however, or it will become wet and difficult to handle.

FREEZING

Sponge cakes and soft-iced cakes freeze well and can be stored over a period of months. Fruit cakes can also be frozen, but rich types are better stored in a cool, dry atmosphere.

SPONGE CAKES

Uncooked cake mix can be stored for up to 6 weeks in an airtight container in the freezer. A cooked sponge cake should be frozen as soon as it has cooled. Wrap it in clingfilm and freeze it for up to 4 months.

FRUIT CAKES

A fruit cake can be frozen in the same way as a sponge cake. It is not necessary to freeze a rich fruit cake, however, and the freezing process actually inhibits the development of the flavour.

SOFT-ICED CAKES

Cakes coated with a soft icing, such as buttercream or whipped cream, are particularly suitable for freezing. They should be opened frozen, un-wrapped until firm to avoid spoiling the icing. When firm they should be wrapped very carefully in several layers of foil or in an airtight, rigid container, as cream-based mixtures tend to absorb flavours from foodstuffs around them if exposed to the air.

HARD-ICED CAKES

These do not freeze well – royal icing, for example, may crack during freezing and become crumbly during defrosting.

DEFROSTING

SOFT-ICED CAKES

The packaging should be removed before defrosting. Allow 6 to 12 hours for the cake to defrost.

BASIC CAKE RECIPES

Successful cake decorating relies on successful cake making. There is no point in spending hours elaborately decorating a cake that has not been well made and properly baked. By following a few simple rules and using a good recipe, you can ensure a good result every time. It is particularly important to know your oven, and make any minor adjustments to baking times and temperatures that are necessary. The recipes given in this section are for traditional sponge and fruit cake mixes, and these are the cakes which are used for the many decoration techniques which follow. You may have your own tried and tested recipes and you can, of course, use these instead. This section also gives advice on how to cut cakes in order to achieve the largest number of portions. Lastly, a brief guide to common faults in cake making is included right at the end of the chapter.

RULES FOR BAKING

A few basic rules apply to baking, which when observed, remove many of the uncertainties and help to avoid possible mistakes.

First, read the recipe through from start to finish. Then, make sure that all the ingredients are available; if you have not got all the ingredients to hand, do not try to substitute any or adjust the quantities, but choose another recipe instead.

Next assemble all the ingredients and if possible leave them in the kitchen for about an hour to reach the same temperature, prepare the utensils; grease and line the baking tins; weigh out all the ingredients accurately, sifting, grinding, grating or chopping as necessary. Everything should be ready when baking commences.

Switch on the oven to pre-heat it to the correct temperature.

Stocking the larder Keep your store cupboard stocked with the basic baking ingredients, but make sure that you do not over-buy; everything should be fresh.

Oven temperatures The temperatures indicated for each of the recipes are for regular ovens, where the heat source lies on either side, or at the top or bottom, of the oven. Fan-assisted and fan ovens work on a different principle, and the heat is circulated by a fan, which gives the same temperature throughout the oven, because there is little variance in heat, cakes are inclined to bake more quickly and to dry out. It may be necessary, therefore, to reduce the oven temperature but please consult the literature accompanying your appliance for exact instructions.

Oven thermometer An accurate oven is essential for successful baking. It should be well insulated and draught-proof, as a discrepancy of a few degrees in the temperature can have a disastrous effect. Regular checking with an oven thermometer helps avoid this.

Baking and testing Cakes must always be baked in a pre-heated oven. Never open the door before at least three-quarters of the cooking time has elapsed, otherwise the delicate structure may collapse.

A cooked cake should have risen well, be slightly domed in the middle and have a golden colour; it should be shrinking very slightly from the sides of the tin.

To test for readiness, lightly press a finger on the centre of the cake which should feel quite firm and springy. If the impression of the fingerprint remains, bake for a few minutes more. You may also test by inserting a skewer or wooden toothpick in the centre of the cake and withdrawing it gently; it should be dry and clean. If any mixture still adheres, the cake needs further cooking. (See also the What Went Wrong and Why? guide on page 25.)

Quick Cake Mix

This 'all-in-one' cake recipe is almost as moist as a Victoria Sandwich but firmer, so more suitable for cutting into novelty cake shapes. It is ideal for children, who often dislike rich fruit cake, and can be made even more appealing if you add their favourite flavouring. Choose one of the variations below or experiment with your own choice of flavouring ingredients.

Cakes made from Quick Cake Mix can be kept for up to 3 days in the refrigerator and up to 2 months if frozen, provided they are not iced. Thaw frozen cakes in the refrigerator and do not ice stored cakes until the day before they are to be eaten.

> *225g/8oz soft margarine*
> *225g/8oz caster sugar*
> *5 eggs*
> *275g/10oz self-raising flour*
> *½ tsp baking powder*
> *1 tbsp milk*

1 Set the oven at 170°C/325°F/Gas 3. Grease a tin and line it with greased nonstick baking paper or greaseproof paper. Place all the ingredients in a bowl and beat well with an electric whisk or wooden spoon for 1 to 2 minutes until evenly blended. (Don't beat mixture any more than necessary.)

2 Turn the mixture into the prepared tin and bake for the time stated in recipe, until it is well risen and the surface feels just firm to the touch.

3 Leave the cake in the tin for 5 minutes then turn it out onto a wire rack. Peel off the lining paper and leave the cake to cool completely. Wrap in foil until ready to ice.

VARIATIONS

Chocolate Substitute 50 g/2 oz cocoa powder for 50 g/2 oz of the flour.

Orange or Lemon Add the grated rind of 1 orange or lemon. Substitute 1 tbsp of juice squeezed from the fruit for the milk.

Coffee and Walnut Dissolve 2-3 tbsp instant coffee powder or granules in 1 tbsp boiling water. Use in place of the milk. Stir in 50 g/2 oz chopped walnuts.

Cherry and Coconut Add 50 g/2 oz chopped glacé cherries and substitute 50 g/2 oz desiccated coconut for 25 g/1 oz of the flour.

Spicy Fruit Add 50 g/2 oz mixed dried fruit and 2 tsp ground mixed spice.

Pastel Stir in 1 tsp blue, red or green food colouring, depending on the child's favourite.

Cup Cakes

Quick Cake Mix can be used to make cup cakes. The mixture based on 225 g/8 oz fat and 275 g/10 oz flour as given will yield about 48 small cakes. The mixture should be divided between greased patty tins or paper cake cases and baked at 180°C/350°F/Gas 4 for about 25 minutes, until the cakes are risen and golden brown. Cool the cakes on a wire rack, then store them in an airtight container. The cooked cakes can be frozen and defrosted as required.

In addition to the variations given, the following flavouring ingredients can be added to the mixture.

Coconut Add 75 g/3 oz desiccated coconut and substitute 3 tbsp orange juice for the milk.

Chocolate Chips Fold 100 g/4 oz chocolate cooking chips into the prepared mixture.

BASIC VICTORIA SANDWICH AND ONE-STAGE MIXTURES CHART

EGG QUANTITY AND TIN SIZE	OVEN TEMPERATURE	APPROX. COOKING TIME
2-egg quantity is sufficient for:		
2 x 18cm/7in sandwich tins	180°C/350°F/Gas 4	20 minutes
20 paper cases	180°C/350°F/Gas 4	15-20 minutes
1 x 20cm/8in (900ml/1½pt) ring tin	170°C/325°F/Gas 3	30-35 minutes
450g/1lb loaf tin	170°C/325°F/Gas 3	35-40 minutes
900m/1½pt pudding basin	170°C/325°F/Gas 3	50 minutes
1 x 15cm/6in round tin	170°C/325°F/Gas 3	40 minutes
3-egg quantity is sufficient for:		
2 x 20cm/8in sandwich tin	180°C/350°F/Gas 4	20-25 minutes
30 paper cases	180°C/350°F/Gas 4	15-20 minutes
1 x 18cm/7in round tin	170°C/325°F/Gas 3	55 minutes
1 x 28 x 18cm/11 x 7 in slab tin	170°C/325°F/Gas 3	35-40 minutes
1 x 900g/2lb loaf tin	170°C/325°F/Gas 3	50-55 minutes
1 x 23cm/9in (1.5 litres/2½pt) ring tin	170°C/325°F/Gas 3	40-45 minutes

To give a finished cake with a depth of approximately 5cm/2in use:

EGG QUANTITY	TIN SIZE	OVEN TEMPERATURE	APPROX. COOKING TIME
2	15cm/6in round	170°C/325°F/Gas 3	40 minutes
3	18cm/7in round 15cm/6in square	170°C/325°F/Gas 3	55 minutes
4	20cm/8in round 18cm/7in square	170°C/325°F/Gas 3	1 hour
5	23 cm/9in round 20cm/8in square	170°C/325°F/Gas 3	1¼ hours
6	25cm/10in round 23cm/9in square	170°C/325°F/Gas 3	1¼ hours
8 plus extra 100g/4oz flour	28cm/11in round 25cm/10in square	170°C/325°F/Gas 3	1½ hours
10 plus extra 150g/5oz flour	30cm/12in round 28cm/11in square	170°C/325°F/Gas 3	1½-1⅔ hours

Victoria Sandwich Cake

This is a fairly firm, yet moist cake. It can be left plain or flavoured in many ways, such as by adding grated lemon or orange rind, coffee or cocoa powder. Chopped nuts or glacé fruits and various sweet spices can also be added. You can experiment to find your favourites, although there is a list of variations at the end of the basic recipe.

A Victoria sandwich is often sandwiched together with jam, but it can also be iced with glacé icing, buttercream or frosting.

The basic Victoria sandwich mixture is very useful for larger cakes as it keeps well for several days in an airtight container. It freezes well, too. There are many shapes to bake the mixture in, so follow the chart as an easy guide to quantities and cooking times.

> 175g/6oz butter or margarine, softened
> 175g/6oz caster sugar
> 3 eggs, beaten
> 175g/6oz self-raising flour
> milk

1 Set the oven following the information given on the chart. Cream the butter and sugar together until light and fluffy. The mixture should drop easily from the spoon or whisk if tapped against the side of the bowl.

2 Add the beaten egg a little at a time, beating well between each addition, so that the egg is absorbed into the mixture. Sift the flour and fold it into the mixture. Add a little milk to give a dropping consistency.

3 Spoon the mixture into the prepared tins. Level the surface, then make a slight dip in the centre. Bake until cakes are well risen, golden and firm to the touch (see chart for timings).

4 Allow the cakes to cool slightly in the tins, then transfer to a wire tray. Invert the tins over the cakes and leave until completely cold. This helps to keep the cakes moist while cooling.

VARIATIONS

Chocolate Replace 1 tbsp flour with 1 tbsp cocoa powder for every 1-egg quantity.

Coffee Add 1 tsp instant coffee powder for each 1-egg quantity. If using coffee granules dissolve them first in a little hot water.

Lemon or Orange Omit the milk. Add 1 tsp grated rind for each 1-egg quantity, plus a little juice to mix to a dropping consistency.

Nut Add 50-75 g/2-3 oz chopped nuts to the basic mixture.

Dried or Glacé Fruits Add 50-75 g/2-3 oz sultanas, chopped glacé cherries or chopped crystallized ginger to the basic mixture.

Chocolate chip Add 50 g/2 oz chocolate dots or chips to the basic mixture.

Coloured Pink, green or yellow food colouring may be added to the mixture. Add several drops, as required. A marbled effect can be achieved by spooning alternate coloured mixtures into a cake tin, then swirling them lightly with a skewer.

One-stage Victoria Sandwich

This uses basically the same ingredients as the Victoria sandwich, in the same proportions, and it makes a lighter cake than the Quick Cake Mix. The main difference is that soft tub margarine is used instead of butter or block margarine. This means that the creaming stage of the butter and the sugar is unnecessary, but extra raising agent must be added to compensate for this. Allow 1 tsp baking powder for every 3-egg quantity or for 2-egg quantity use ½ tsp.

This recipe is not suitable for making large cakes as extra flour is necessary and the Quick Cake Mix should be used instead.

> 175g/6oz soft margarine
> 175g/6oz caster sugar
> 3 eggs
> 175g/6oz self-raising flour
> 1 tsp baking powder

1 Set the oven following the information given in the chart. Place all the ingredients in a bowl and beat well for 1-2 minutes until evenly mixed.

2 Spoon the mixture into the prepared tin, level the surface and bake, following the timings given on the chart.

VARIATION

Lemon or Orange Add grated rind of 1 lemon and 1 tbsp juice. See also the variations for Victoria Sandwich Cake.

Whisked Sponge Cake

This is a very light sponge cake made by whisking eggs and caster sugar in a bowl over hot water. Once this mixture turns to a pale thick foam, sifted plain flour is very carefully folded in. No extra fat is added, so once baked this mixture does not keep well and is best eaten on the day of making, or the following day.

> 3 large eggs
> 75g/3oz caster sugar
> 75g/3oz plain flour

1 Set the oven following the information given in the chart. Put the eggs and sugar in a bowl over a pan of simmering water. Using a hand-held electric mixer or rotary whisk, whisk the eggs and sugar until thick, pale and foamy; about 5 minutes. Remove from the heat and continue whisking for a further 3-4 minutes until the mixture is thick enough to hold the trail of the whisk.

2 Sift the flour, then fold it into the egg mixture a little at a time, until it is evenly dispersed.

3 Pour the mixture into the prepared tins and bake according to the chart. The cake is cooked when it has just started to shrink away from the sides of the tin and springs back when pressed lightly with a finger.

4 Cool slightly, then turn the cakes out onto a wire rack. Invert the tins over the cakes and leave until completely cold. This helps to keep the cakes moist.

Swiss Roll

1 A Swiss roll is made from the Whisked Sponge Cake mixture, but baked in a tin that measures 34 x 24 cm/13½ x 9½ in. Line the tin with greaseproof or waxed paper that extends about 2.5 cm/1 in above the edge all the way round. Grease the lining paper well.

2 Set the oven at 220°C/425°F/Gas 7 and bake the Swiss roll for 7-8 minutes until risen and springy to the touch.

3 While the cake is baking, lay a clean, damp tea towel on the work surface, cover it with a large sheet of greaseproof or waxed paper and sprinkle liberally with caster sugar.

4 Invert the cake onto the sugared paper. Quickly peel off the lining paper and trim off the edges of the cake. Make an indentation with the back of a long-bladed knife across one of the short edges. Use this to start rolling the cake, ensuring the greaseproof or waxed paper is in between each rolling of cake, and using the tea towel as a guide for rolling up the cake.

5 Wrap the Swiss roll in the tea towel and cool it on a wire rack until cold. When cold, unwrap the roll carefully and spread it with whipped fresh cream, buttercream or jam. Roll up again and dust with caster sugar. If using only jam as a filling, this may be spread on the hot cake and rolled up straightaway.

VARIATIONS

Chocolate For each 2 egg-quantity replace 15 g/½ oz flour with 15 g/½ oz cocoa powder.

Coffee Add 2 tsp instant coffee powder with each 2 egg-quantity used.

Lemon or Orange Add the grated rind of a lemon or an orange with the sugar.

WHISKED SPONGE MIXTURES CHART

EGG QUANTITY AND TIN SIZE	OVEN TEMPERATURE	APPROX. COOKING TIME
2-egg quantity fills:		
2 x 18cm/7in sandwich tins	190°C/375°F/Gas 5	10-15 minutes
20 sponge drops or fingers	200°C/400°F/Gas 6	7-8 minutes
15cm/6in round tin	190°C/375°F/Gas 5	25 minutes
3-egg quantity fills:		
2 x 20cm/8in sandwich tins	190°C/375°F/Gas 5	10-15 minutes
18cm/7in round tin or		
15cm/6in square tin	190°C/375°F/Gas 5	30-35 minutes
Swiss roll tin:		
34 x 24cm/13½ x 9½in	220°C/425°F/Gas 7	7-8 minutes
900g/2lb (1.7 litres/2¾pt)		
loaf tin	190°C/375°F/Gas 5	20-25 minutes
23cm/9in (1.5 litres/2½pt)		
ring tin	190°C/375°F/Gas 5	20-25 minutes
4-egg quantity fills:		
6 x 20cm/8in discs greaseproof		
or waxed or non-stick paper	190°C/375°F/Gas 5	8-10 minutes
20cm/8in round tin or		
18cm/7in square tin	190°C/375°F/Gas 5	30-35 minutes
For larger cakes, use the following:		

TIN SIZE	EGG QUANTITY	OVEN TEMPERATURE	APPROX. COOKING TIME
23cm/9in round			
20cm/8in square	5	190°C/375°F/Gas 5	30–35 minutes
25cm/10in round			
23cm/9in square	2 x 3	190°C/375°F/Gas 5	15–20 minutes
28cm/11in round			
25cm/10in square	2 x 4	190°C/375°F/Gas 5	15–20 minutes
30cm/12in round			
28cm/11in square	2 x 5	190°C/375°F/Gas 5	15–20 minutes

Genoese Sponge

This is basically a whisked sponge cake, but melted butter is added after the flour to give a more moist, richer cake, which has improved keeping qualities. To make a slightly softer sponge, some of the flour is replaced by cornflour.

> *3 eggs*
> *75g/3oz caster sugar*
> *65g/2½oz plain flour*
> *15g/½oz cornflour*
> *40g/1½oz butter, melted and cooled*

1 Follow the method and cooking instructions given for Whisked Sponge Cake, but fold in the melted butter after the flour.

USING THE CHART

This chart is designed as an easy guide to show you how much cake mixture is required for various tin sizes.

The basic quantity of mixture is known as a 3-egg quantity, and is easily divisible. For example, for each egg you use 25 g/1 oz caster sugar and 25 g/1 oz plain flour. So, if a recipe says a 4-egg quantity, use 4 eggs, 100 g/4 oz caster sugar and 100 g/4 oz plain flour. For larger mixtures (greater than 4-egg quantity), it is necessary to whisk the mixture for 10 minutes over hot water, and then up to 5 minutes off the heat to achieve the required consistency. The finished cake in each case will be about 5-6 cm/2-2½ in deep.

For the very large cakes (25 cm/10 in and upwards) it is best to prepare and cook the mixture in two halves. This is practical for several reasons. First, you would need an extremely large mixing bowl to mix the quantity of eggs. Secondly, the volume is frequently reduced when large amounts are mixed. Finally, the baking time is very short if the mixture is made like a sandwich cake – only 15-20 minutes for each cake.

Madeira Cake

Madeira cake is useful for all the cakes which involve a lot of cutting and shaping before the marzipan and icing are added. In order to achieve good angles and curves the cake should be compact in texture and able to withstand pressure while remaining moist and tasty. The ingredients listed below are for an 18 cm/7 in square cake.

175g/6oz unsalted butter or
margarine
175g/6oz caster sugar
2 eggs
175g/6oz self-raising flour
75g/3oz plain flour
1 tbsp lemon juice

1 Set the oven at 180°C/350°F/Gas 4. Cream the butter or margarine, which should be at room temperature, with the sugar until light and fluffy.

2 Add the eggs one at a time, following each with a spoonful of self-raising flour. It is a good idea to break each egg into a small bowl or cup, beat it lightly with a fork and then add it to the creamed mixture. Beat thoroughly.

3 Sift the rest of the flour together and fold it gently into the creamed mixture, using a large metal spoon in a figure of eight movement. When all the flour is incorporated, the mixture should have the consistency of lightly whipped cream. Then add the lemon juice.

4 Turn the mixture into a greased and lined tin. Smooth the top with a wooden spoon and bake for 1 hour. Leave the cake in the tin to cool for about 5 to 10 minutes. Then turn the cake out on to sugared paper to cool and remove the lining paper.

Light Fruit Cake

A fruit cake is not as light as a sponge cake, so it does not need to be beaten as much. The dried fruit soaks up the alcohol or orange juice and is plumped out during baking – the result is a very moist cake, like a madeira.

225g/8oz butter or margarine
225g/8oz caster sugar
4 eggs, lightly beaten
225g/8oz plain flour
225g/8oz dried mixed fruit,
soaked overnight in ¼ cup sherry
or orange juice.

1 Set the oven at 170°C/325°F/Gas 4. Prepare a 20 cm/8 in round cake tin.

2 Cream the butter or margarine, which should be at room temperature, with the sugar until light and fluffy.

3 Add the eggs a little at a time. If the mixture starts to separate, add 1 tablespoon of the weighed flour.

4 Stir in the soaked fruit. Gently fold in the flour, using a metal spoon in a figure of eight movement, until it has all been incorporated.

5 Turn the mixture into the tin, smooth the top, make a dip in the centre of the cake mix with the spoon, and bake for 1½ hours. Leave the cake in the tin to cool before turning it out.

KEEPING QUALITY
Light fruit cake keeps well for a short period of time. This type of cake is best stored in an airtight container for 2–3 days before it is eaten, allowing the flavour to develop to the full.

It will keep well for up to 2 weeks in this way or it can be frozen for longer storage. The cake can be frozen whole, or it can be cut into slices and these can be individually wrapped in film before packing and freezing together.

Rich Fruit Cake

This is suitable for Christmas or other celebration cakes, and although it may be eaten without any icing or decoration, it is usual to cover it first with a layer of almond paste, then with a royal icing or fondant icing.

Any fruit cake improves with keeping and it is best to make it at least three months before required, although it will keep for up to a year if wrapped and stored correctly.

No alcohol is added to this cake mixture before cooking, although if you have time to soak the dried fruits in a little brandy, rum or sherry before cooking, this will plump the fruit and make the cake more moist. Fruit may be soaked for up to three days. Any spirit left over when the fruit is strained should be kept and poured over the cake once it is cooked.

Spirit can be added as frequently as wished after cooking. Simply warm a little spirit in a small saucepan. Make a series of holes in the surface of the cake with a fine skewer and pour the spirit over. Leave until completely absorbed, then wrap the cake securely in greaseproof or waxed paper and foil. Then place in a large airtight container or polythene bag and seal. Store in a cool dry place.

Follow the chart for quantities of ingredients, tin sizes, oven temperatures and cooking times.

Preparing the Cake Mixture

1 Set the oven at the selected temperature, following the chart. Line the correct cake tin with a double thickness of greaseproof or waxed paper or non-stick paper.

2 Sift the flour, spices and salt together. Quarter or chop the glacé cherries and mix together with all the dried fruits. Cream the butter and sugar until light and fluffy.

3 Add the eggs, one at a time, beating well between each addition. Add the almond essence, black treacle (molasses) and grated rind of orange and lemon with the eggs. If it looks as though the mixture is 'splitting' or 'curdling', add a large spoonful of the dry ingredients and beat well to give a smooth mixture once again. Fold in the flour, then the fruit until well mixed.

4 Transfer the mixture to the prepared tin and level the surface, then make a slight dip in the cake so that the outer edge is slightly higher. The cake will rise more in the centre during cooking and this counteracts that rise, giving a flatter surface to the cooked cake. For large cakes, wrap several thicknesses of brown paper or newspaper around the tin and secure with string.

5 Bake for the suggested time, but always check the cake about 15-30 minutes before the end of the cooking time, depending on the size of the cake, as all ovens vary slightly. If the cake is becoming too brown on the surface, cover it with a layer of foil, or greaseproof or waxed paper.

6 To test if the cake is cooked, insert a skewer into the centre of the cake. The skewer will come out clean if the cake is cooked. If the mixture is still soft and uncooked in the centre it will stick to the skewer.

7 Allow the cake to cool in the tin. When cold, remove from the tin and peel off the lining paper. If you like, add some spirit at this stage. Prick the surface of the cake with a skewer. Warm a few spoonfuls of brandy or other spirit and pour over the cake. Wait until completely absorbed, then wrap the cake. The spirit can be added at frequent intervals during storage.

Alternative Rich Fruit Cakes

The basic rich fruit cake recipe is a very stable one and the variety of dried fruits which are used can be varied. Aim to include the same total quantity of dried fruits but take advantage of the many types which are available.

For example, chopped dates, dried apricots, dried pears or dried peaches can be added in small quantities to give a slightly different flavour. The tougher pears and peaches should be soaked for a few hours first, then drained very well. Ready-to-eat prunes can also be chopped and added to the mixture, to give a particularly dark, rich result; do not add too many or the cake will resemble a pudding.

Crystallized fruits can also be used to flavour such cakes. Pineapple, angelica or ginger can be chopped and added, although the ginger should be added in small quantities. Crystallized fruits are complemented by nuts, such as brazils or walnuts, which can be roughly chopped to provide an alternative texture.

These variations may not be suitable for a traditional wedding cake but they can be used for birthday or anniversary cakes, or for other less-formal celebration cakes.

BASIC CAKE RECIPES ◆

RICH FRUIT CAKE CHART

Round tin	18cm/7in	20cm/8in	23cm/9in	25cm/10in	28cm/11in	30cm/12in	33cm/13in
Square tin	15cm/6in	18cm/7in	20cm/8in	23cm/9in	25cm/10in	28cm/11in	30cm/12in
Ingredients							
Flour, plain	175g/6oz	225g/8oz	375g/13oz	450g/1lb	550g/1¼lb	675g/1½lb	850g/1lb 14oz
Mixed spice, ground	½tsp	¾tsp	1tsp	1½tsp	2tsp	2½tsp	3tsp
Cinnamon, ground	¼tsp	½tsp	¾tsp	1tsp	1¼tsp	1½tsp	1 ½tsp
Nutmeg, ground	¼tsp	½tsp	¾tsp	1tsp	1¼tsp	1½tsp	1½tsp
Salt	½tsp	¾tsp	1tsp	1tsp	1tsp	1½tsp	2tsp
Glacé cherries	75g/3oz	100g/4oz	150g/5oz	175g/6oz	225g/8oz	300g/10oz	350g/12oz
Currants	200g/7oz	300g/10oz	425g/15oz	500g/1lb 2oz	625g/1lb 6oz	800g/1¾lb	1kg/2¼lb
Sultanas	175g/6oz	225g/8oz	375g/13oz	425g/15oz	550g/1¼ lb	675g/1½lb	850g/1lb 14oz
Raisins	175g/6oz	225g/8oz	375g/13oz	425g/15oz	550g/1¼lb	675g/1½lb	850g/1lb 14oz
Cut mixed peel	50g/2oz	60g/2½oz	75g/3oz	100g/4oz	150g/5oz	200g/7oz	275g/9oz
Butter	150g/5oz	200g/7oz	300g/10oz	350g/12oz	450g/1lb	550g/1¼lb	675g/1½lb
Sugar: caster or soft brown granulated or light brown	150g/5oz	200g/7oz	300g/10oz	350g/12oz	450g/1lb	550g/1¼lb	675g/1½lb
Eggs	3	4	5	6	9	12	14
Almond essence	½tsp	½tsp	1tsp	1tsp	1tsp	1½tsp	2tsp
Black treacle	1½tsp	1½tsp	1tbsp	1tbsp	1tbsp	4½tsp	2 tbsp
Orange, grated rind of	½	½	1	1	1	1½	2
Lemon, grated rind of	½	½	1	1	1	1½	2

Oven temperature 150°C/300°F/Gas 2, reducing to 140°C/275°F/Gas 1 halfway through cooking for the larger cakes (25cm/10in and above).

| Cooking time (hours) | 2-2½ | 2-2½ | 2-2½ | 3-3¼ | 3-3½ | 3½-3¾ | 4-4¼ |

CUTTING THE CAKE

Wedding cake is traditionally served in 2.5 cm/1 in square pieces, or 5 x 1 cm/2 x ½ in slices. The information in this table will help you calculate what size cake to make based on the number of guests invited. Do not forget extra pieces to send to absent friends and relatives.

If you are making cake for a very large gathering, either a wedding or celebration, or some other function, then the number of servings required can be made up by baking and icing an additional, large square cake which is not decorated. The cake should be made at the same time as the decorated one and it should be of equal quality. It should be covered with the same basic icing but there is no need to add the final decoration.

This 'spare' cake is particularly useful at weddings as it can be cut in the kitchens, ready to bring out immediately the main tier of the displayed cake is taken away for cutting. This trick will ensure that there is plenty of cake for all guests and for posting to others who are absent.

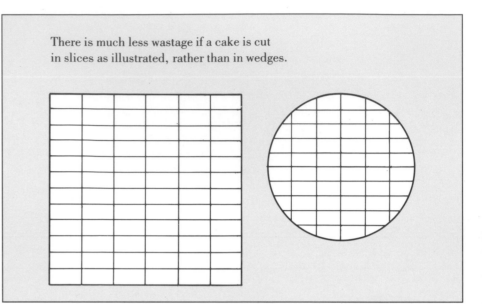

There is much less wastage if a cake is cut in slices as illustrated, rather than in wedges.

Size of cake	No of slices (fruit cake)	No of slices (sponge cake)
13cm/5in round	14	7
13cm/5in square	16	8
15cm/6in round	22	11
15cm/6in square	27	14
18cm/7in round	30	15
18cm/7in square	40	20
20cm/8in round	40	20
20cm/8in square	54	27
23cm/9in round	54	27
23cm/9in square	70	35
25cm/10in round	68	34
25cm/10in square	90	45
27.5cm/11in round	86	43
27.5cm/11in square	112	56
30cm/12in round	100	50
30cm/12in square	134	67

WHAT WENT WRONG AND WHY?

If the recipe is followed closely, the ingredients weighed accurately and the oven cooks correctly, then baked cakes should be perfect every time. However, everyone has the occasional disaster and it is useful to try and determine just what went wrong, if only to avoid repeating the mistake!

Cake sunk in the centre

- Mixture too soft, using too much liquid or too little dry ingredients.
- Too much raising agent.
- The oven door was opened too early in the cooking process, or the cake was under-cooked.
- Too cool an oven so the centre did not rise.

Fruit sunk towards the base of the cake

- Too much raising agent.
- Damp fruit or sticky glacé fruits.
- The oven door was opened or banged whilst the cake was rising.

The cake has peaked and cracked

- Insufficient creaming of fat and sugar.
- The cake tin was not large enough.
- The cake was cooked too near the top of the oven.

The cake is dry

- Insufficient liquid or eggs.
- Over-cooked.
- Too much raising agent was used.

Uneven, coarse, open texture

- The egg and sugar was insufficiently creamed together.
- The oven was too hot.
- Too much baking powder was used.

Heavy, close texture

- Insufficient raising agent used.
- Too much liquid used.
- Overstirring when folding in the flour to whisked sponges.
- Eggs and sugar insufficiently whisked to trap air.

Heavy base layer with Genoese mix

- The melted butter was too hot when it was folded into the whisked mixture.
- The fat was unevenly folded in.

Cake Rescue Remedies

Cake that has gone terribly wrong does not necessarily have to fill the bin. For a special occasion it is best to start again and make another cake, however there is a good chance that at least part of the failure can be eaten.

Economical Truffles Cake which is over-cooked can be trimmed and the dry, but edible, part reduced to crumbs. Moisten the crumbs with rum, sherry or fruit juice, then bind them with melted chocolate to make a simple truffle mixture. Shape the truffles and coat them in cocoa powder.

Ring Cake A sunken round cake can sometimes be turned into a successful ring cake. Cut out the soggy, sunken centre and discard it. Cover the ring of cooked cake with icing, frosting or whipped cream, depending on the type of cake, and add suitable decorations.

Cake Shapes Burned or soggy areas of an oblong or square cake should be trimmed off and discarded. The remainder of the cake can be cut into various shapes, either using cutters or with a knife to give small squares, oblong or diamond-shaped pieces. These can be coated in icing and decorated.

Fruit Cake Cream Soggy fruit cake is the most difficult of disasters to use successfully. Small pieces can be crumbled into glass dishes and dressed with a little dry sherry, then allowed to stand, covered for several hours. The plump, very moist crumbs should be topped with whipped cream and served as a dessert.

COVERING AND FILLING CAKES

Almond paste (marzipan)

This is a mixture of ground almonds and sugar mixed together with beaten egg. Almond essence or orange flower water may be added to heighten the flavour. It is sometimes used on its own as a cake covering and, if wished, toasted to give an attractive finish. Almond paste is particularly good for modelling shapes. It absorbs most colours well, but because it is basically yellow in colour some food colourings do not give a good final result. A whiter paste can be made by adding egg whites only to bind the mixture. This can be made by two methods; a cold mixture bound with eggs, or a hot mixture with boiled syrup.

Glacé icing

This is the simplest of all icings, made from icing sugar and water. It can be flavoured with coffee or chocolate to give a richness and density that white icing lacks. It can also be coloured by adding a few drops of edible food colouring. When poured directly over a cake, glacé icing gives a smooth shiny coating that sets hard on the surface while remaining soft underneath. The coating may be left undecorated, or piped with designs in contrasting coloured glacé icing or buttercream.

Fudge icings and frostings

These are made from a variety of ingredients, frequently incorporating egg whites, butter, sugar and cream. The similarity between these two groups is that they are mixed over direct heat or hot water, or have the basis of a hot sugar syrup. The icings are therefore very soft and can be swirled to give a decorative effect. Once cold they set firm on the surface, remaining soft underneath.

Buttercreams

These are soft, creamy icings made from butter. The simplest one is made from butter and icing sugar beaten together until light and fluffy. French buttercream (crème au beurre) is a smooth, pipeable icing made with unsalted butter. Marshmallow buttercreams are particularly light and fluffy.

Buttercreams are used as fillings as well as icings, and they are frequently spread over the sides of a cake, as a base for decoration, such as chopped nuts, grated chocolate or desiccated coconut. They also pipe very well.

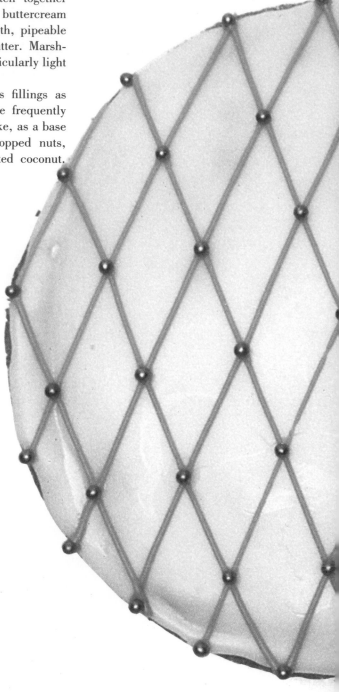

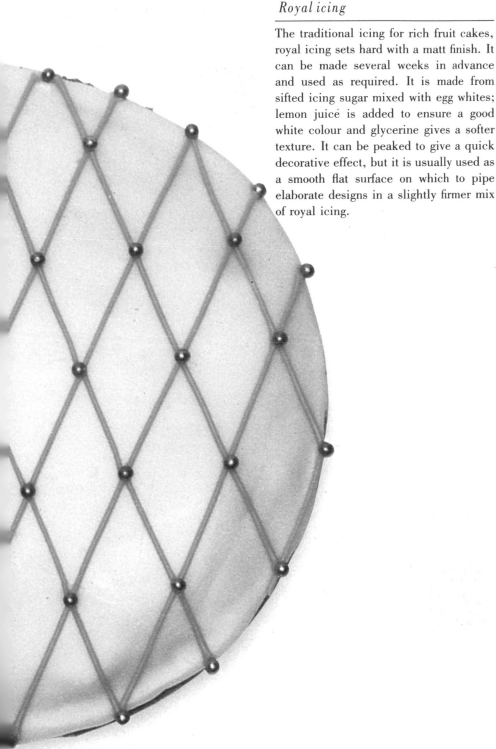

Royal icing

The traditional icing for rich fruit cakes, royal icing sets hard with a matt finish. It can be made several weeks in advance and used as required. It is made from sifted icing sugar mixed with egg whites; lemon juice is added to ensure a good white colour and glycerine gives a softer texture. It can be peaked to give a quick decorative effect, but it is usually used as a smooth flat surface on which to pipe elaborate designs in a slightly firmer mix of royal icing.

Chocolate icings

A simple icing in itself, chocolate can also be mixed in many ways to give deliciously rich icings. Melted chocolate can also be used effectively to decorate cakes.

Moulding icings

There are many ways of preparing this type of icing, some more difficult than others. With experience you will decide which of the recipes best suits your needs and it is a good idea to use that particular icing as much as possible.

Traditional fondant icing is perhaps the most difficult moulding icing to make, but it is extremely versatile. It is made from a sugar syrup that is boiled to a precise temperature (a sugar thermometer is invaluable), then cooled by working it with a palette knife until it can be kneaded by hand. The resulting icing is opaque white, which hardens as it cools, but, unlike royal icing, it remains soft to the bite. The icing can be rolled out or softened to a pouring cosistency with a little extra sugar syrup and poured directly over a cake. It gives a very good finish to a cake and extra decoration can be made by using a firmer mixture for moulding shapes. Piped designs in royal icing can also be added.

There are several easy fondant recipes which require no cooking and can be used in the same way as the traditional fondant. Commercially prepared fondant is also available from cake decorating suppliers and supermarkets, although the best quality is obtained from specialist shops.

The other moulding icings are much simpler alternatives to traditional fondant, but they can be used in the same way.

MARZIPAN AND ALMOND PASTE

The difference between marzipan and almond paste is in the proportion of almonds used. Marzipan has to have at least 25 per cent almonds — anything less than this, and it is called almond paste. Neither uses nuts other than almonds.

Marzipan has been used for centuries by confectioners. Its name means 'the bread of Mars'. It should be smooth and as malleable as potter's clay. It can be used in baking, in macaroons and biscuits, for covering and sandwiching cakes, and for making marzipan fancies and colourful cake decorations.

Marzipan can be nutty white or yellow in colour. Traditionally bakers use artificially coloured yellow marzipan for wedding cakes, because it looks as good and rich as egg yolk. Today, naturally coloured white marzipan is becoming more popular as many cooks prefer not to use artificial colouring. Commercial marzipan is made by blanching and pounding the almonds, and passing them several times through granite rollers. The almonds and sugar are then roasted together.

Colouring Marzipan

*I*t is easier to colour white marzipan than the commercially produced yellow variety. The artificial yellow colouring distorts some food colours, in particular purple, which tends to become a dull brown colour.

Add a very small amount of liquid or paste food colour to white marzipan. Dip a cocktail stick in the food colour and streak the marzipan. Knead the marzipan thoroughly until the colour is evenly distributed.

With practice you will soon be able to judge how much colour needs to be added to produce a particular shade.

Coloured marzipan is used mainly for modelling work, although it can be put to good use as a colourful cake covering (see pages 30/31 and 138 to 211).

Cooked Almond Paste

This is a quick-drying paste that is not oily. It keeps well for several weeks in the refrigerator, but if possible, make it about 24 hours before it is required. Store it in an airtight container or a double wrapping of clingfilm. If it dries, moisten it with a little egg white. Cooked almond paste tastes better than the uncooked variety and it has a smoother texture because the sugar is dissolved in water before it is used.

> 450g/1lb granulated sugar
> 150ml/¼pt plus 4 tbsp water
> large pinch of cream of tartar
> 350g/12oz ground almonds
> 2 egg whites

1 Put the sugar and water into a large pan over a very low heat. Stir with a metal spoon until all the sugar has dissolved.

2 When the sugar has completely dissolved, add the cream of tartar and bring the syrup to the boil. Boil rapidly without stirring until it reaches the soft ball stage (115°C/240°F on a sugar thermometer).

3 Stop the boiling process quickly by plunging the base of the saucepan into a bowl of cold water. Stir in the ground almonds.

4 Stir in the egg whites. Return the pan to a low heat and stir until the mixture thickens slightly.

5 Turn the mixture out onto a marble slab or work surface, lightly sprinkled with icing sugar, and work it with a spatula until it begins to cool and thicken.

6 As you work the paste, sprinkle over a dusting of sifted icing sugar, to prevent it sticking to the work surface.

7 When the paste is cool enough to handle, knead it with your hands. It will take up to half its weight in added icing sugar used to dust the surface during kneading. The finished paste should feel dry to the touch. Be careful not to add too much sugar at a time, or the mixture will become too dry and will crumble when rolled out or worked. The more sugar you add, the harder you will have to work to disperse the oils produced by the almonds.

8 Store the cooked almond paste in an airtight container, thick polythene bag or clingfilm.

Uncooked Marzipan or Almond Paste

This traditional marzipan tends to be oily and crumbly, a little like short pastry, when you roll it out. Because it is un-cooked, it is not advisable to store it for more than two or three days before use. If you do have to store it, wrap it tightly in clingfilm, and put it in a cool part of the refrigerator. You can also freeze it for up to six months. If you are using uncooked marzipan to cover a cake which is to be kept, add a tablespoon of alcohol to act as a preservative. The quantities below are sufficient for covering a 23 cm/9 in round cake.

450g/1lb caster sugar, sifted
450g/1lb icing sugar, sifted
450g/1lb ground almonds
1 tbsp rum, brandy or whisky, or
a few drops of lemon juice or
orange flower water (optional)
2 large or 3 small eggs, or 4
yolks only

1 Combine the two sugars. Add the ground almonds and mix thoroughly. Make a well in the centre and add the rum or other flavouring.

2 Gradually add the lightly beaten eggs and stir with a wooden spoon or spatula to form a stiff paste. You may not need all the egg. If the paste is too soft, it will be difficult to handle.

3 Gather the mixture together with your hands and knead it until it is well combined.

4 Continue to knead the marzipan lightly on a sugared work surface until it is smooth. Avoid over-kneading, or it may become greasy.

5 The finished result – an evenly tex-tured and malleable paste. Store it in an airtight container or a double wrapping of polythene or clingfilm.

COVERING CAKES WITH MARZIPAN

For Royal Icing

A common problem with cakes covered in marzipan and then royal icing is that the icing becomes discoloured by the marzipan beneath. This happens usually because there is too much oil in the marzipan and it has not been allowed to dry thoroughly before being covered with icing. Allow the cake plenty of time to dry and use a cooked, not uncooked, marzipan.

This problem does not occur with bought marzipan. If possible, choose white or naturally coloured marzipan.

1 Always turn the cake over to decorate it, so that the flat base becomes the top. What is now the base of the cake may be concave or convex. Either slice off the rounded part if it is concave or fill the hollow with marzipan if it is convex.

2 Roll a long, thin sausage of marzipan and stick it round the base of the cake with jam or egg white by pressing it in to the cake with a palette knife. This will both seal the edges of the cake to the cake board and help the cake to keep longer.

3 Sprinkle the work surface with icing sugar. Roll out the marzipan, using spacers as a guide to even thickness and the right width, which should be a little more than the cake top.

4 Turn the marzipan over, sprinkling more icing sugar beneath it if necessary. The smoother rolled side of the marzipan is the 'right' side. Brush a circle of warm apricot jam or egg white the same size as the diameter of the cake on the 'wrong' side of the marzipan. Alternatively, brush the cake with jam. Apricot is generally used rather than other jams because it does not dominate the flavour of the marzipan.

5 Place the cake top down on the marzipan. Cut the marzipan closely round the cake.

6 Turn the cake the right way up, being careful not to leave finger marks in the marzipan. Trim off any excess marzipan from the bottom sausage. Ensure that the sides of the cake are smooth, filling any small holes with pieces of marzipan.

7 Roll out a strip of marzipan about 5 mm/¼ in thick for the sides of the cake. The length of the strip should be three times the diameter of the cake. Measure the depth of the strip to fit the sides. Make sure that the work surface is well dusted with icing sugar. Turn the marzipan over, so that the smoother side is face down. Brush the marzipan with warm apricot jam.

8 Roll the cake along the marzipan, pressing it into position. If you have miscalculated, and you need to add a little extra marzipan, it will not show if the joins are neat.

9 If you are covering a square cake, measure the sides of the cake and cut two pieces to fit. Attach them to opposite sides of the cake and measure the two remaining sides plus the thickness of the marzipan before cutting and fitting. This will give you 90-degree corners. Otherwise follow the instructions for the round cake.

10 Now the cake is completely covered smooth it carefully with the heel and palm of your hands. A smooth, flat coating of marzipan will provide the perfect base for a professional coating of smooth, royal icing.

For Fondant Icing

If you intend to finish your cake with fondant rather than royal icing, a slightly different technique for putting on the marzipan is involved. The marzipan needs to be rounded at the corners and edges, because the fondant is applied to the top and sides of the cake in one process. Use warm apricot jam or egg white to hold the marzipan in position.

Fondant icing does not become discoloured by marzipan in the way that royal icing does, so either natural or coloured marzipan can be used.

1 Turn the cake upside down, so that the flatter surface becomes the top. Trim the sides if necessary and fill any holes with marzipan dampened with egg white. Roll a long, thin sausage of marzipan for the base of the cake, paint the edge of the cake with egg white and attach the marzipan.

2 Press the marzipan on to the cake with a palette knife to secure it. Do not use your fingers.

3 Turn the cake the right way up and place it on a sheet of greaseproof paper. Moisten the cake all over with egg white.

4 Roll out a square of marzipan large enough to cover the top and sides of the cake, allowing a little extra.

5 Pick up the marzipan right-side up. Use one hand to pick up the marzipan and the other to help drape it over the cake.

6 Hold the marzipan up from beneath with one hand and smooth it down with the other towards the raised hand to exclude air bubbles.

7 Once the top is flat, flare out the corners. Make sure you do not stretch the marzipan too much, or it will crack and craze. Smooth and fit the corners using the palm of your hand before you fit the sides. Make sure the sides are flat and not pleated or creased.

8 Use the warmth of your hand to help smooth off the marzipan and ensure it is well fixed to the cake.

9 With a palette knife trim the marzipan to the base of the cake making a neat edge all the way around.

ROYAL ICING

Working with royal icing is one of the most skilful aspects of cake decorating. It is used both for covering the cake and for piping decorations.

Royal icing, or glacé royale, as it is also known, is made by beating together sugar and egg whites. The action of beating incorporates millions of minute air bubbles into the mixture, and it is this that gives it its texture. Well made royal icing can be easily cut with a sharp knife.

The slightest trace of egg yolk or grease, however, will break down the egg white and prevent it from becoming properly aerated, no matter how much you beat it. Always make absolutely sure that the bowl used to mix the icing is grease-free by washing it out with hot, soapy water, rinsing it under hot water and then standing it upside down to drain. Let it dry off by itself. If you need to dry it quickly, use a freshly washed tea towel.

Mixer Royal Icing

You can also make royal icing in a mixer. It will save you a lot of hard work, but you will not be able to judge the consistency with the same accuracy. Always keep the beater on the lowest speed – if you beat it fast you will incorporate too much air into it and large bubbles may appear as you coat the cake. You will also shower the kitchen in icing sugar.

The basic principle is the same as for making the icing by hand. The following photographs show the technique using dried egg powder – pure albumen – egg substitute, or a boosted albumen.

> 15 g/½ oz albumen powder
> (or 7 tsp)
> 75 ml/3 fl oz water
> 450 g/1 lb icing sugar, sifted

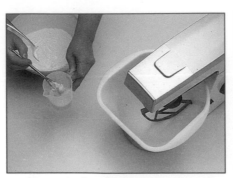

1 First mix the albumen into the water. The resulting liquid will be sloppy and lumpy and give off a strong smell. Do not give up and throw it away! Albumen does have a strong smell. It has a very long shelf life and the smell does not mean it has gone off. Do not try to whisk out the lumps of coagulated albumen. Leave it for at least 15 minutes, or a couple of hours if possible, to dissolve.

2 Sieve the albumen and water mixture into a mixing bowl. Add half the sugar and beat it until it is smooth, remembering to wipe down the sides of the bowl frequently to incorporate any sugar that may be sticking to it. Then add the rest of the sugar and, if you are using pure albumen, beat it for 12-14 minutes. If you are using boosted albumen, about 4 minutes is long enough to achieve the correct consistency. Boosted albumen contains a foaming agent that helps it reach the right consistency much quicker than normal egg white, and therefore it needs less beating. If you overbeat it, your icing will be very hard and flinty.

3 The right consistency is reached when the icing stands up in soft peaks. Seal and store the icing as for handmade icing.

Ingredients for Royal Icing

Egg white

It is a good idea to break and separate the eggs you are going to use for royal icing two or three hours before making it, or even the night before. This will allow some of the water to evaporate from the white, which increases its viscosity and makes a stronger icing. Place the egg whites into a grease-free bowl and cover with a dampened cloth to prevent them completely drying out.

Albumen powder

Reconstituted albumen powder can be substituted for fresh egg white in royal icing. Use it according to the manufacturer's instructions, but the ratio is generally 15g/½oz albumen powder to 75 ml/3 fl oz water to 450 g/1 lb sugar.

Sugar

The amount of icing sugar you need is impossible to specify exactly, because it depends on the quantity of egg white. Sift the sugar twice through a fine sieve to ensure that the icing is perfectly smooth. This is vital if you intend to use the icing for piping.

Additional ingredients

A squeeze of lemon juice both whitens royal icing and gives it more elasticity but once it has set, the lemon juice tends to make it more brittle, and liable to crack when you cut the cake. Therefore, only add lemon juice to icing which is to be used for piping, but not for covering the cake.

Adding 1 teaspoon glycerine per 450 g/1 lb icing sugar makes the icing a little softer. Only add glycerine to icing for covering the cake, not for piping. Never add more glycerine, or you will prevent proper drying of the icing coatings. This can have disastrous results if, for example, the weight of an upper tier causes the icing to subside.

Hand-made Royal Icing

Royal icing made by hand often has a better consistency than that made in a mixer, because you can judge by the feel of it when to add more sugar and when the icing is ready. However, this method is hard work!

If the icing is to be used for coating the cake only, weigh out the correct amount and put it in a clean bowl, then add 1 teaspoon glycerine per 450 g/1 lb icing. This will help to give an icing that will cut without splintering.

> *1 egg white, at room temperature*
> *about 350g/12oz icing sugar,*
> *sifted twice just before using*
> *strained juice of ½ lemon*

1 Break up the egg white with a palette knife, making sure that both the knife and the bowl are free from grease. A palette knife cuts and aerates the white more effectively than a metal spoon.

2 Very gradually add the sugar, working each addition in well with the palette knife before adding the next. Only add half a tablespoon at a time. If you add it too quickly and do not beat it enough in between additions, the result will be too much sugar in the icing, and this will give it a dull yellowish colour. Stir frequently round the sides of the bowl to incorporate the sugar sticking to it, and every time you do so, scrape off the knife on the edge of the bowl to stop sugar building up on the blade. If you do not do this, the sugar crystals which are not mixed in will harden and block the nozzles.

3 As you add more sugar the icing thickens until you can pull it into a peak when you lift the knife out of it. Once the icing is stiff enough to hold a peak, add a squeeze of lemon juice. If this wets the icing too much, incorporate a little more sugar. The lemon juice will give the icing a smoother, creamier feel. Remember that a firmer consistency is needed for piping borders, and a softer consistency for line work.

4 To store the icing, you must protect it from moisture. Carefully wipe out the sides of the bowl with a clean sponge cloth to remove every particle of sugar.

5 Take a piece of clingfilm and press it right down on to the icing, smoothing it to eliminate any air bubbles. Put another layer of clingfilm across the top of the bowl and seal the bowl in an airtight container. You can store it in this way for up to two weeks. Do not put the icing in the fridge because it will absorb moisture, and this spoils its consistency.

Colouring Royal Icing

*I*t is difficult to achieve strong royal icing colours, such as Christmas red, royal blue, moss green or black, with the standard food colours widely available in general grocers. Better colours are achieved with food colours designed for the purpose available from specialist cake decorating sources.

Food colours come in several forms — as liquid, powder, syrup or paste. Powder can be extremely messy to use. Paste colours maintain the consistency of the royal icing, and are the most suitable. Take care not to overthin icing with weak liquid colours.

In order to achieve a bright red or true black, it is important to allow the colour to 'wet out' in the icing — that is, to leave the icing to stand for 20-30 minutes while the strength of the colour develops.

COVERING CAKES WITH ROYAL ICING

Leave the marzipan for two or three days for the surface to harden slightly before you ice the cake. If you are working in damp conditions, you may have to put the cake in an airing cupboard or a warm dry place.

Make up the royal icing with a sufficient quantity to give the cake three coats. Give the cake top a coat with the freshly made icing, which should be well aerated from beating. Always keep the bowl of icing covered as you work. Let the top dry for about six hours or, better still, overnight before you start to work on the sides. Do not try and hurry the drying process – if you dry it in a low oven the icing will discolour, and it may crack as the cake expands and contracts.

In this instance only, it does not matter if air bubbles are present, as the first layer of icing serves to provide a foundation on which subsequent finishing coats are applied.

1 Place the cake on a turntable. Put the equivalent of two or three spoonfuls of icing in the centre of the cake with a palette knife. The blade of the knife should be about 20 cm/8 in long.

2 With a paddling motion, spread the icing towards the sides of the cake. Turn the cake as you tilt and rock the blade of the knife in the icing being careful to even it out and eliminate any air bubbles.

3 Smooth round the cake in a fan pattern, turning the cake and drawing the knife out from the centre to the edges. Flatten the fan pattern in two or three sweeps, using the turntable and keeping the knife still.

4 Take a straight-edge or a ruler, longer than the diameter of the cake. Hold it at either end, tilt it at an acute angle to the cake and pull it smoothly across the surface, to the edge of the cake. Pivot the straight-edge so that its other long edge is in contact with the icing and push it gently away from you. You should have icing sticking only to one face of your straight-edge. Maintain an even and steady pressure with both hands as you move the straight-edge over the cake.

If after one sweep, you have not got a smooth surface, repeat the process.

If you still have not got a smooth top after three or four attempts remove as much icing as is practical, beat the mixture and start again from Step 2. Do not despair since the first coat need not be immaculate.

5 When working on the sides of a cake use a stainless steel smoother to remove the excess icing. A plastic one might bend with the weight of the icing. Hold the smoother at an angle against the side of the cake and rotate the turntable. As the icing piles up on the smoother, scrape it off into the bowl of unused icing.

6 To cover the sides, take some icing on the palette knife and rock it backwards and forwards on the cake as you rotate the turntable. Keep the knife in the icing so that it is pushed forwards on to the marzipan to eliminate any air bubbles. Repeat the process until the sides are completely coated and have a reasonably smooth finish.

7 Smooth the sides of the cake in one continual sweep. Start with both hands on the furthest side of the cake, holding the smoother in one and the turntable in the other.

8 Rotate the turntable towards you so that your hands meet up at their starting point. When the circle is completed, pull the smoother off gently towards you.

9 Go round once more with the smoother to neaten the join between the sides and the top of the cake.

10 If you have not had time to allow the top to dry, omit Step 9, because you may spoil the clean edge. Allow the icing to dry and use a very sharp knife gently to carve away the rough edge of icing at the join. Apply the second and third coats in the same way.

11 To cover the cake board, put some icing on the board with your palette knife and turn the table, dragging the icing round it for about 10 cm/4 in. Repeat the process all around the board.

12 Use the smoother to finish off and stop the icing building up around the sides of the cake. Hold the smoother still and rotate the turntable with your other hand, smoothing all around the board in one sweep.

13 Hold the palette knife at an angle to the board and rotate the turntable to trim off any icing the smoother has pushed over the edge.

Rough Icing

If you are icing a cake for the first time and are unable to get the icing smooth, you can always turn it into rough icing. This method is also useful if you want to ice a cake in a hurry.

1 Put the royal icing on the cake as before and use a paddling motion with the palette knife to bring it out to the edges of the cake. Pull up peaks of icing all over the cake with a flat knife.

2 Alternatively, use a slightly damp but not wet piece of foam rubber sponge. This will give a lighter, more delicate texture than the knife.

Rough icing is particularly suitable for Christmas cakes where the textured surface is used to resemble snow.

FONDANT ICING

Fondant is used for both icing cakes and making cake decorations. It has a softer more moulded look than the stiff, formal royal icing.

Uncooked Fondant

Uncooked fondant is the easiest fondant to make and several different recipes are included. This does not have the elasticity or fine texture of cooked fondant but it is easy to work with and rolls out rather like short pastry. It can be made by hand or in a mixer. Do not use a hand-held mixer as it may not be strong enough.

> 2 tbsp liquid glucose
> 1 egg white
> 675-900g/1½-2lb icing sugar, sifted
> juice of half a lemon
> 1½ tsp glycerine
> flavouring and colouring as required

1 Soften the glucose over hot water. Put the egg white into a mixing bowl, add about half the icing sugar and beat well until the mixture begins to stiffen. Add the lemon juice and beat again.

2 Add about 225g/8oz icing sugar to the mixture. Beat thoroughly until all the icing sugar is well incorporated.

3 Add the glycerine and glucose and continue beating in more icing sugar until the mixture has thickened. Incorporate the flavouring.

4 Once the paste is stiff, sift some icing sugar onto a work surface. Tip out the mixture onto it and knead it, adding more sugar, until it loses all signs of stickiness.

5 Test to see if the paste is ready by pressing it firmly with your fingers. If your fingers are sticky, you need to add more sugar.

6 This fondant can be used straight away, but it is better to leave it overnight before coating the cake. Wrap it tightly in a double layer of clingfilm and seal it in an airtight container.

Continental Fondant Icing or Sugar Paste

This is a superb fondant, but it is quite difficult to make. You will need a marble slab and plenty of muscle power – a good half hour's work is involved. If you are not confident enough to attempt this recipe, then it is best to use one of the icings which are easily prepared.

> 450g/1lb granulated sugar
> 1tbsp liquid glucose
> 150ml/¼pt water

1 Wet a marble slab. Put the sugar and glucose into a saucepan. To measure out liquid glucose by the tablespoon, put the jar of glucose into a basin of hot water until it becomes thin and runny.

2 Stir in the water over a gentle heat. As you bring the sugar to boiling point stir continuously with a wooden spoon and wash down the sides of the pan with a dampened pastry brush to stop sugar crystals from forming.

3 When the syrup has reached a temperature of 115°C/240°F, 'soft ball' stage, plunge the base of the saucepan into cold water to stop it cooking further.

4 Pour the syrup in a spiral motion from the pan onto the marble slab. Marble is the best surface for the speedy cooling of the syrup. You can use an ordinary work surface, but the syrup will take longer to cool.

5 To aid cooling, sprinkle the syrup with cold water from a pastry brush. As it cools, the syrup turns whitish in colour. Do not be tempted to work it before it has cooled, or it will become tough and sugary.

6 When the syrup has completely cooled, take a damp metal scraper and begin lifting the edges of the syrup and folding them in towards the centre.

7 Then work in a figure of eight motion, turning the outside edges of the syrup into the centre all the time. Carry on working for about 5 minutes until it is glossy and viscous and has a creamy-oloured tinge.

8 After a while you will probably find the syrup is easier to stir with a long-handled spatula, so that you can put more pressure on it as you mix.

9 The mixture will gradually become thick and opaque and you will need to use both hands to continue mixing. At this stage it is often easier to go back to the metal scraper to lift it and turn the fondant.

10 The mixture will quite quicky become white and crumbly and too thick to work at all. It will take up to 20 minutes of hard work to get to this point.

11 Moisten your hands and work the crumbled fondant into a ball. Knead it for 5–10 minutes until it is completely smooth and free from lumps. You can complete this process using a food mixer with a dough hook.

12 Wrap the fondant tightly in cling-film and store it in a sealed container in the fridge. It will keep for up to four weeks.

This fondant can be used in two ways — either as a cold fondant or a cooked fondant. To make a cold rolled fondant, or sugar paste, add a little icing sugar to the fondant and simply roll it out to cover a cake.

To make a cooked fondant, which is used for fondant fancies or fondant centres for chocolates, put the fondant in a double boiler over a low heat to break it down. Add stock syrup (page 58) until the consistency has thinned enough to coat the back of a wooden spoon. Now it is ready to use. Pour it over your cake, as you would glacé icing.

Mallow Paste

This icing sets firm and is particularly good for modelling or moulding flowers. The quantity given is sufficient to cover an 18 cm/7 in cake.

> 2tsp gelatine
> 2tsp white fat
> 3tbsp water
> 500g/1lb 2oz icing sugar, sifted
> colouring, as required

1 Place the gelatine, fat and water in a bowl over a saucepan of simmering water and heat gently until dissolved.

2 Place three-quarters of the sugar in a bowl, then pour in the gelatine mixture and work together with fingertips until a smooth paste is formed, adding as much of the remaining sugar as necessary.

3 Colour as wished and store as for satin icing.

Satin Icing

This is very similar to easy fondant icing, but the fat content gives it a particularly smooth finish, hence its name. The quantity given is sufficient to cover a 23 cm/ 9 in cake.

> 50g/2oz butter, margarine or
> white fat
> 2tbsp lemon juice
> 2tbsp water
> about 675g/1½lb icing sugar,
> sifted
> colouring as required

1 Put the fat and liquids in a saucepan and heat gently until the fat has melted. Add about one-third of the sugar and stir over a low heat until dissolved.

2 Increase the heat slightly and cook until the mixture just begins to boil. Remove from the heat.

3 Stir in another one-third of the sugar and beat well until evenly mixed. Turn the mixture into a mixing bowl.

4 Add sufficient of the remaining sugar to mix the icing to a firm paste. Dust the work surface with icing sugar and knead the icing until it is smooth.

5 Add a few drops of food colouring, if wished, and knead well until the icing is evenly coloured. Wrap the icing in a polythene bag or clingfilm, and place in an airtight plastic container. The icing will keep for several weeks in the refrigerator. To use, allow it to soften at room temperature then knead it until it is smooth.

COVERING CAKES WITH FONDANT ICING

Cold rolled fondant or sugar paste has a big advantage over royal icing because it can be used to cover a cake in a single operation. In an emergency, it may even be applied without marzipan, though the results may not be very satisfactory. Marzipan the cake and leave it for two or three days for the surface to harden. When rolling out a fondant, make sure that you do not have too much icing sugar on the work surface, or it will cause the paste to dry out. Use only enough icing sugar to prevent the fondant from sticking.

1 To colour the fondant, dip a cocktail stick into the food colouring and draw it across the surface of the fondant a number of times. Do not dig holes in the fondant, or you may introduce pockets of air which do not become apparent until the fondant has been rolled out ready for the cake.

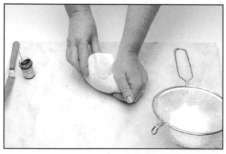

2 Knead the fondant in a circular motion to distribute the colour evenly. For a marbled effect, stop kneading before the colour has spread evenly throughout the piece of paste.

3 To test that you have an even colour, cut the fondant ball in half. If it is full of deeply coloured swirls and lines, you will need to knead it again, as the colour is not evenly distributed. Knead and test again – the results should be perfect.

4 Use alcohol or water to fix the fondant to the marzipan. Many people use brandy or rum for flavour, or sherry for economy. The alcohol helps to sterilize the surface of the cake and improves the flavour. The cake should be placed on a sheet of waxed paper to stop the work surface getting sticky. Moisten the cake all over – if you leave any spaces uncovered, air bubbles may form there. Remove the paper and put the cake on the work surface on a dusting of icing sugar.

5 Roll out the fondant icing on a surface lightly dusted with icing sugar. Lift the fondant and support it over both hands.

6 Drape the fondant over your right hand and arm. Put your other hand inside the fold of the fondant so that you can support it flat on both hands and arms.

7 Lay the fondant over the cake so that the side furthest away from you touches the work surface. Smooth it carefully over the top of the cake. The technique is the same as for covering a cake with marzipan.

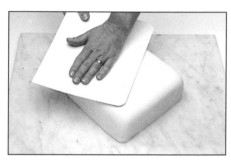

8 To obtain a really smooth glossy finish to the fondant icing use a large plastic smoother. Press down firmly and move it from side to side across the cake.

9 For the sides of the cake, hold the cake steady with the large smoother to avoid fingermarks. Using a smaller-handled smoother with a bevelled edge, smooth over the sides and round the corners of the cake.

10 The smoothing process may create a few air pockets on top of the icing. If it does, prick them with a pin, going diagonally through the fondant to the marzipan. Smooth the top again once the air has been pushed out.

Crimpers are used to make border patterns in fondant icing RIGHT. They are simple to handle and create a very consistent, attractive effect.

11 Push the cake to the edge of the work surface using a smoother, and then support the base of the cake on the palm of your hand. Hold it over the cake board and quickly withdraw your hand, allowing the cake to drop on to the board below. Adjust the cake to its final position using the smoothers. Note that the cake is secured to the board with a piece of fondant placed in the centre just before the cake is put on to it. When it is in place, press down on the top of the cake with the large smoother to flatten the ball of fondant and secure the cake.

12 While the fondant is still soft, crimp the cake. Crimpers, marzipan nippers or clippers are useful tools for impressing a pattern into fondant icing. They are available with nine different patterns. Draw out the design you want to use, and pin the paper pattern to the cake, then copy the design onto the cake. Remove the pattern and put a ribbon round the cake as a guide for maintaining a horizontal line. Remember not to release the crimpers too quickly or pull them away too fast or you will tear the fondant. They are very easy to use, and with half an hour's practice on a piece of fondant you will be skilled enough to produce quite a professionally decorated cake.

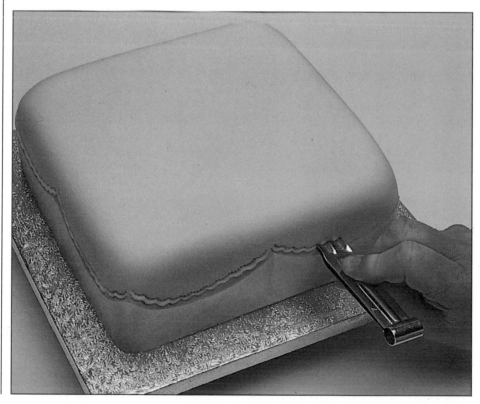

Glacé Icing

Glacé icing is simple and no cooking is involved. It is most suitable for sponges, small cakes and iced fancies. It sets very quickly and must be used while still warm. This quantity will cover an 18 cm/ 7 in cake or about 18 small cakes.

> 150g/5oz icing sugar
> about 1 tbsp warm water
> flavouring and colouring as
> required

1 Sift the icing sugar into a bowl and beat the warm water into it a little at a time until the required consistency is reached.

2 The consistency of glacé icing is important. It should be just thick enough to coat the back of a spoon so that it pours evenly onto the cake.

3 Add your chosen colouring and flavouring. Colouring paste is better than liquid colour because it does not affect the consistency of the icing. Paste colours are much stronger and more vibrant than the liquid varieties. They should be added sparingly with the tip of a cocktail stick.

Rich Orange Icing

> 100g/4oz icing sugar, sifted
> juice of 1 orange
> 1tbsp Stock Syrup (page 58)
> or water

1 Put the icing sugar with the orange juice in a small pan over a gentle heat and mix in the stock syrup or water to a creamy consistency. (Use stock syrup if possible because it gives a richer gloss to the finished icing than water.)

2 Pour over the cake. Candied orange peel softened in hot water, and thoroughly dried, makes an attractive decoration.

Real Chocolate Icing

Real chocolate icing is luxuriously rich. If it tends to get too stiff, you can either beat it over a pan of warm, but not hot, water, or add Stock Syrup (page 58).

> 175g/6oz plain chocolate, broken
> into small pieces
> 100g/4oz unsalted butter, cut into
> pieces
> 1 tbsp liquid glucose
> 2-3 tsp brandy or water

1 Put the chocolate, butter and liquid glucose in a double saucepan or a bowl over hot water and stir until smooth and completely melted.

2 Add the brandy or water and stir. Remove from the heat and allow to cool until almost set but still spreadable.

Buttercream

Buttercream is a simple combination of butter and sugar, beaten together to lighten it and eliminate any greasiness. The butter should be pale coloured. This can be used as a filling or as a topping.

> 100g/4oz unsalted butter,
> softened
> 175g/6oz icing sugar, sifted
> flavouring as required

1 Beat the butter until it is light and fluffy and then add the icing sugar a little at a time, until it is all incorporated. An electric mixer will save you a lot of hard work here. Alternatively use a balloon whisk to begin with to get the butter fluffy, and then a rotary whisk for incorporating the sugar.

2 The finished buttercream is thicker and stiffer than whipped cream, but light and white.

3 Buttercream can be left plain, or flavoured with vanilla, lemon, orange, chocolate, coffee, mocha or mint. To flavour it with chocolate, as here, mix in melted chocolate, which gives a smoother taste and finish than adding cocoa powder.

Crème au Beurre

Crème au beurre will keep in the fridge for a week or two, but it must be brought to room temperature and re-beaten before being used.

> 225g/8oz lump sugar
> 60ml/2½ fl oz water
> pinch of cream of tartar
> 6 egg yolks
> 350g/12oz butter

1 Put the sugar, water and cream of tartar in a saucepan and stir over a low heat until the sugar has completely dissolved. Wash the sides of the pan with a pastry brush dipped in cold water, to make sure no crystals are left sticking to it. Raise the heat and boil rapidly without stirring until the syrup reaches 115°C/240°F.

2 While the syrup is cooking, whisk the egg yolks until they are fluffy. Then, beating constantly, pour the boiled syrup in a thin stream onto the yolks. The mixture will become thick and light as it cools. Leave to cool completely.

3 Beat the butter to a light creamy consistency, then beat in the sugar and yolk mixture.

Custard Buttercream

> 50g/2oz sugar
> 150ml/¼pt milk
> 2 egg yolks, well beaten
> 175-225g/6-8oz unsalted butter, softened
> flavouring as required

1 Put the sugar and milk in a pan and bring to the boil, stirring. Pour it onto the yolks, stirring, and return the mixture to the pan. Cook very gently until thickened; *do not boil.*

2 Cream the butter well, then whisk in the custard a little at a time.

3 For a rich chocolate crème au beurre, beat 100 g/4 oz melted and cooled unsweetened milk chocolate and 3 tbsp cognac into the finished cream.

Continental Buttercream

This is cold cooked custard mixed with creamed butter. Either use packet custard or follow the recipe below, which is light but rich in flavour.

> 300ml/½pt milk
> 175g/6oz caster sugar
> 6 egg yolks
> 1 egg
> 350g/12oz unsalted butter

1 Put all the ingredients except the butter in a double saucepan and whisk over a low heat until the custard coats the back of a wooden spoon. Pour the custard into a cold basin, lay a piece of greaseproof paper or clingfilm directly on the surface of the custard and leave to cool.

2 Remove the paper or film. Beat the butter until it is quite light and soft, then work the cold custard into the butter.

Flavourings

*T*hese should be beaten into the finished buttercream until well blended.

Vanilla ½ tsp vanilla flavouring.

Lemon 1 tsp lemon juice with a little finely grated rind. Do not use the rind if the buttercream is to be piped.

Orange 1½ tsp orange juice with a little finely grated rind.

Chocolate 1 tbsp cocoa powder or 50 g/2 oz melted chocolate.

Coffee 1½ tsp instant coffee powder dissolved in ½ teaspoon hot water.

Mocha 1 tsp instant cocoa powder and 1 tsp instant coffee powder.

Mint 2 drops peppermint oil with a little green food colouring.

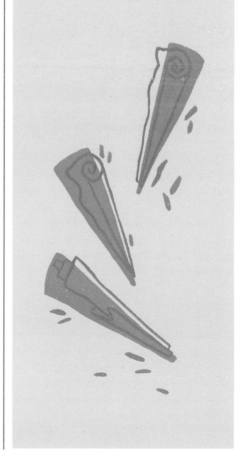

American Buttercream

> 225g/8oz butter (or half butter, half margarine), softened
> 150ml/¼pt milk
> ½ tsp salt
> 2 tsp vanilla essence (or rose water or orange flower water)
> 900g/2lb icing sugar

1 Put the butter, milk, salt and vanilla essence in a mixing bowl with half the sugar. Mix slowly, gradually incorporating the remaining sugar. Continue beating until light and fluffy.

2 Add flavourings, essences, colourings or liqueurs as required. Cover with a damp cloth and keep in a cool place until ready to use.

Bavarian Chocolate Cream

> 300 ml/½ pt plus 2 tbsp milk
> 40 g/1½ oz sugar
> 25g/1oz chocolate
> 1 egg
> 2 egg yolks
> 6g/¼oz cornflour
> a few drops of vanilla essence
> 1½ tsp gelatine

1 Put the 300 ml/½ pt milk, sugar and chocolate in a pan and bring it to the boil, stirring.

2 Mix the egg and yolks with the corn-flour and vanilla essence and pour the milk mixture into it. Stir over a gentle heat until thickened.

3 Warm the remaining milk and dis-solve the gelatine in it, then stir this into the custard and allow to cool.

4 For a richer cream whip 150 ml/¼ pt whipping cream with 15 g/½ oz caster sugar until fairly stiff, then fold it gently into the cooled custard.

The buttercreams illustrated here are (anticlockwise from top): Chocolate Crème au Beurre (p.43), Continental Buttercream (p.43) and American Buttercream (left). The cake is decorated with the Chocolate Crème au Beurre, walnuts and chocolate shavings.

FROSTINGS

These have the texture of marshmallow and they spread and swirl easily. They set quickly so have your utensils and cake decorations ready before you start.

American Frosting

This frosting is easily flavoured and coloured. In order to make it successfully, however, it is best to use a sugar thermometer. The quantity given is sufficient to cover the top and sides of a 23 cm/9 in sandwich cake. Half quantity is sufficient to cover a 23 cm/9 in ring cake.

> 350g/12oz granulated sugar
> 150ml/¼pt water
> 2 egg whites
> pinch of salt or cream of tartar
> flavourings and colourings as
> required

1 Place the sugar and water in a saucepan and heat gently until dissolved. Bring to the boil and boil steadily, without stirring, for about 10-15 minutes, to soft ball stage: 116°C/240°F. Remove the sugar syrup from the heat.

2 Whisk the egg whites with the salt or cream of tartar until stiff. Slowly pour the sugar syrup onto the egg whites, whisking all the time until cool and thick. As this takes 5-10 minutes, it is best to use a hand-held electric mixer.

3 Add any chosen flavourings and colourings, and use at once.

VARIATIONS

Lemon or other citrus fruits Beat in the grated rind of a medium lemon with 1 tbsp juice. Add a few drops of colouring if liked.
Coffee Whisk in 2 tbsp instant coffee powder dissolved in 2 tsp hot water.
Chocolate Whisk in 4 tbsp cocoa powder dissolved in 2 tbsp hot water.
Caramel Substitute soft brown sugar for the granulated sugar.

Seven-minute Frosting

This takes its name from the speed with which it is prepared. It is similar in texture to American Frosting, but it can be made without a sugar thermometer. The quantities given are sufficient to cover an 18-20 cm/7-8 in cake.

> 1 egg white
> 175g/6oz caster sugar or soft
> brown sugar
> 2 tbsp hot water
> pinch of salt or cream of tartar

1 Put all the ingredients in a bowl over a saucepan of hot water.

2 Whisk until the mixture thickens sufficiently to stand in soft peaks; this should take about 7 minutes using a hand-held electric mixer. Use at once.

VARIATIONS

Any flavourings should be added at the beginning with all the other ingredients. Follow the flavours for American Frosting, but use only *half* the amount.

Jam Frosting

Sufficient to cover a 20 cm/8 in cake.

> 3 egg whites
> pinch of salt
> 4 tbsp jam, warmed and sieved

1 Whisk the egg whites and salt until stiff enough to stand in peaks.

2 Whisk in the jam and continue to whisk for a further minute. Use this frosting at once.

A ring cake decorated with American Frosting and a loaf cake covered with Caramel Frosting. Instructions for making sugar bells can be found on page 134.

A hand-held electric mixer gives best results at all stages when preparing Marshmallow Buttercream.

Marshmallow Buttercream

A light and fluffy icing made by beating softened butter into a meringue mixture. The meringue can be made either by whisking egg whites and icing sugar over simmering water until stiff, or by boiling a sugar syrup to the hard ball stage and adding that to stiffly whisked egg whites. Both versions can be flavoured in the same way as buttercream and Crème au Beurre.

Recipe 1: sufficient to fill and top a 20 cm/8 in sandwich cake

> 2 egg whites
> 100g/4oz icing sugar, sifted
> 150g/5oz butter, softened
> flavouring as required

1 Place the egg whites and sugar in a bowl over a pan of simmering water. Whisk for 5-7 minutes until the mixture is thick and white.

2 Remove from the heat and continue whisking until cool.

3 Beat the butter until fluffy, then fold in the meringue mixture. Flavour as liked and use at once.

Recipe 2: sufficient to fill and cover a 20-23 cm/8-9 in cake

> 225g/8oz granulated sugar
> 100ml/4 fl oz water
> 4 egg whites
> 225g/8oz butter, softened
> flavouring as required

1 Place the sugar and water in a saucepan and heat gently until the sugar has dissolved. Bring to the boil, and boil until the syrup reaches the hard ball stage: 121°C/250°F.

2 Meanwhile, whisk the egg whites until stiff. As soon as the syrup is ready, pour it in a thin stream onto the egg whites, whisking all the time.

3 Continue to whisk until the mixture stands in stiff peaks. Leave to cool.

4 Beat the butter until fluffy, then fold in the meringue mixture. Flavour as liked and use at once.

VARIATIONS

The following quantities are used for recipe 1; for recipe 2 use double the amounts given.

Lemon or orange Add grated rind ½ lemon or orange and 1 tbsp juice.
Chocolate Add 50 g/2 oz melted chocolate, cooled.
Coffee Add 2-3 tsp coffee essence or instant coffee powder dissolved in a little hot water.
Praline Add 3-4 tbsp praline (page 59).

Fondant Buttercream

This is a good way of using up leftover fondant icing, use any one of the different recipes. It has a creamy texture similar to Crème au Beurre. The quantity given is sufficient to fill and cover a 20 cm/8 in cake.

> 175g/6oz fondant icing
> 1-2 tbsp Stock Syrup (page 58)
> 175g/6oz butter, softened
> flavouring as required

1 Warm the fondant with the syrup, in a bowl over hot water, until it is soft enough to beat.

2 Beat the butter until fluffy, then beat in the cooled fondant.

3 Flavour as liked and use at once.

To decorate
the sides of a cake

The sides of a cake can be spread with a buttercream, then left smooth, swirled with a knife or combed with an icing comb. If, however, a further coating, such as chopped nuts, is required the cake may first be spread with either apricot glaze or buttercream. For gâteaux, Crème au Beurre or fresh cream is usually used.

Spread the sides of the cake with a thin layer of buttercream or brush with apricot glaze.

Spread the chosen coating on a sheet of greaseproof or waxed paper and, holding the cake between the palms of your hands, gently roll it over the coating until evenly covered.

Sometimes a cake may be too delicate for this, in which case, the coating ingredient must be pressed against the sides of the cake using a palette knife.

Suitable coatings include: chopped nuts; toasted coconut; chocolate vermicelli; grated or chopped chocolate.

Fudge Icing

The basic recipe is a smooth fudge icing that turns golden during cooking, so don't worry and think you've spoiled it! The quantities given are sufficient to cover an 18-20 cm/7-8 in ring cake or a 20 cm/8 in sandwich cake.

> 150ml/¼pt single cream or
> soured cream
> 225g/8oz caster sugar
> 100g/4oz unsalted butter

1 Place the cream and sugar in a saucepan and heat very gently until the sugar has dissolved.

2 Increase the heat and boil the mixture for about 15 minutes, until it reaches the soft ball stage: 116°C/240°F. Stir frequently to prevent the mixture sticking to the pan. If you don't have a sugar thermometer, a small spoonful of the mixture should form a soft ball when dropped into cold water.

3 Leave to cool for about 2 minutes, then beat in the butter, a little at a time. If the icing starts to look oily, add an ice cube and beat vigorously until it has melted; this will return the icing to a good consistency.

4 Coat the cake, allowing the icing to run down the sides and using a palette knife as little as possible, or allow to thicken and spread over the cake.

VARIATIONS

Chocolate Beat in 50 g/2 oz plain chocolate, broken in pieces, with the butter.
Nut Beat in 25-50 g/1-2 oz finely chopped toasted nuts.
Coffee Beat in 1 tbsp instant coffee powder dissolved in 1 tsp hot water.

Lemon Fudge Icing

The quantities given in this recipe are sufficient to cover an 18cm/7in cake

40g/1½oz butter
2 tbsp lemon juice
225g/8oz icing sugar, sifted
grated rind of ½ lemon

1 Melt the butter and the lemon juice in a saucepan over a gentle heat. Bring to the boil.

2 Remove from the heat, add the sugar and lemon rind and beat well. Allow to cool slightly, then use at once.

VARIATIONS

Caramel Substitute milk and brown sugar for the lemon juice and icing sugar. Omit lemon rind.
Coffee Substitute milk for the lemon juice; add 1 tbsp instant coffee powder. Omit lemon rind.
Chocolate Substitute milk for the lemon juice; add 1-2 tbsp cocoa powder. Omit lemon rind.
Orange or lime Substitute orange or lime juice and rind for the lemon juice and rind used in the main recipe.

CHOCOLATE ICINGS

There are many different chocolate icings to make, but the easiest one is simply melted chocolate, though this does set hard and it is rather difficult to cut unless you use a hot knife.

Very simple icings can be made by just adding a little butter or fresh cream to melted chocolate. This softens the chocolate, making it more manageable and sometimes suitable for piping. Spirit, particularly rum, is often added.

Buttercream and Creme au Beurre can be flavoured with melted chocolate and glace icing can be made with some sifted cocoa powder in addition to the icing sugar.

CHOICE OF CHOCOLATE

There are many types of chocolate available and it may be confusing when it comes to deciding which one you should use for what purpose. Basically, chocolate can be divided into three categories.

Chocolate cake covering This is usually found in the baking section of the supermarket. It is not a true chocolate bar, but melts and spreads easily and is perfectly acceptable for everyday cakes and children's cakes. It is also slightly softer in texture than a true chocolate bar and is, therefore, easier to grate or to make into chocolate curls.

Cooking chocolate This is available in bars and as drops. It is very good for all icings and chocolate cookery.

Superior dessert chocolate An expensive choice, which should be used only for very special icings.

Right: In these step-by-step pictures, the milk and butter are warmed before the chocolate is added. The finished Chocolate Frosting is spread over the ring cake (below). Darker, Mocha Icing covers the plain round cake (far right).

Ganache

This is one of the richest chocolate icings imaginable! It is made from chocolate and double cream, which are melted together, then mixed to a dark, smooth icing. It can be spread as it is, or whipped to lighten it and increase the volume. Liqueur or spirit may be added as desired. Once whipped, Ganache pipes extremely well. The quantity given is sufficient to fill and cover a 20 cm/8 in cake.

250ml/8oz double cream
225g/8oz plain chocolate

1 Heat the cream to just below boiling. Remove from the heat.

2 Break the chocolate into small pieces and add to the cream. Leave for several minutes until the chocolate has melted. Beat well, then leave to cool.

3 If wished, whip the cooled chocolate icing until pale and doubled in bulk. Add spirit as desired. Use at once.

Mocha Icing

This is a very dark chocolate icing, flavoured with coffee. Pour it over a cake and allow it to flow down the sides. Use a palette knife as little as possible to spread it and it will set to a glorious shine. The quantity given is sufficient to cover a 20-23 cm/8-9 in cake.

100g/4oz caster sugar
3 tbsp cocoa powder
2 tbsp water
1 tsp instant coffee powder
75g/3oz butter

1 Heat the sugar, cocoa, water and coffee in a saucepan over a gentle heat, stirring all the time with a wooden spoon, until the sugar has dissolved.

2 Bring to the boil and simmer for 1 minute, remove from the heat.

3 Beat in the butter and allow to cool sufficiently to coat the back of a wooden spoon. Use at once.

Chocolate Frosting

This is a spreadable icing that can be swirled to give a decorative, yet quick finish to a cake. The quantity given is sufficient to cover a 20 cm/8 in cake.

100g/4oz plain or milk chocolate
25g/1oz butter
5 tbsp milk
300g/10oz icing sugar

1 Melt the chocolate and butter in the milk in a saucepan over a gentle heat.

2 Remove the pan from the heat. Add the icing sugar and beat well. Allow to cool before using.

QUICK AND EASY DECORATIVE TOPPINGS

These step-by-step pictures show how a plain loaf cake can be transformed by decorating it with meringue. The piped meringue is browned and fresh fruit completes the decoration.

Apart from icings, there are many simple yet highly effective ways of decorating a cake, using whipped cream, meringue or dredged icing sugar.

DECORATING WITH FRESH CREAM

Fresh cream makes a very good filling and 'icing' for a whisked sponge cake, transforming it into something quite special.

Double cream is the best cream to use as it whips well and holds its shape when piped. Whipping cream has a low fat content and is less firm than double cream. It can be used for spreading, but is not as good for piping. There are commercial cream substitutes in powder form, which pipe very well when reconstituted with milk.

Both cream and cream substitutes are piped through a large star nozzle rather than the smaller icing nozzles.

Whipped cream may be used as the finished covering of a cake. For the sides it can be smoothed or serrated using an icing comb, or used as a base for another covering, such as chopped nuts or sponge finger biscuits. The addition of fresh fruit on the top of the cake adds colour and texture. The fruit can be arranged on the surface and glazed with apricot glaze, then piped with whirls of whipped cream, or the cream can be the main decoration with a little fruit for added colour.

To whip fresh cream Place the cream in a bowl and, using a hand-held electric mixer or a balloon whisk, whisk the cream until it forms soft peaks. Be careful not to overwhip the cream as it will become very thick and granules will appear giving a slightly curdled appearance. This texture cannot be remedied.

Meringue

> 2 egg whites
> pinch of salt
> 100g/4oz caster sugar

1 Whisk the egg whites with the salt until stiff. Add the sugar a spoonful at a time, whisking thoroughly between each addition until a thick white meringue mixture is formed.

2 Use the meringue at once. Spread the sides of the cake with a thin layer of meringue. A thicker layer can be used as insulation for an ice-cream filling.

3 Spread the top of the cake with an even layer. Place the remaining mixture in a nylon piping bag fitted with a large star nozzle and pipe a decorative pattern.

4 Place the cake in the oven for 2-3 minutes until golden. Add any further decorations.

5 A meringue-covered cake is best eaten straightaway, but if it has an ice cream filling, it can be kept in the freezer for an hour or two until you are ready to serve it.

DECORATING WITH ICING SUGAR

Dredged icing sugar is the easiest decorative topping. Spoon a little icing sugar into a sieve and sift it over the surface of the cake. Use a palette knife to lightly score the surface with diagonal lines to create a simple pattern.

More elaborate results can be achieved by sprinkling the icing sugar over a doily, then carefully removing the doily.

Cocoa powder or drinking chocolate powder can be used as a second sprinkling to give a more intricate design.

DECORATING WITH MERINGUE

Meringue mixture pipes very well and effectively, and can be used in a similar way to fresh cream as a decoration. It should be browned very quickly for 2-3 minutes in a preheated oven. Any other decoration, such as whipped cream or fresh fruit, should be added afterwards.

Ginger Cream Filling

300ml/½pt Confectioner's
Custard (right)
50g/2oz preserved ginger, finely
sliced
grated lemon rind
2-3tsp ginger syrup
2 tbsp whipped cream

1 Put the custard with the ginger and lemon rind into a bowl, stir in the ginger syrup and fold in the cream.

2 If the filling is too thin, add some cake crumbs. Pineapple may be substituted for ginger.

Crème Pâtissière

This quantity is sufficient for filling and topping a 20 cm/8 in sponge.

2 egg yolks
50g/2oz caster sugar
15g/½oz cornflour, sifted
20g/¾oz plain flour, sifted
300ml/½pt milk
1 egg white
3 or 4 drops vanilla essence

1 Break up the yolks in a bowl, add the sugar gradually and cream well. Add the sifted flours with half the milk.

2 Bring the remaining milk to the boil and pour onto the egg mixture. Blend and return to the saucepan. Stir over the heat until the mixture reaches boiling point, then set aside.

3 Whip the egg white until stiff. Take about a quarter of the thickened cream from the pan and fold the whipped egg white gently into it. Then return the mixture to the pan and cook over a gentle heat for 3 to 4 minutes, folding the mixture occasionally and adding the vanilla essence. Turn it out into a basin to cool.

Confectioner's Custard

300ml/½pt milk
6tsp cornflour
2 egg yolks
½tsp vanilla essence
25g/1oz caster sugar

1 Warm the milk gently and blend in the cornflour. Bring to the boil, stirring and simmer for 5 minutes. Take the pan off the heat and allow to cool.

2 Stir in the egg yolks and vanilla essence. Do not be tempted to add the yolks before the custard has cooled, as they will curdle and start to cook.

3 Stir in the sugar, return to the heat and cook gently for a few minutes, without allowing it to boil. Once the sugar has dissolved, cover the pan and leave it to cool.

Moulding Icing

This is great fun to use as it can be moulded to any shape (rather like plasticine) making all sorts of novelty cakes well within the cakemaker's grasp! And if you are not happy with the shape you've moulded simply re-knead and start again.

Moulding icing also makes a softer (and far quicker) alternative to Royal Icing as a cake covering and is ideal for those who prefer a softer texture – although it will eventually set hard too.

Once made, wrap the icing tightly in foil or polythene and keep for up to 24 hours. Cornflour, rather than icing sugar, is used when rolling and shaping, as it helps produce a smoother surface and excess can easily be dusted off with a paint brush once the icing has hardened.

The liquid glucose or golden syrup are added to the mixture to prevent crystallization and keep the icing pliable.

2 egg whites
4tbsp liquid glucose or 2tbsp
golden syrup
900g/2lb icing sugar, sifted
colourings as required
cornflour for dusting

1 Place the egg whites and liquid glucose or golden syrup in a bowl. Gradually add the sifted icing sugar, working with a wooden spoon until the mixture is too stiff to stir.

2 Knead it into a firm ball. (You may find it easier to turn the mixture out onto a work surface and knead in the sugar as it becomes stiff.)

3 Dot the icing with food colouring, if using, and knead it in on a surface dusted with cornflour.

4 If you find that the icing is too soft when you roll it – losing its shape and becoming sticky – knead in more icing sugar. If it's too dry and has a tendency to crack, brush the icing with a little water and re-knead it.

Gelatine Icing

This is another variation on the types of fondant icing which can be used. This recipe and the one which follows are particularly easy alternatives.

> 4 tbsp water
> 15g/½oz gelatine
> 2 tsp liquid glucose
> 450g/1lb icing sugar
> cornflour

1 Put the water in to a small bowl and add the gelatine. Leave to soak for 2 minutes.

2 Stand the bowl over a saucepan of water.

3 Heat the water to simmering. Stir the gelatine all the time until all the lumps have dissolved and the liquid is clear. Remove the bowl from the pan and leave to cool for 2 minutes.

4 Add the liquid glucose to the gelatine mixture and stir until dissolved. Leave to cool for 2 minutes.

5 Place the sugar in a mixing bowl, then add the gelatine mixture and stir with a wooden spoon. If the mixture is a little wet, add more icing sugar.

6 Stir sufficient cornflour into the mixture in order to allow the icing to be worked like bread dough.

7 To store the icing wrap it tightly in a plastic bag. Any air coming into contact with the surface of the icing will cause it to get dry and hard, making it impossible to use.

Colouring Gelatine Icing

If the icing is to be coloured, the colour can be added to the warm gelatine mixture making it easier to incorporate into the icing. However, adding the colour in advance does mean that the colour may be darker than you had expected by the time you use the icing.

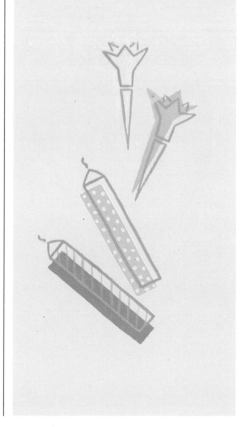

USEFUL BASIC RECIPES

Stock Syrup

This is simply sugar dissolved in water, which can be flavoured with liqueur or spirit, and is used to moisten sponge layers before assembling them with fresh cream or icing. It is also used to soften fondant icing so that it can be poured over a cake. Stock syrup may be stored in the refrigerator for several weeks in a screw-top jar or other container.

100g/4oz granulated sugar
150ml/¼pt water

1 Place the sugar and water in a saucepan and dissolve gently.

2 Bring to the boil and boil for 1 minute. Flavour with any liqueur or spirit to the desired strength.

Apricot Glaze

This is frequently spread over a sponge or sandwich cake before the layer of icing is applied. The sticky glaze ensures there are no loose crumbs that could stick to the icing and spoil the finished effect. It is also used to attach decorations to a cake, such as desiccated coconut or chopped nuts, to attach almond paste to a rich fruit cake, and as a glaze for fresh fruits on a gâteau.

225g/8oz apricot jam
2 tbsp water
squeeze of lemon juice

1 Place the jam, water and lemon juice in a small saucepan. Heat gently until the jam has dissolved, then boil for 1 minute. Strain and cool.

2 Any spare glaze can be stored in the refrigerator in a screw-top jar for several weeks. Warm the glaze gently to re-use.

VARIATION
Redcurrant glaze Replace the apricot jam with redcurrant jelly. Omit the water. No need to strain.

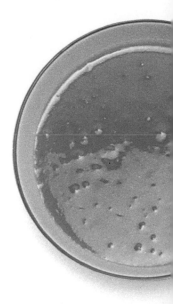

Praline

A delicious mixture of whole, unblanched almonds toasted with sugar to form a caramel. The caramel is usually finely chopped or ground and may be used as a decoration, or to flavour buttercreams or fresh whipped cream.

> 100g/4oz unblanched whole
> almonds
> 100g/4oz caster sugar

1 Place the almonds and sugar in a saucepan over a very low heat. Stir continually until the nuts are toasted and the sugar has caramelized to a rich golden colour.

2 Lightly butter or oil a baking sheet and pour the praline over the sheet. Leave until completely cold, then break into pieces.

3 Finely chop or grind the praline, or place in a thick plastic bag and pound it with a rolling pin. The praline may then be sieved if wished. Store in an airtight container.

Caramel

Sugar syrup can be boiled until it reaches a golden caramel colour. Once this has set hard the caramel can be broken into tiny pieces and used very effectively as a decoration. With a gas hob it is possible to put only sugar into a pan and heat it gently until caramelized. But with an electric hob, this is more difficult, so it is better to make a strong sugar syrup first and then boil it to a caramel stage.

> 100g/4oz caster or
> granulated sugar
> 3 tbsp water

1 Dissolve the sugar in the water in a saucepan over gentle heat. Bring to the boil and boil to a golden caramel.

2 Pour the caramel onto a buttered or oiled baking sheet and leave until set hard. Break into tiny pieces.

3 This does not store well, so make only sufficient for the decoration.

4 Caramel may also be used as a coating, rather like an icing. In this case, pour it directly onto the sponge layer and leave until starting to set. Mark out the portions of the cake with an oiled knife, otherwise the cake will be impossible to cut when the caramel is hard.

SIMPLE DECORATING TECHNIQUES

This section demonstrates the simpler methods of decorating cakes, with soft fillings and coatings, including very easy designs with a dusting of icing sugar and more elaborate piped buttercream coverings. If you are a beginner, you will find here an introduction to some of the basic techniques and tools of cake decoration.

The techniques are simple but create attractive effects, and include diamond marking, cobweb icing and feather icing, grooving, swirling and peaking, two ways to decorate a Swiss roll and coating sponge with soft fondant icing. All the cakes are ideal for afternoon tea or even to celebrate an informal festive occasion.

Attempting these decorations will give you practice in using some of the basic tools of the trade – the turntable, palette knives, cake combs, piping bags and food colour – and at the same time help you develop skills which can be applied to the more complicated aspects of cake decorating.

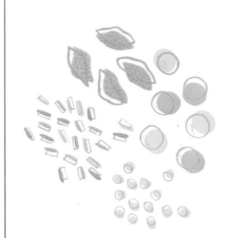

EQUIPMENT AND DECORATIONS

The techniques covered in this section require only fairly basic cake decorating equipment. The turntable is the most expensive item illustrated here, but if you are planning to take up cake decorating it is worth having from the very beginning.

1 *A heavy-duty metal turntable. Cheaper models are available in plastic.*
2 *Food paste colours*
3 *Crystallized violets*
4 *Crystallized rose petals*
5 *Angelica*
6 *Glacé cherries*
7 *Piped sugar flowers*
8 *Real chocolate strands or vermicelli*
9 *Silver and coloured balls or dragees*
10 *Piping bag stand, with two filled piping bags and nozzles*

11 *Thick paintbrushes, for cleaning up around a partially finished cake.*
12 *30 cm/12 in spatula*
13 *10 cm/4 in spatula or palette knife*
14 *Stainless steel rolling pin*
15 *Stainless steel profiled-edge scraper, for special effects on the side of a cake*
16 *Plastic scraper, for 'combing' the side of a cake*
17 *Parchment piping bag triangles*

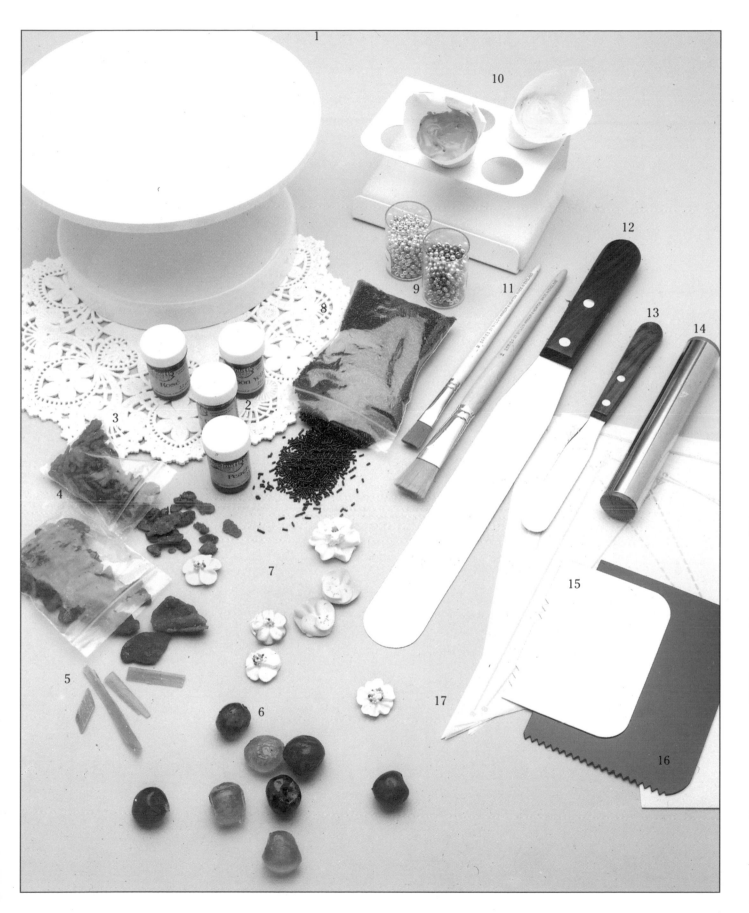

A VARIETY OF USEFUL CUTTERS

There is a fantastically wide range of biscuit and aspic cutters available in all sorts of shapes, such as numbers, alphabet, animals and geometric shapes. The best definition comes from metal cutters, though some plastic ones are available. Cutters are used frequently to stamp out marzipan and rolled moulding icings, and can also be used as templates for run-out designs.

BOUGHT CAKE DECORATIONS

Use almonds (whole, blanched, rubbed or flaked), preferably toasted; hazelnuts (whole, blanched or chopped), preferably toasted; shelled walnut halves; shelled pecan halves and shelled and skinned pistachios (whole or chopped).

To toast nuts, either place them on a baking sheet in an even layer and put under a medium grill, turning from time to time, until evenly browned, or place them in the oven at 180°C/350°F/Gas 4 for about 10 minutes until evenly browned. This is also the way to loosen skins from hazelnuts. After toasting, allow the nuts to cool a little, then place them in a paper bag and rub between the palms of your hands until the skins flake off.

To skin pistachios, almonds and walnuts, bring to the boil in a minimum of cold water, drain immediately and drop into cold water. Drain again. With almonds, simply rub the skins off. For pistachios and walnuts use a small sharp knife to remove the skins. Leave the nuts to dry on absorbent kitchen paper.

Coconut is available as desiccated or as long thread. It is useful for coating the sides of cakes. It can be toasted to a light golden colour by placing it in a shallow tin and baking at 180°C/350°F/Gas 4 for 10 minutes.

Small biscuits can be used to cover the sides of cakes or to give an extra decoration to the top of a cake, for example, florentines, sponge finger biscuits, brandy snaps, cigarellas.

Chocolate coffee beans have a chocolate centre or a liquid coffee centre. Chocolate vermicelli is useful for coating the sides of cakes.

Crystallized rose and violet petals are commercially prepared and sold loose or in small tubs.

Mimosa balls are small yellow flowers of the Mimosa bush, also commercially crystallized.

Dragées are available in silver and other colours, as well as in a range of sizes.

Small sweets or candies look particularly good on children's novelty cakes.

Icing flowers are available from specialist suppliers and are sold individually.

Leaves, such as scented geranium, lemon balm and strawberry, may be used as decoration, either plain or sugared.

Chocolate decorations can be made at home, but small pieces of chocolate or chocolate sweets can also be used as decoration.

Sugar strands, hundreds and thousands and other sugared decorations are available in tubs from supermarkets.

Edible food colourings are available in liquid and paste form, as well as in felt-tipped pens, which are ideal for fine details. Add food colouring to icing a drop at a time.

Apart from glacé cherries, angelica and ginger, there are many crystallized fruits available either in boxes or loose, from specialist confectioners.

INEDIBLE CAKE DECORATIONS

A selection of inedible cake decorations is illustrated here. The more conventional decorations for celebration cakes include wedding bells and horseshoes, keys for 18th and 21st birthdays, cupid for an engagement or valentine, and a variety of flowers. For sporting birthday cakes, there are tennis rackets, golf clubs and footballers. For children, there are animals, robots and a toy train with a candle on each carriage. The rosette is made from a laced ribbon – when the laces are pulled, the ribbon loops up into the rosette shape.

The range is almost infinite. You can, after all, put anything you like on a cake.

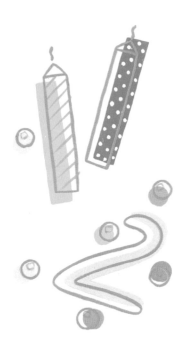

DECORATING CAKES WITH FRESH FRUIT

The colours and textures of fruits, especially soft fruits and some of the tropical varieties, finish off a cake beautifully. Take care in preparation to cut even-shaped pieces and brush them with apricot or redcurrant glaze when using fruit as a complete covering to stop it drying out. Single pieces of fruit need not be glazed when used as additional decoration. Drained, canned fruit can also be used when fresh fruit is unavailable.

CHERRIES AND REDCURRANTS
Use on or off the stem, either plain or coated in sugar.

ORANGE SEGMENTS
Cut the white pith away from the orange with the peel. Use a sharp knife to remove each segment from the skin which holds the orange together. Do this over a small bowl to catch all the juices. You can also make decorative twists from orange, lime and lemon slices.

JULIENNE STRIPS OF ORANGE, LEMON OR LIME
Pare the rind from the fruit with a vegetable peeler and cut it into very fine strips with a sharp knife or pair of scissors. If wished, bring to the boil in cold water, drain at once and plunge into cold water, drain again and dry on kitchen paper.

PEACHES, NECTARINES AND PLUMS
Stone and slice these fruits and dip them in lemon juice to prevent discoloration.

STRAWBERRIES AND RASPBERRIES
Use whole, hulled or unhulled, halved or cut into slices.

BANANA AND APPLE
Remember to dip sliced banana and apple in lemon juice to prevent discoloration. Add these ingredients to a cake shortly before it is to be served.

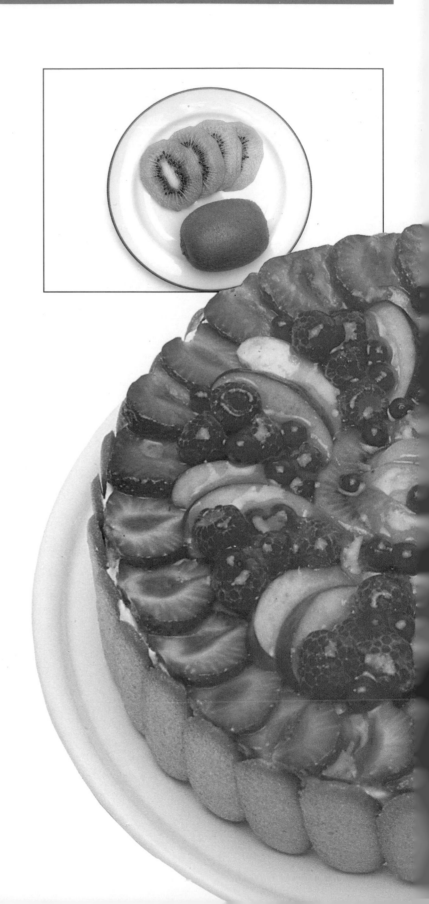

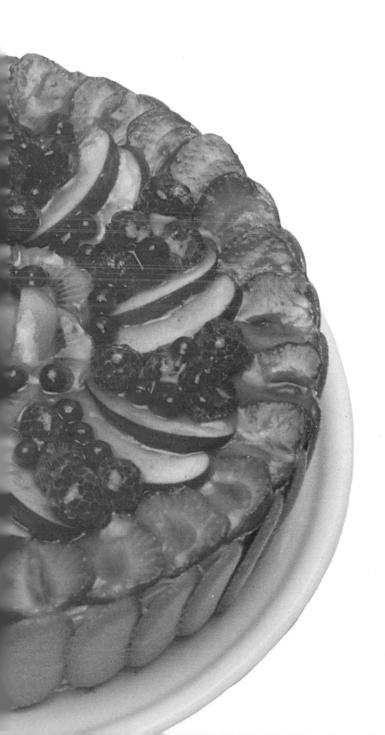

DECORATING SPONGES

Over the following dozen or so pages you will discover a wide variety of ways in which simple sponge cakes can be transformed into decorative centrepieces. All the methods and techniques are fairly simple and, with a little patience, perfect results can be achieved every time.

FILLING

A Victoria sandwich is traditionally filled with whipped cream and jam, either strawberry or raspberry, for a good contrast in flavour.

Spread one half of the cake with cream, and the other with jam, using a flat palette knife. Do not try to spread them one on top of the other. Sandwich the two halves together.

COATING THE SIDES OF THE CAKE

Buttercream makes a very good coating for the sides of a sponge cake. It is particularly useful for a sandwich cake because it covers the join and gives a smooth finish. The cake can then be rolled in silver balls, chocolate, nonpareils, chopped nuts, muesli or finely chopped glacé fruit.

1 Smooth the buttercream round the sides of the cake with a palette knife.

2 Fill your palm with chopped nuts or golden praline and brush the nuts against the buttercream all round the base.

3 If you want to coat the sides of the cake completely, spread a layer of the decoration on paper and roll the cake in it.

DUSTING

1 For a very pretty dusting on top of the cake, cover it with a paper doily and gently tap icing sugar from a sieve onto the cake.

2 Remove the doily very carefully, lifting it straight upwards, or you will spoil the pattern beneath. Use this technique, too, with home-made stencils. If you are giving the cake as a present for example, you can stencil the person's name over the top.

The cake features chocolate vermicelli around the base, a piped rope of Bavarian Buttercream around the edge, and segments of crystallized orange on the top. Simple decorations such as these can make the plainest cake very special.

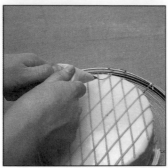

Glacé Icing is easily applied to a sponge cake; here the cake is decorated with quilted icing.

USING GLACÉ ICING

This very simple icing is used to decorate sandwich or sponge cakes. It can be coloured and flavoured in many ways; if adding a liquid flavouring, such as a liqueur, omit an equivalent amount of the water. The quantity given in the basic recipe will cover the top and sides of a 20 cm/8 in cake; use half the quantity for the top only.

Apart from its use as a coating, glacé icing may be piped, using a plain or writing nozzle (no 2 or no 3). However, it is not firm enough to make rosettes and whirls. Piped rosettes or swirls of buttercream may be added to an iced cake for further decoration.

TO COAT THE TOP OF A CAKE

Place the cake on a plate or board. If desired, brush the top with a thin layer of Apricot Glaze (page 58).

Pour or spoon the icing onto the centre of the cake. Using a palette knife, spread the icing carefully to the edges. Dip the clean palette knife in hot water and smooth the icing.

Tap the plate gently on the work surface to release any air bubbles and give a smooth finish. Burst any small air bubbles with a pin, then leave to set for at least 1 hour.

An alternative method of coating the top of a cake is to make a greaseproof or waxed paper collar about 1 cm/½ in deeper than the cake. Wrap the collar tightly round the cake and secure with a paper clip. Pour the icing on to the cake and spread it to the edges. Leave the icing to set before carefully removing the collar.

If decorations are to be added, press these into the icing before it sets completely. If piped icing is to be added, pipe it on when the base coat is completely set.

TO COAT THE TOP AND SIDES OF A CAKE

Follow the basic rules for coating the top, but allow the icing to flow down the sides and carefully smooth it with a wetted palette knife. Once the icing is set the excess may be scraped from the plate or board. An alternative method is to place the cake on a wire rack over a plate or piece of greaseproof or waxed paper, and allow the excess icing to drip through. Once the icing is set, the cake can be carefully removed from the rack.

QUILTED ICING

Use a no 2 or no 3 plain or writing nozzle and pipe parallel lines 1–2 cm/½–¾ in apart over the set base coat. Always start with a central line and pipe either side of it. Turn the cake and pipe another series of parallel lines at an angle to the first, thus producing a diamond pattern.

Press a small flower or dragée on to the icing at each intersection. Leave to set. Contrasting coloured icings should be used to give a bold effect.

FEATHER ICING

Make the glacé icing and reserve about 2 tablespoons of it. Colour this a contrasting colour or, if liked, colour each tablespoon of icing a different colour.

Make one or two small greaseproof paper piping bags (page 90) and insert a no 2 or no 3 plain or writing nozzle. Fill with the reserved icing.

Coat the top of the cake with remaining icing. While still wet, pipe parallel lines in coloured icing, about 2.5 cm/1 in apart, across the cake. Using a skewer or wooden cocktail stick, *quickly* draw it across the cake at right angles to the piped lines. Turn the cake and draw the skewer in the opposite direction between the first series of markings. Leave to set.

Feather Icing is easy and it is attractive on both large or small cakes.

COBWEB ICING

Follow the directions for feather icing above, but instead of parallel lines, pipe circles of icing about 2.5 cm/1 in apart. Draw the skewer across the piped lines at regular intervals, starting at the outside edge and working towards the centre. If liked, draw the skewer in the opposite direction between the first series of markings. Leave to set.

FLAVOURING GLACÉ ICING

Glacé icing can be flavoured and coloured in many ways, as already mentioned. The following suggestions are the most usual variations which are used but exercise your imagination to create your own favourite icings. Remember that liquid flavourings must be used in place of water, *not* in addition to it.

Vanilla Use 1 tsp vanilla essence in place of the same amount of water.
Orange, lemon, lime, grapefruit or other fruit juice Substitute strained fruit juice for the measured amount of water.
Coffee Dissolve 1 tbsp instant coffee powder in the measured water.
Chocolate Substitute 2 tbsp sifted cocoa powder for an equal quantity of icing sugar.
Liqueur Substitute your chosen liqueur for an equal amount of water. Use at least 1 tbsp liqueur, but increase this if wished.
Adding colouring Add just a few drops of the appropriate colouring. It is best to drop the colouring off a cocktail stick to avoid adding too much at once.

The sides and top of this cake have been decorated with buttercream, combed with a serrated comb, and a strip of golden praline laid around the base. The spiral effect on the top has been made by putting the cake on a turntable and holding a palette knife over it like the arm of a record player while the cake is rotated.

ROSETTES

1 To make rosettes, fill a large piping bag with buttercream and use a star nozzle (no 15). Pipe the rosettes in a circular motion, one at a time – if you try to pipe them continuously, they will turn into scrolls.

2 Finish decorating the cake with green glacé cherries, cut into segments and positioned on the sides between the rosettes. Make a flower shape of glacé pineapple with a yellow glacè cherry for its centre on the top.

PEAKING

1 Cover the top of the sponge with butter icing and use a palette knife to pull it up into peaks.

2 Sprinkle the top with coloured strands and add a gold ribbon for a festive effect.

DIAMOND MARKING

1 Cover the sides of the sponge with chocolate vermicelli and spread the top with chocolate buttercream. Make a diamond pattern by pulling a skewer through the buttercream as shown.

2 Pipe simple shells round the edge of the top of the cake using a star nozzle (no 11 or 12) and chocolate buttercream.

Simple decorating techniques can produce attractive results. The chocolate cake above is diamond marked with a border of piped shells.

BUTTERCREAM DECORATIONS

Buttercream is a smooth spreadable icing, which can be easily made into an effective pattern. The illustrations here highlight the many simple ways in which the buttercream can be used to create patterns. The starting point for all these is to spread an even layer of buttercream on the cake.

1 Use a fork to make a circular design on a round cake, or straight or wavy lines on a square cake. If wished, mark the cake into sections with a knife.

2 Using a palette knife, work the icing from side to side, slightly overlapping the lines made by the knife each time.

3 Using a palette knife, start from the centre of the cake and make swirls to the edge, each time overlapping the previous swirl.

4 Use a palette knife to make a general swirling pattern.

Buttercream also pipes very well and can be used in many ways to give a decorative effect. All of the piped designs shown opposite are achieved by using a star nozzle. The size of the nozzle can be varied according to the result that is required.

1 Straight parallel lines in one or more contrasting colours.

2 Rosettes in lines or circles, in one or more contrasting colours.

3 Large shells or rosettes around the edge of the cake.

4 A lattice effect over the surface of the cake.

5 Scrolls on each marked portion of the cake.

6 Pipe elongated loops from the centre to the outside edge of the cake and fill each loop with jam.

SWIRLING

1 As well as a palette knife, you can use a cake comb to create all sorts of patterns in buttercream. Hold the comb against the side of the cake as you rotate it on a turntable, or move it from left to right across the top to make waves, as here.

2 Pipe stars round the edge of the cake and finish it off with a white satin ribbon.

Always make a generous quantity of buttercream when decorating cakes like the one shown below. A lot of buttercream is scraped off as the pattern is made.

GROOVING

1 Use a cake comb with chocolate buttercream to create this complicated looking effect very simply. Rotate the cake on a turntable and move the comb sideways to make undulations. Be careful when you get back to the beginning of your pattern not to make a ridge. Use a deeply grooved comb on the sides of the cake.

2 Pipe a rosette in the centre, and beading around the top and bottom edges of the cake.

USING FONDANT ICING FOR FINE RESULTS

These techniques are commonly used with glacé icing; here you can see how they can be applied to fondant. Fondant icing does not set on the surface quite as rapidly as glacé icing, so it does allow more time for piping.

COBWEB ICING

1 Pour the fondant over the top of the cake. Pipe concentric circles of chocolate icing, fondant or melted chocolate on the fondant. Start from the centre and work outwards. When the circles are completed, draw a skewer across the cake from the centre outwards, dividing it into quarters. Draw the skewer from the edge of the cake inwards, dividing it into eighths.

2 Brush the sides of the cake with a little egg white or apricot glaze. Use a palette knife to press green coloured coconut onto the sides of the cake.

FEATHER ICING

Here the feather icing technique which was earlier discussed for glacé icing is applied to fondant icing.

1 Pour the fondant over the top of the cake. The cake can have a marzipan base. Pipe straight lines of chocolate icing, fondant or melted chocolate across the cake. The best way of keeping the lines parallel is by working from the centre outwards. Starting at the centre of the cake, draw a skewer through the lines in the opposite direction, leaving a double space between the lines. Turn the cake round and repeat the process in the other direction creating a feather pattern.

2 Brush the sides of the cake with a little egg white or apricot glaze and use a palette knife to press green coloured coconut all round the cake.

VARIATIONS ON FEATHER ICING

Feather icing can be used in a variety of ways, on both large or small cakes. The basic technique can be used on square cakes as well as on round ones. Fondant icing gives a fine result and enables the simple decoration to be incorporated as part of a more elaborate design.

Square or oblong cakes can be topped with feather icing, working diagonally across the cake instead of parallel to the sides. The feather technique can be used on one area of the cake, for example across opposite corners, leaving a central band of plain icing. Flower decorations or a piped message can be added to the plain band of icing when the base coat is thoroughly dry.

Vary the idea of feathering a round cake
by piping a circle of icing round the top of the cake about 5 cm/2 in in from the edge. Complete the feathered decoration within the band, leaving the centre of the cake free for adornment.

Always plan the design before you ice the cake, drawing a pattern to follow so that you know exactly what you are aiming to achieve once the cake is coated in fondant.

To colour coconut for the cobweb-iced cake above, rub a little food colour onto your fingers and work them through the coconut. This method gives a good even colour.

SPLIT SPONGES

TRIANGULAR TOP

1 Spread one half of a Victoria sandwich with buttercream and pipe two rows of shells around the edge. Cut the second cake in half horizontally with a very sharp serrated knife and use the bottom slice. Dredge the top with icing sugar, making a pattern through a doily. Cut it carefully into three. Position the three pieces on top of the cake with a cake slice. They will project like wings. The top cake can be left whole but the pieces will not balance as lightly on the cream.

2 Pipe lines of cream shells over the joins. Decorate the top with split almonds, angelica and a cherry in the centre.

HALVED TOP DECORATION

1 Spread one half of a Victoria sandwich with buttercream. Draw a line over the cream with a skewer to give the half-way mark. Pipe a double row of butter-cream shells around half the cake, piping them more heavily in the middle than at the sides. Do the same around the other half if you want to create a butterfly effect with the finished cake.

2 Dredge the top of the second layer with icing sugar and cut it in half. Mark a decorative pattern in the icing sugar with a skewer as shown.

3 Being careful not to touch the top of the cake with your fingers, which leave prints, place the two halves in position on top of the buttercream shells using a cake slice.

4 Pipe a line of buttercream shells across the join and decorate with cherries or angelica.

DECORATING CAKE ROLLS

Cylindrical cakes are usually made with sponge mixture which is rolled up but they can also be made by baking a fruit cake mixture in a cylindrical tin. Here, the base for the decorations is a plain Swiss roll mixture.

1 Cover the Swiss roll with buttercream, taking it down the sides. Leave the base and the ends uncovered.

2 Press chocolate vermicelli onto the bottom half of the sides of the cake. Pipe ridges along the top with a star nozzle or mark ridges with a fork.

3 Pipe a line of shells across the centre of the cake and decorate it with walnuts, cherries or angelica.

YULE LOG

This traditional Yule log decoration makes a simple, but attractive Christmas cake.

1 To make the ends of the log look like sawn wood, roll out a thin square of creamy yellow fondant icing and brush it with brown food colour diluted in water. Cut the paste into strips. Join the strips up into a continuous length and roll up.

2 With a very sharp knife, cut two thin slices off the roll. Set the roll aside.

3 Flatten the slices to merge the strips into one, and create a pattern of rings to resemble those in a piece of wood. Cut the circles to fit the ends of the cake.

4 Fix the circles to the ends of the cake with chocolate buttercream. Cover the sides with forked buttercream.

5 For the sawn-off branches, roll a fat sausage of brown marzipan about 1.5 cm/¾ in thick. Cut the ends off at 90 degrees to the roll and then cut it in two with a diagonal cut.

6 Position the diagonal ends in the buttercream. Cut two small circles from the fondant icing roll to cover the ends of the branches. Cover the branches with buttercream and use the back of a fork to create bark as before.

7 Finish the decoration with a robin and an axe and sift the cake with icing sugar for a snowy effect.

COATING AND PIPING WITH FONDANT

COATING SIMPLE FANCIES

To make simple fondant icing to cover fancies, break down a Continental or Australian Fondant (pages 36/37) with Stock Syrup (page 58).

Melt the fondant in a basin over hot water. Do not let the water boil, or the shine will be lost from the cooled fondant. It may take 15 to 20 minutes to melt. Add enough stock syrup to make a soft flowing icing that will coat the back of a spoon. It is important not to stir the icing too vigorously, or you will incorporate air bubbles.

Fancies can be cut from slabs of sponge to any shape. Popular shapes are diamonds, squares, circles and hearts. To ensure clear shapes, always wipe the knife or cutter to remove any traces of cake between each cut. Coat the fancies with warm apricot jam and, for a more professional finish, cover them with marzipan.

1 Dip the cake into the fondant. The marzipan or apricot glaze will prevent crumbs getting into the fondant. Push the cake right down, so that the sides are evenly coated.

2 Using a fork, and being careful not to put your fingers in the icing, lift the cake out of the fondant.

3 Set it on a wire rack. The fondant will level itself out on the cake and any excess will drip off the bottom. You can scrape this up afterwards, warm it and use it again.

4 Finish the cakes by setting them in paper cups when dry, and piping a design on the top. You can also use fondant for piping (overleaf), melted down and mixed with a little stock syrup to make it quite runny.

COATING A ROUND CAKE

Prepare the cake by glazing it with warm apricot jam and/or marzipan. Melt the fondant in a basin over hot water and add stock syrup to thin it down if necessary.

1 Stand the cake on a wire rack and pour the fondant carefully onto the centre of it. Give it a fairly thick coating so that it will run over the sides of the cake. The excess will drip through.

2 Use a palette knife to smooth over the top and sides of the cake. Tap the wire rack a few times on the work surface to settle the icing. As it settles, it will drip off the base. It is important to use a wire rack, so that the fondant does not build up at the bottom of the cake.

COATING A SQUARE CAKE

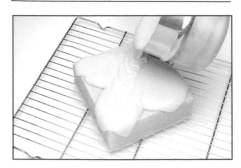

1 Prepare the fondant as for a round cake, and stand the square cake on a wire rack. Pour the fondant over the cake from corner to corner in a diagonal cross.

2 Use the palette knife to push the fondant from the centre of the cake to the sides and down the edges, working fairly fast before it starts to set. Tap the wire rack on the work surface to settle the fondant and dislodge any air bubbles.

PIPING WITH FONDANT

1 Add a little melted chocolate to some fairly runny fondant and pipe it straight from the piping bag, cut off at the point to give a fine line. Some chocolate piping designs are shown on pages 136/137. Embroidery pattern books are also a good source of ideas for attractive designs.

2 A more complicated design is piped on the round cake, using five colours of fondant. To stop the petals flowing into each other, pipe alternate petals and wait for them to set slightly before piping the petals in between.

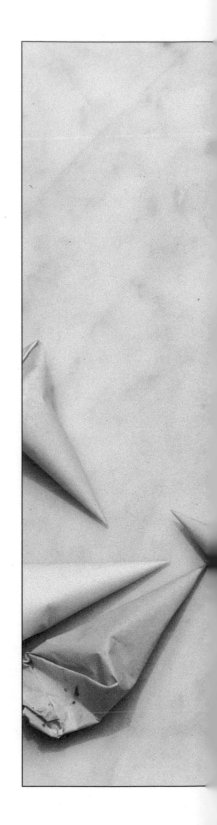

Fondant is piped straight from the bag without a nozzle. It can be used to create fairly intricate effects as shown here.

ELABORATE DECORATING TECHNIQUES

This chapter explains and illustrates some of the more complicated techniques of cake icing. They are perfected by practising and a good way to do this is on a polystyrene cake dummy. Try out the different piping techniques on it and this will help you choose your cake design, by giving you a chance to discover which types of decoration you like and find easy.

This section opens with the fundamentals that must be acknowledged: starting with the essential equipment and how each item should be used. The effects that can be achieved are illustrated with step-by-step guidance to ensure success. Making lace, run-outs, piping flowers and borders are all included, and finally making templates for positioning pillars on tiered cakes and assembling tiers is outlined.

EQUIPMENT

The equipment illustrated opposite is a selection of items used in the preparation of elaborately decorated cakes.

1 Heavy-duty icing turntable
2 Plaster wedding cake pillars
3 Plastic wedding cake pillars, with hollow centres for wooden skewers
4 Polystyrene cake dummy for practising and display purposes
5 Wooden skewers
6 A selection of shaped 4 cm/½ in thick cake boards and thin cake cards
7 Large flexible plastic icing smoother for fondant icing
8 Small stainless steel scraper for royal icing
9 Small flexible plastic smoother
10 Stainless steel straight edge for applying royal icing
11 Short spatula for general mixing and filling work
12 Handled smoother for fondant icing – an alternative to the large flexible smoother
13 Silver banding for cakes and cake boards

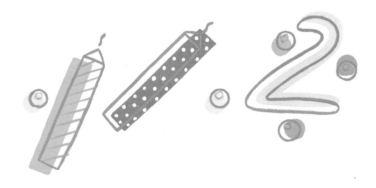

SPECIALIST EQUIPMENT

The illustration shows a collection of tools that are used for creating the elaborate decorative designs which follow in this chapter.

1 Cotton-coated floristry wire

2 Modelling tools (from left to right): paddle and U shape (no 4); Shell and blade (no 2); Cone and star tool (no 5); Ball tool (no 3); Dog bone shape (no 1)

3 Stainless steel scriber, for marking patterns onto icing

4 Nozzle cleaning brush

5 Fine-pointed tweezers

6 Cranked handle palette knife

7 Set of crimpers

8 Stainless steel rolling pin

9 Selection of fine paintbrushes

10 Selection of edible food colour pens

11 Strong paste food colours

12 Dry colour

13 Frill or flounce cutter

14 Flower cutters (top row from left to right); Briar rose; Serrated rose leaf; Blossom-shaped plunger cutters; (bottom row from left to right) Rose petal or Azalea petal cutters; Star or rose calyx cutters

15 Selection of 1 cm/½ in aspic cutters

16 Flower nails

17 Selection of graduated biscuit cutters

18 Hollow plastic bell-shaped moulds

19 Selection of numeral cutters

20 Artificial stamens

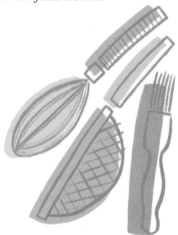

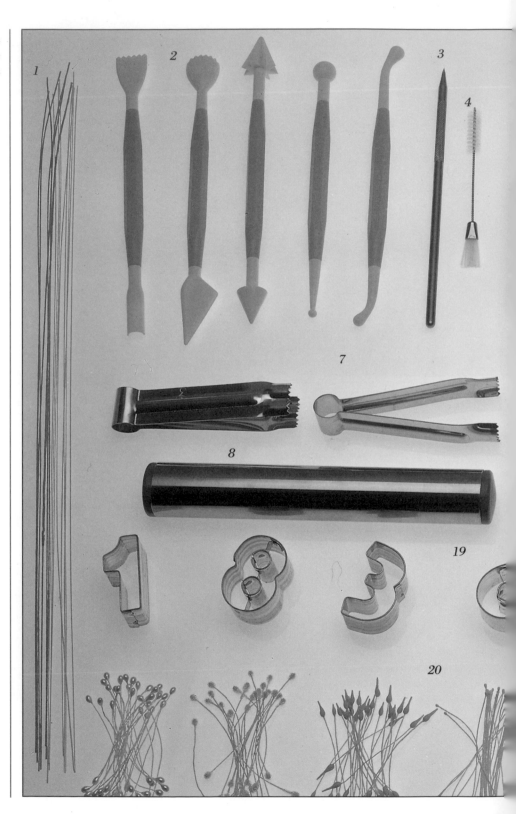

PIPING BAGS

For intricate decorating work, paper piping bags are essential.

If you are doing multi-coloured work or using different nozzles, have several piping bags ready. The metal syringe-type piping equipment is not suitable for delicate cake decorating as this type of equipment does not give fine results and it is not easy to achieve precise movements.

Nylon and cotton piping bags are too large for this type of work. However most good suppliers sell ready-made grease-proof paper piping bags.

MAKING A PIPING BAG

Making paper piping bags for fine decorative work is not difficult. Use either greaseproof or waxed paper or use packs of ready-cut paper.

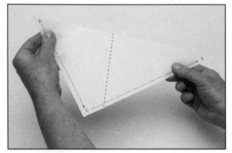

1 Cut a 25 cm/10 in square of greaseproof or waxed paper. Fold it in half diagonally to make a triangle. Mark points (A), (B) and (C) in the corners as illustrated.

2 With the point of the triangle (C) facing towards you and holding the triangle at points (A) and (B), fold (B) round and back over (A).

3 Hold point (A) firmly and pull point (B) towards you to complete the cone shape. Take point (B) round to point (C).

4 To secure the piping bag, fold in the loose ends over the top edge and staple them together.

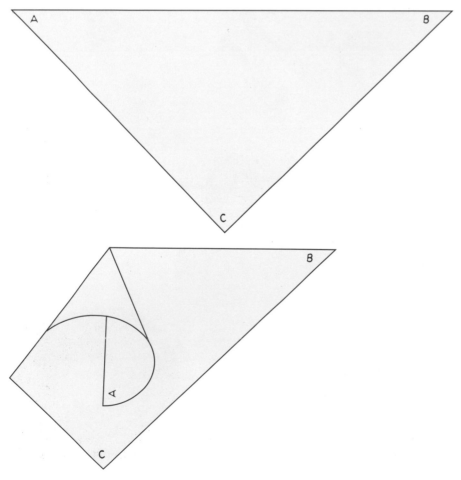

FILLING A PIPING BAG

1 Cut off the tip of the piping bag and insert the required nozzle. Take care not to cut off too large a portion of the tip.

2 Hold the piping bag in your left hand with your thumb at the back.

3 Using a palette knife, fill the bag half to two-thirds full. Push the icing down into the back of the bag against your thumb. Take care not to overfill as the icing may overflow from the top or the bag may burst.

4 With your thumb, push the back of the bag right down over the icing.

5 Carefully fold the sides of the bag in towards the centre, then fold over the top, pushing the icing down gently towards the tip. Fold over one corner again, making a pad to push with your thumb.

TIP

*H*ave a damp cloth at hand to wipe the nozzle in between pipings and to help stop the tube getting clogged with hardened icing. If using several bags to decorate a cake, always cover the tips of them when not in use with a damp cloth, or stand them nozzle downwards in an icing bag stand filled with a dampened sponge.

HOLDING A PIPING BAG

1 Hold the piping bag between your middle and index fingers and push with your thumb.

2 Place the tip of the nozzle in position over the work, before beginning to push the icing through the bag. Pressing down with your thumb on the folded part of the bag, squeeze out the icing. Pressing with and releasing your thumb will cause the icing to flow, then stop. Because the icing continues to flow after the pressure has stopped, you must release the pressure on the bag before you reach the end of the line to be piped. If you watch carefully to see how the icing flows, you will quickly learn to judge the pressure and movement required.

3 Once you have mastered piping straight lines, try using a star nozzle for shells. Position the nozzle on the surface where you want to pipe the shell. Without moving the bag, push out the icing. Once the shell has formed, pull the bag back to form a tail. Pipe the next shell so that it just overlaps the first one.

IDENTIFYING ICING NOZZLES

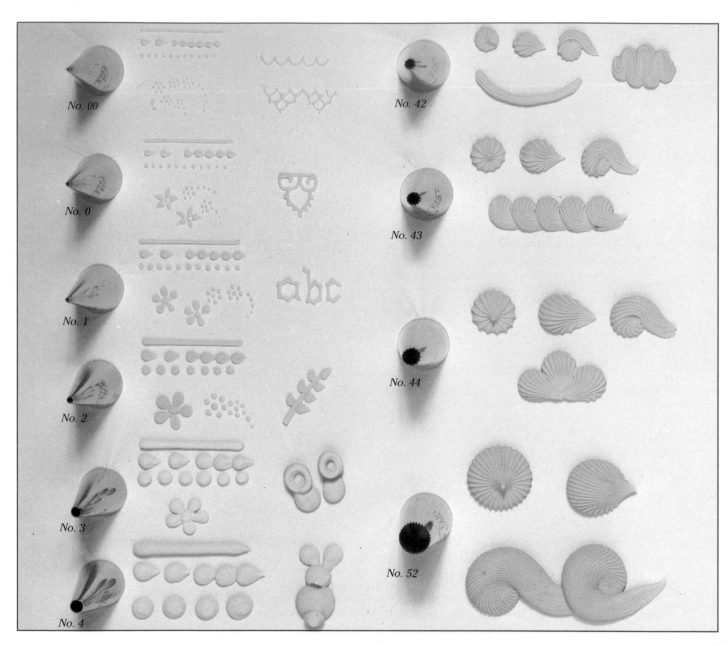

There are many different kinds of icing nozzle on the market. Different manufacturers use different numbers to designate the widths of the nozzles, but smaller numbers always refer to finer nozzles. The choice of nozzle sizes is also very much a matter of personal preference. The photographs above and right illustrate the most popular nozzles and the effects which can be achieved when using them. Experiment with types of nozzles and different designs before deciding which you prefer. It is a good idea to perfect one or two techniques and to use them regularly rather than to achieve inferior results by always using a different nozzle.

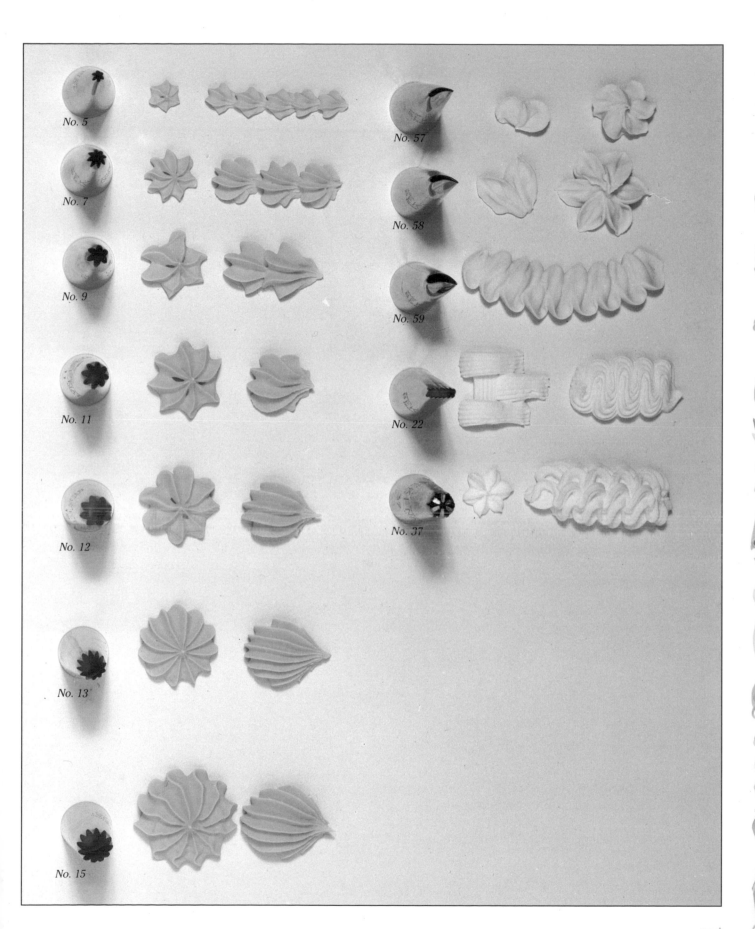

No. 5

No. 7

No. 9

No. 11

No. 12

No. 13

No. 15

No. 57

No. 58

No. 59

No. 22

No. 37

PIPING TECHNIQUES

The consistency of the icing is the most important factor in piping. It should not be too stiff – it must be light and fluffy, and it must hold a peak.

STARS

Stars can be piped with nozzles nos 5, 7, 9, 11, 12, 13 or 15. Hold the bag, fitted with the appropriate nozzle, perpendicular to the surface to be iced. Press on the bag to release the icing, then pull it up gently to form a point and a star shape.

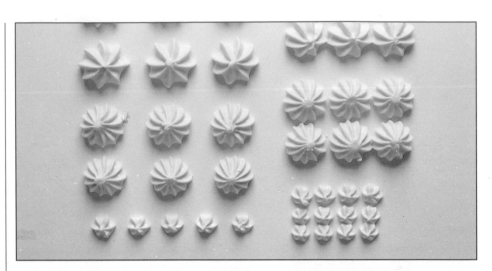

ROSETTES

You will need nozzles nos 42, 43 and 44. These rosettes are made with fine rope nozzles, which have shallower indentations than the star nozzles. With the bag held perpendicular to the surface to be iced, pipe a circle. Lift the nozzle slightly, apply pressure, bring it round to the centre and release the pressure as you tail it off.

SCROLLS

Pipe scrolls with fine rope nozzles, as for rosettes, but instead of tailing off into the circle, come out of it, creating a C- or an S-shape. For a C-shape, work in an anti-clockwise motion. For an S-shape, take the nozzle round clockwise. You can make attractive patterns by combining the C and the S, and if you twist the nozzle as you pipe, you will get a rope effect.

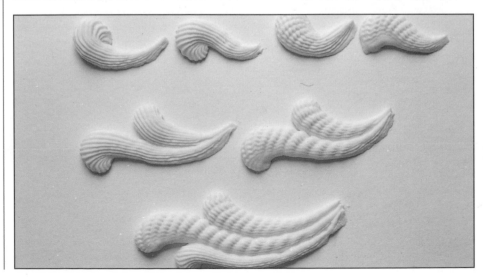

ALTERNATING SHELLS

You will need nozzles nos 5 and 13. Follow the instructions for shells, but take the point down at an angle of 45 degrees. Pipe a second row of shells beneath the first, taking the points up. Start with your piping nozzle at the tail of the upper shell for a plait effect.

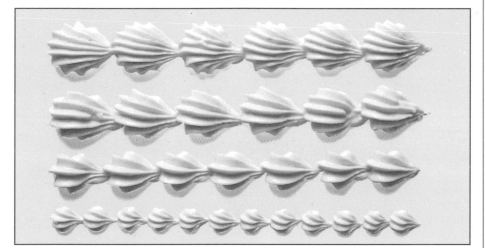

SHELLS

You will need to use nozzles nos 13, 11, 8 and 5. Rest the appropriate nozzle on the surface where you want to pipe the shell. Push out the icing without moving the bag. Once the shell has formed, pull the bag back to form a tail. Position the bag to form the next shell so that it just overlaps the tail of the one in front.

FLEUR DE LYS

This shape can be piped with a shell nozzle no 13 (above) or fine rope nozzle nos 44, 43 or 42 (below), or you can even use a plain round nozzle for a smooth effect. First pipe a shell with a long tail. Then pipe an S-shape scroll to the left and a C-shape scroll to the right. You can pipe the flowers in the same way. Pipe one set of petals, and overpipe the second set.

STRAIGHT LINES

You will need nozzle nos 4, 3, 2, 1 and 0. Touch the surface where you want to pipe. Lift the tube and apply pressure so that the icing flows out in a straight line. Drop it down at the other end of the line after you have released the pressure and the icing has stopped flowing. Do not attempt to pipe a straight line by dragging the nozzle along the surface of the cake or waxed paper. All you will succeed in doing is damaging the fine edge of the nozzle and indenting the surface of the cake. The nozzle must be lifted off the surface. It is best to practise on a sheet of paper to get a feel for the way in which the icing flows.

Overpiping is a classic piping technique. It is difficult and requires a very steady hand. By piping straight lines of varying widths touching each other, you can create a classic three-dimensional effect. Let each line dry before you begin on the next.

TRELLIS

You will need nozzle no 1. Pipe one set of parallel lines, then overpipe a second either at right angles for squares, or with both sets of lines on the diagonal for diamonds. Use another width nozzle for overpiping to create a different effect.

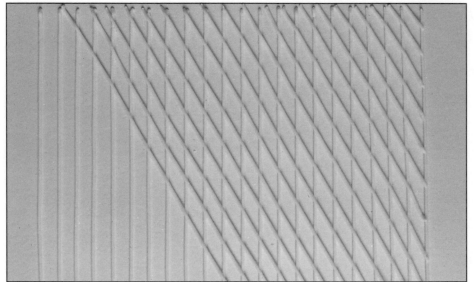

ZIGZAGS

You will need nozzles nos 42, 5 or 3. These can be piped in a continuous line with any shaped nozzle. Until you are more confident, you may find it easier to stop and start at each point – this will give a very definite V-shape to the zigzag.

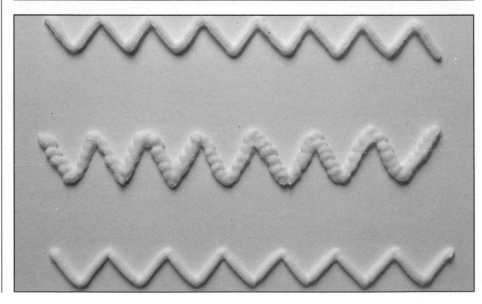

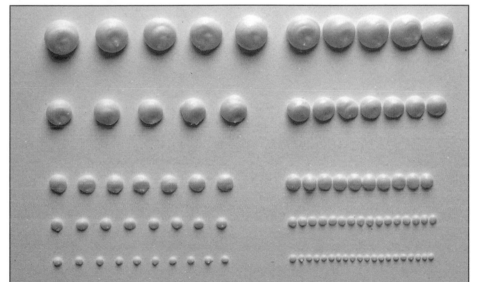

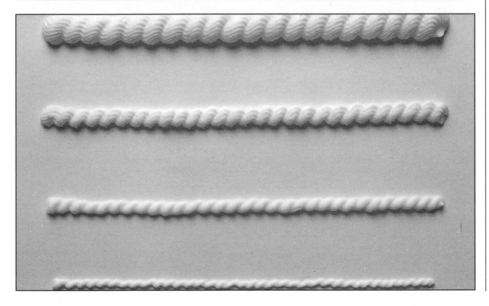

RAISED TRELLIS OR NETS

You will need nozzles nos 43, 3, 2 and 1. This is a style that was very popular a couple of decades ago. It has rather gone out of fashion because it is time-consuming. You can build up from the base with trellis work, but it is quicker and just as effective to pipe an oval scroll with a fine rope nozzle and cover it. Anchor the icing, twist the nozzle to form a rope as you apply the pressure, then release the pressure and taper off. Overpipe with a fine round nozzle, making parallel diagonal lines. Overpipe again in the opposite direction. You can build up the net by overpiping with de-creasing nozzles in different directions.

DOTS AND BEADS

You will need nozzles nos 4, 3, 2, 1 and 0. The difficulty with piping dots and beads is disguising the take-off point, which will tend to make a tail. This is harder to dis-guise, the bigger the bead you are piping. Using constant pressure keep the point of the nozzle stationary in the bead until it is the size required. Release pressure on the bag after piping the bead and then take off gently to the side. Correct any mistakes with a slightly dampened brush once the bead is nearly dry by gently pressing any projecting point down into the mass of icing. The larger beads are almost always used for over-piping, that is adding dotted features to plain, shell or star icing.

TWISTED ROPE

You will need nozzles nos 44, 43, 42, and 5. Twisted rope can be piped with a plain writing nozzle or a shell nozzle as well as a rope nozzle. The trick is to twist the bag as you are piping. Keep constant pressure on the bag. To avoid varying the width of the rope, hold the bag at an angle and rotate it as you go.

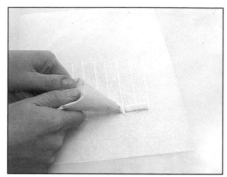

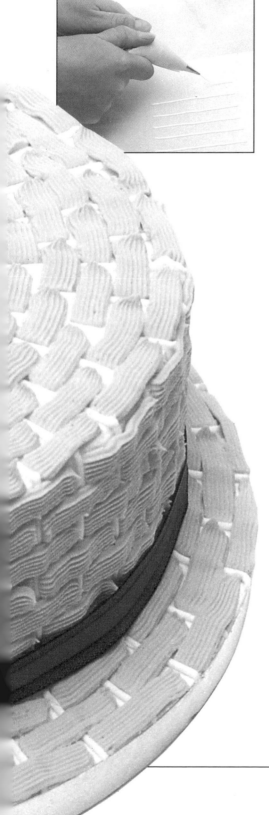

BASKET WEAVE ICING

This is actually quite easy to do and gives a very professional finish to a cake. You will need two icing nozzles – a basket or ribbon nozzle and a plain nozzle (no 2 or no 3).

Give the cake a basic flat coat of royal icing – it does not matter if this is slightly uneven as it will be totally covered by the basket work.

With an icing bag fitted with the plain nozzle, pipe a series of vertical parallel lines around the cake at regular intervals. Leave to dry.

With a second icing bag fitted with the basket or ribbon nozzle, start the horizontal weaving at the base of the cake. Hold the nozzle at the side of one vertical line and squeeze out a ribbon of icing. Lift it over the second vertical line and finish at the side of the third vertical line. Start the next strip at the other side of the third vertical line. Repeat this all the way round the base of the cake.

Start the next row of weaving, but make sure you begin the piping at the second vertical line. Continue around the cake, building up the woven appearance.

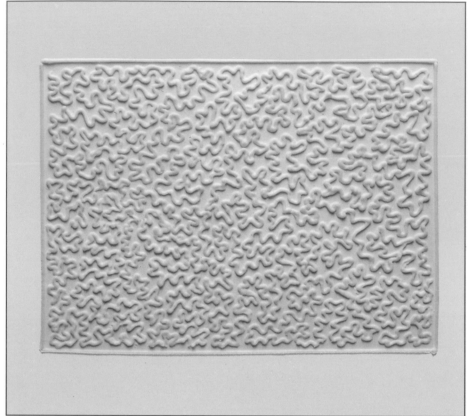

CORNELLI

You will need nozzle no 1. Cornelli or scribbling is an attractive texturing technique achieved by piping a maze of W-shapes and M-shapes in a continuous line but at random over a confined space. Use a fine nozzle and avoid moving in straight lines — you should not be able to see where the work begins or ends.

This is a comparatively easy technique which can be used to create a very professional-looking finish. It can be used on the flat surface of a cake, to fill scallop shapes, for example, or it can be used as a border on the rounded edge of fondant iced cakes.

EMBROIDERY

Embroidery work makes a very attractive decoration for the side of a cake. The illustration shows a complete pattern and then the elements that make it up. Use nozzle no 0 or 1 and pipe a row of blue built-up circles 2.5 cm/1 in apart. Pipe two similar circles above the first, two below the second and so on, alternating throughout the pattern. This is a reliable method of achieving an even pattern. Pipe a forget-me-not between each group of built-up circles. Finally add the leaves with green royal icing.

Again, this is not a difficult technique but it is one which demands concentration and patience.

MAKING LACE

Lace is always the last decoration to be added to a cake because it is so fragile and breaks so easily. Take great care when handling lace or when moving a cake with lace attached.

Designs for lacework are simple and varied. Several designs are included towards the end of the book in the chapter on templates (pages 218-249). Alternatively you can design your own lace. Patterns with several joins are stronger than those where the lines cross in only one or two places.

Lace is piped separately onto waxed paper, left to dry, then carefully lifted off and attached to the cake with fine lines of royal icing. To achieve a perfect result you must allow plenty of time for this work.

1 Choose a pattern and copy it 40 to 80 times on to a 15 cm/6 in square piece of greaseproof paper, depending on the size of the lace. Use a sharp pencil or fine felt tip pen. Each piece of lace is 1 cm/½ in wide, so it is easy to work out how much you will need. Six sheets with 40 to 80 pieces of lace will be enough for a three-tiered wedding cake. It is a good idea, however, to pipe half as many pieces again as you will actually need if you are a beginner, because you are likely to break several pieces.

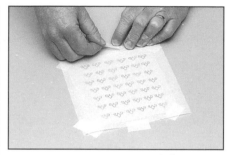

2 Tape the four corners of the grease-proof paper securely to a work surface or large board. Tape a larger piece of waxed paper over the pattern with masking tape. Only use a couple of pieces so that you do not disturb the piped lace too much when you remove the tape.

3 With nozzle no 0 or 1, pipe the lace in any direction that feels comfortable. Ensure that each piece of lace has a flat bar where it is to be attached to the cake. Wipe the end of the nozzle with your fingers or a damp cloth between each piece of lace to ensure clean lines. For particularly elaborate lace, use different coloured icing for different sections of each piece. The bar should be the same colour as the icing on the cake.

4 If you make a mistake, it can be corrected with a fine paintbrush. The paintbrush should be slightly dampened, but not wet.

5 Leave the lace to dry for at least two hours or overnight if possible. Do not put the lace in the oven to dry as the waxed paper will melt into the icing.

6 To remove the lace, curl the waxed paper over the index finger of your left hand. The lace will begin to release. Slide a cranked palette knife under the piece of lace and gently lift it off. Never try to remove lace with tweezers, as the slightest pressure will break the lace. The lace is now ready to attach to the cake.

MAKING MOULDS AND SHAPES IN TRELLIS AND LACE

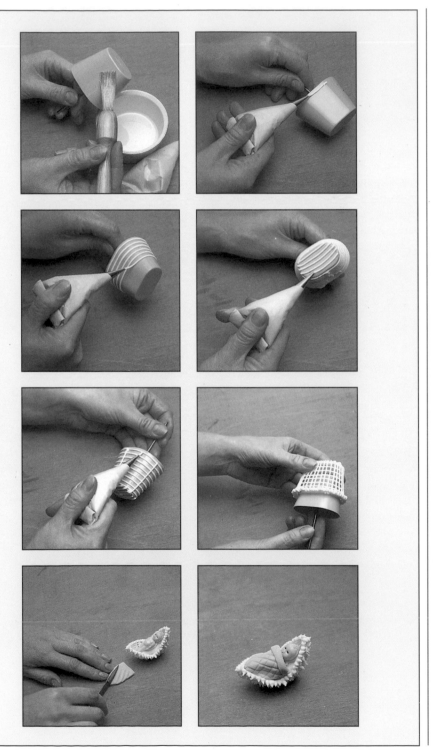

This takes quite a bit of practice, but some very pretty decorations and effects can be achieved. Start with simple shapes, such as small tartlet tins, patty tins and boat-shaped moulds. Special icing moulds are available as well.

Lightly grease the mould with oil. Using a no 2 icing nozzle, pipe trellis or lace work over the surface of the mould. Strengthen this with several lines piped around the outside edge.

Leave the icing to dry for at least 24 hours, then carefully remove the shape from the mould. Store between crumpled tissue paper or cotton wool in a rigid airtight container.

Other shapes, such as boxes or cots, can be built up by piping rectangles or squares for the sides and base on to non-stick paper. Fill these in with trellis or lace work and once they are absolutely dry secure the pieces together with a little icing. The pieces may need to be supported in position by placing crumpled absorbent kitchen paper around them. They should be left until the icing joins are quite firm before attempting to move them.

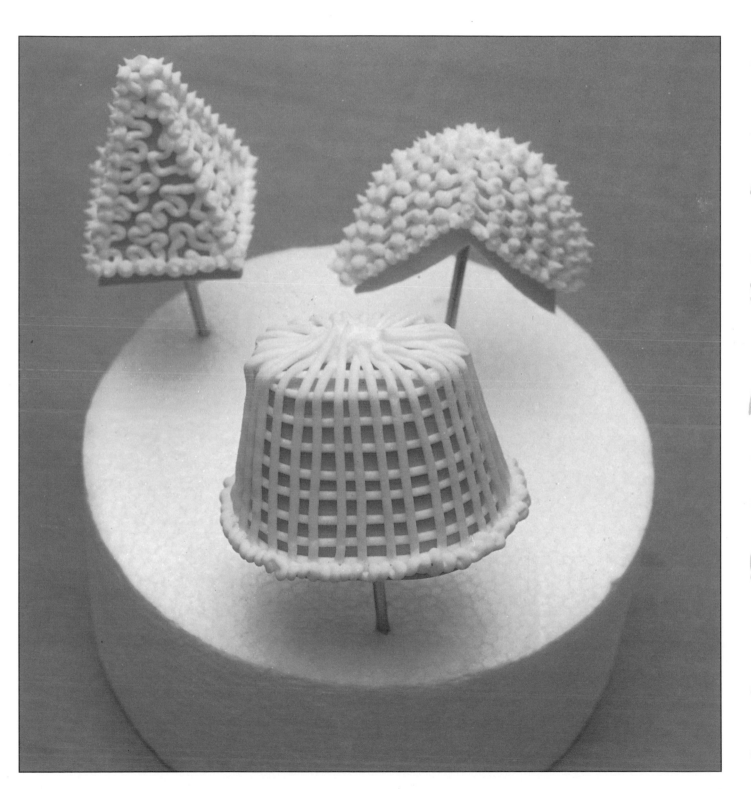

RUN-OUTS

This technique involves piping an outline and flooding it, giving a good flat shape with cleanly rounded edges. It is also called flooding or running. The run-outs are usually piped on waxed paper, left to dry, then lifted off and used to decorate the cake. However, in some cases, it is simpler to pipe run-out designs directly onto the cake, especially if the design is a figure or fairly complicated shape.

ICING FOR RUN-OUTS

When you make up royal icing for run-outs, it should be to normal piping consistency. It should not be too moist or the icing will not set quickly and will be too weak. Make it in the normal way, then thin it down a little with egg white or water. If you use egg white, the icing will be stronger, but it may take up to a week to dry. It is better to use water and add it, literally, a drop at a time. Use an eye dropper to get the consistency exactly right. Do not beat the icing as you are adding the water because you will incorporate too much air. Just stir it gently.

Add enough water so that your icing is of a piping consistency. To judge the amount of water to add to the icing, swirl the knife in the bowl and count steadily to 10 as the ripples subside. The icing should just have found its own level as you get to 10.

Icing collars, filigree pieces and designs that are subsequently lifted before placing in position are always piped onto waxed paper, over an outline. The outline obviously acts as a guide, but its other purpose is to stop the flooded icing from contracting as it dries – not to stop it spreading. It will only spread if your icing is too runny.

It is important to dry run-outs as quickly as possible in order to get a good sheen or surface finish. The airing cupboard is often a good place.

PIPING A RUN-OUT

1 The first step in making a run-out is to secure a piece of waxed paper to a board over the outline you want to fill in. Attach a tag to the paper on which the outline is drawn, so you can easily slide it out from the waxed paper afterwards. Do not use greaseproof or silicone paper as a substitute for waxed, as it may wrinkle. Put the paper waxed side up to facilitate the release of the run-out when it dries. Use masking tape, which pulls off more easily than conventional sticky tape, to secure it. Wrenching away a piece of adhesive tape may break your run-out. Do not tape right around the waxed paper – you may trap air underneath and the damp icing on top will cause the paper to lift and buckle the run-out as it dries. Secure the paper only at the corners.

2 If you are piping a collar, or anything with a hollow middle, make a small cut in the shape of a cross in the centre of the paper to relax the natural tension in the fabric of the paper.

3 Pipe the outline carefully following the line of the pattern on the tracing beneath.

4 Fill a piping bag with flooding icing, but do not cut the hole in the bottom until you are ready to make the run-out, or the icing will pour straight out of it. Make sure that the hole you cut is not too big, or you might lose control. A nozzle is not necessary for flooding.

5 Start close to your outline, but do not touch it with the bag, or you may break it. Keeping the tip of the bag in the icing to reduce the chance of air bubbles forming, allow the icing to flow out, moving the bag backwards and forwards.

6 When you have almost filled the whole area, use a paintbrush to push the icing right to the edge of the line, so that it just spills on to it.

7 Make sure there are no air bubbles in the icing by gently tapping the board.

8 Remove the pattern from beneath the paper by the tag. If you are making a whole series of run-outs, you can use the same pattern each time. Leave the run-outs to dry.

9 Once a run-out is dry, you can remove it from the paper by working a **cranked palette knife** (one with a thin angled blade) underneath it all the way round, or by peeling the paper off the back, taking care not to break the run-out. With a large collar, the easiest way to peel off the backing is to pull it down, away from the run-out over the edge of the work surface.

MONOGRAMS AND NUMERALS

1 The important thing to decide here is which part of the design should be the most prominent. Pipe the back of the design first.

2 In the monogram 'NC', the visible parts of the C are piped first, because the N lies on top of it.

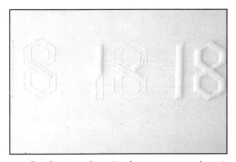

3 In the number 8, the crossover bar is slightly raised, so this should be piped last. Do not try to do it all at once, or it will merge into a completely flat shape.

BUTTERFLIES

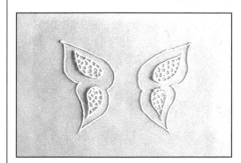

1 First pipe the inside of the wings with cornelli or other fine piping work. Then pipe the outline of the wings and flood first the bottom part and then the top.

2 When the wings are dry, pipe a tear-drop-shaped piece of icing for the body. Attach the wings to it while it is still wet, and support them with cotton wool balls until they have set in position. Use stamens for antennae, but remember that they are not edible.

FLOWER

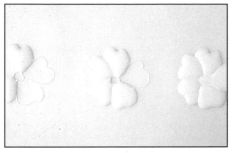

As for the maple leaf, work on opposite sides of the flower, which will not touch each other, before flooding the inside petals. When all five petals are dry, pipe in the centre.

ROSE

Start from the back of the design and work forwards, building it up in layers. As each step dries, fill in the next. Then finally fill in the centre petals.

BELLS

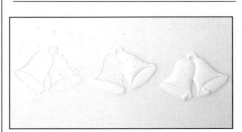

Pipe the insides of the bells first, and allow them to dry. Then pipe the top of the underneath bell. When that has dried, pipe the uppermost bell. The result is three-dimensional.

LEAVES

For holly and rose leaves, pipe the outline, flood half the leaf, and let it dry, then flood the other half. The maple leaf is piped in four parts, allowing each to dry separately, to give a veined effect.

SHIELD AND OVAL

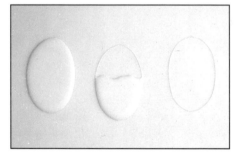

These are simple designs that can be adapted to many occasions. Pipe the outline, then flood the centre. To give the shield a frame, the flooding goes upwards but not over the outline.

BRIGHTLY COLOURED RUN-OUTS

As a contrast to the delicate run-outs shown on the previous pages, here we see how the same technique can be applied to jolly designs, often using several colours. Elaborate run-outs can be made by tracing motifs from Christmas cards or other pictures. You can also use the trace-off templates shown at the end of the book.

It is important to trace the drawing accurately and to plan the colours which you intend to use carefully – remember the result is intended to be jolly, not messy.

When using more than one colour in a run-out, always allow one section to dry completely before starting on the next to prevent the colours from running into each other.

Once dry, these run-outs can be outlined again or extra piping can be used to improve the definition of the shape. Fine details can be painted on with liquid food colouring, or pastes thinned with a little water, or drawn with coloured icing pens.

PIPED FLOWERS

You will need nozzle no 57, 58 or 59. Piping flowers is no more difficult than the other techniques described here, though the results look very sophisticated. To give the petals strength you will need to work with slightly thicker icing than that used for piping shells. Flowers can be piped onto either a cone or onto squares of waxed paper stuck with icing on an icing nail.

You will need a petal nozzle, which is basically flat with a slightly scooped opening where the icing is squeezed, but with one end slightly wider than the other to give flare to the petals.

ROSE

1 Take a cone of marzipan, making sure it has dried thoroughly before you start to work. Pipe a tight little centre to the rose with nozzle no 57, 58 or 59 by putting the thick end of the nozzle down onto the marzipan and piping all round the tip of the cone. Rotate the cone in the hand which is not holding the piping bag to do this. Leave the icing to dry between steps.

2 For the next layer, pipe three tiny petals, each one going a third of the way round the cone and slightly overlapping the one before. Angle the nozzle outwards, to make the petals curve.

3 Starting at the centre of one of these petals, make a second row. Keep the thick side of the nozzle down, and the thin side up. Pipe four or five petals for the outer layer.

If you are making about a dozen roses at a time, the petals on the first rose will be dry by the time you come to the last one – this way you need not stop working.

For a two-tone rose, pipe the outer petals a shade lighter, or darker, than the inner ones. For a variegated rose, streak the icing in the bag with two or more different shades.

Once the roses are dry cut them off the marzipan cones with a sharp knife.

APPLE BLOSSOM

For this technique you will need an icing nail, which is a disc of metal on a spike, nozzle no 57, 58 or 59 and a small square of waxed paper for every flower you pipe. If you have not got an icing nail, you could use the top of a cork stuck onto a skewer.

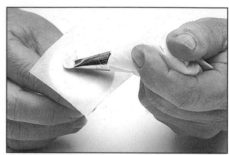

1 Put a dab of icing on the head of the nail and press it into the centre of the waxed paper. Let it dry so that the paper does not slip while you are working.

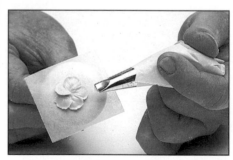

2 Use the petal nozzle with the thick edge towards the centre of the flower. Increase the pressure on the bag as you turn the nail, and slightly lift the thin edge of the nozzle as you form each petal.

3 After you have made the first petal, wipe the end of the nozzle clean. Then tuck the nozzle underneath the edge of the first petal and make another one just as you did before, releasing the pressure before you take it off.

4 Continue until you have five petals. You can decorate the centre of the flower with a little bead of yellow icing wire for stamens.

Hyacinth

Primrose

Pussy willow

Violet

HYACINTH

You will need nozzle no 37. First pipe the stem and the leaves in green icing. Then pipe two rows of tiny flowers, about five in a row, on either side of the stem. When these have dried, pipe a third row directly over the stem, giving a three dimensional effect. Add a final green leaf at the front of the flower.

PRIMROSE

You will need nozzle no 57, 58 or 59. Pipe primroses as for apple blossom, but indent each of the petals slightly as you go. Pipe halfway up the petal, bring the nozzle back down towards you, then continue the curve, making a heart-shaped petal. Pipe five petals, tucking each one just underneath the one before. Pipe the centre with a yellow dot and paint on green stamens.

PUSSY WILLOW

You will need nozzle no 3 or 4. First pipe the branches in dark green or brown. Then, with white icing, pipe teardrop shapes, tailing back to join the ends of the branches. Finally, pipe the little V-shape at the base of each teardrop in brown.

VIOLET

You will need nozzle no 57, 58 or 59. For a violet, pipe three larger purple petals at the top and two smaller ones underneath. A dot of yellow icing forms the centre of the flower.

NARCISSUS

Pipe these as for apple blossom, but make six white petals of a slightly more elongated shape, piping up and down the petal rather than straight round it. With the side of a dampened brush, mark the lines going to and from the centre of the flower. Dot the centre with orange icing. For a daffodil, build up the centre of the flower holding the nozzle vertically. Rotate the icing nail or inedible pipe to a cylinder.

Violet

Narcissus

Apple blossom

Sweet pea

SWEET PEA

Using waxed paper on a piping nail, make the first petal fairly large, using similar techniques as for the apple blossom or pansy. Then pipe the second petal to overlap the first almost completely. The third and fourth petals are piped to the right and left respectively of the first pair.

The centre petal or pod is piped in one motion by holding the nozzle so that the axis of its opening is ranged straight up the centre line of the flower. With the tip of the nozzle held just a little above the petals, squeeze the bag gently, and move the tip towards the top of the flower. Increase the pressure and then draw the tip of the bag towards the starting point, decreasing the pressure as you pipe the return stroke.

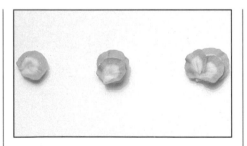

PANSY

Using the icing nail, make the first petal as for the apple blossom. Then pipe a second petal to overlap the first. Exerting pressure and shaking the piping nozzle slightly will help to give each petal a frilly edge.

The third and fourth petals are piped to the left and right sides respectively of the first pair of petals, and each must overlap the edges of the first pair.

After piping the fourth petal, turn the nail through 180 degrees and pipe the final petal, starting from the centre of the flower. This is a large petal which must overlap the sides of the two small petals adjacent to it. It should have a frilly edge.

The key to making successful pansies is to pivot the petal nozzle around a central point, so that the thicker end of the nozzle is almost stationary while the outside edge rotates from the outer edge of the petal.

PIPED BORDERS

Pink forget-me-not

Blue forget-me-not

Hanging rose

Grape

These pretty designs make charming decorations for the side of a cake. You can scribe a line lightly around the cake indicating the position of the border.

The first two are variations using a forget-me-not nozzle (no 37), which you use in the same way as a star nozzle, simply pushing out a small amount of icing. Fill in the centres with yellow, pipe leaves with a fine nozzle, and add a beaded border.

For the hanging rose, start with the stems and leaves. Then pipe the flowers, starting with the back petal. Pipe the next petal to overlap the first slightly, the third tucked underneath it and brought forward, and the fourth the same on the other side. Pipe a green calyx to join the flowers to the stems.

For the grape border, pipe the stems and upper leaves, making tendrils by rotating the tip of the nozzle. Add the grapes, bead by bead, then pipe more leaves.

MAKING DECORATIONS

Choosing and making decorations is not only an important part of cake decorating but it is also one of the most creative, and enjoyable, areas of activity. Whether they are an integral part of the design or added at the last moment as a finishing touch, the decorations must look right on the cake, and not spoil the effect by being out of proportion or made from the wrong material. Edible decorations can be made from marzipan, fondant and moulding icings, modelling or petal paste, sugar and meringue mixes or chocolate. Different effects are achieved with each type of icing or material. Select the type of decoration to comply with your ability and the cake.

In this chapter you will find a wide variety of ideas to suit all types of cake, some more complicated than others. It is important to plan your finished design well and to practise any difficult techniques first.

EDIBLE DECORATIONS

The decorations illustrated here are all edible, and are just some of the enormous range of ready-made cake decorations available from both specialist and non-specialist sources.

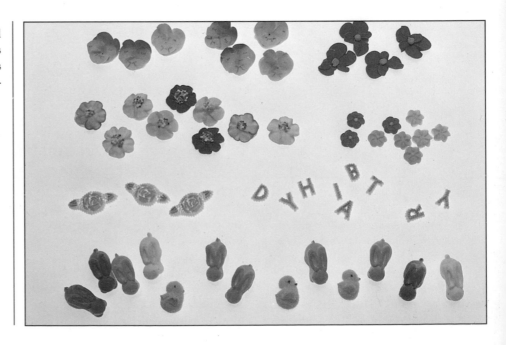

SECURING MOULDED SHAPES

By pressing a cocktail stick into shaped pieces of icing and leaving it to harden, all sorts of attachments can be added to novelty cakes to make them more fun. Discard them before slicing the cake.

Mould the appropriate shape out of the chosen fondant or moulding icing and press a cocktail stick into the end which will eventually lie against the cake. Transfer it to a sheet of nonstick baking paper, wax paper or foil and leave it to dry. This takes about 2 days with home-made icing, but it can take longer if you use the bought variety.

Peel away the paper or foil and press the shape into the cake. If you like, make a hole first with another cocktail stick so the shape slips into place very easily. With delicate shapes it's worth making a 'spare' in case of breakage.

TULLE BUTTERFLIES

These are a clever alternative to making run-out butterflies and they can be very effective when used on the right type of cake. Tulle is a delicate netting available from haberdashery and fabric shops and it usually comes in an assortment of colours. If you have difficulty finding it, rice paper makes a good substitute.

Make a template (see page 250) for the butterfly. Use it to cut out the tulle shapes. Fold the tulle through the centre of the butterfly so it looks as if it is in flight.

Place some Royal Icing (page 32) in a piping bag fitted with a plain nozzle (no 1) and pipe along the underside of the fold. Secure the butterfly to the cake and leave it to set. Using the same nozzle, pipe around the edges of the butterflies as shown.

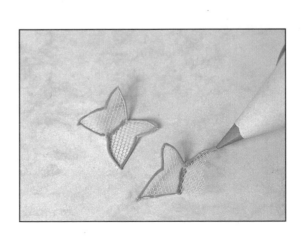

ALMOND PASTE MARQUETRY

This is a very easy, and fun, way to decorate a cake and though it looks very elaborate, it is quite simple to produce. It is based on the ideas of marquetry and mosaics used in furniture and tile design.

Small pieces of different coloured almond paste are arranged in an interlocking pattern to cover the top of a cake. Any design you like can be used and it is a good idea to draw it first. Cut a piece of paper the exact size of the top of the cake, then draw the design on it, deciding how many colours you are going to use and marking the shapes with the appropriate colour. Make a copy of the finished design on greaseproof or waxed paper and cut it into the individual pieces. Arrange these on the original pattern until you are ready to cut out the pieces.

Colour the almond paste by kneading a little colouring into each piece. Have some apricot glaze ready to attach the pieces to the cake.

The sides of the cake should be decorated first; this can be done with one continuous strip of almond paste, or two half strips. Follow the method for covering a cake with almond paste on pages 30/31, or cover with buttercream and a coating such as praline.

Roll out one piece of coloured almond paste on a surface lightly dusted with icing sugar or cornflour and cut out all the pieces in that colour. Repeat with the other colours, then build up the pattern on the cake, attaching each piece with a little apricot glaze and ensuring that all the pieces interlock neatly.

PAINTING WITH FOOD COLOURS

There is a great variety of food colouring and cake decorating materials available in the shops, making it possible to achieve a wide range of decorative effects. The range of colours is constantly being extended, and the quality of colours improving. The most common method of applying colour is to add it to the icing, then apply the icing to the cake. Unfortunately, there are certain circumstances where this produces rather false colours. Leaf green, for example, when added to icing, never produces an authentic leaf colour, no matter how much colour is used. However, leaf green does produce a beautiful and authentic shade of green if the food colour is used as a paint. In fact, by using the colour in this way it is possible to achieve a greater variety of decorative effects.

1 Food colours can be used like any watercolour paint. For example, adding water will make the colour paler and mixing different colours can produce some interesting and exciting shades of colour.

2 In order to make food colours fade into each other, apply the chosen colours to the surface being decorated so that they lie immediately next to each other. Whilst the colours are still wet make gentle brushstrokes across where the colours meet, merging one into the other.

3 To produce wood-grain effect, mix the colour required in a palette or saucer. Using a medium-sized paintbrush, dip the brush into the colour shaking off any excess colouring. The brush should not be too wet. Press the brush down on to a work surface so that the bristles splay out into points. Gently brush across the surface of the icing to produce several lines.

4 To produce a colour wash effect, make sure that the brush is full of colour. If you have to dip the brush too often, you risk creating a streaked effect. Gently brush backwards and forwards until the surface is completely covered. Let the colours dry. Once dry it is possible to paint a design over the wash without disturbing the colour background, as illustrated.

5 When painting certain details or designs on a cake, it might be helpful to have an outline drawn on the cake beforehand using either black food colour or a food colour pen. In either case be sure to let the outline dry completely before filling in the colours, as illustrated.

6 To produce a stippled or marbled effect mix the colours required and make sure the brush is not too wet. Press the brush down vertically on to a work surface so that the bristles splay out into a rough circle of points. Lift the brush and holding it vertically, lightly dot the surface of the icing, as illustrated. In all cases when colour decorating, *practise* on a spare piece of icing before painting the design on to the cake.

If you are painting two different colours directly beside each other or one colour over the top of another as shown, let the first colour dry completely before applying the second. Otherwise the colours will bleed into each other.

MARZIPAN ANIMALS

Marzipan animals make delightful decorations for children's birthday cakes. The basic ideas demonstrated here can easily be adapted to other animals and figures.

Recipes for marzipan are given on pages 28/29; in addition you will need a variety of modelling tools and kitchen equipment.

RABBIT

1 Take a piece of white marzipan the size of an egg and roll out a cone for the rabbit's body. Make an indentation where the tail will fit. Make indentations at the larger end of the cone for the haunches. Roll a small ball of marzipan for the head.

2 Make an indentation with your little finger across the head, and roll it into a dumbell shape.

3 Cut down the length of the thinner end to form the ears. Use the dog bone tool to make indentations in the ears, which you can line with pink marzipan.

4 Indent little holes for the eyes and nose. Fill in the eyes with white royal icing and add a cone of pink marzipan for the nose. Paint black dots for the eyeballs. Try to suggest that the rabbit is looking slightly to one side. With the 'U' tool, indent a smiling mouth.

5 Make a little carrot out of orange and green marzipan. Divide the pointed end of the cone to make the front legs, slightly open them out and fix the carrot between them. Fix the head on the body with egg white, icing or melted chocolate.

SCOTTIE DOG

1 Roll out a sausage of dark brown marzipan about 10 cm/4 in long and 1.5 cm/¾ in thick. Cut off a quarter for the head and mark the remaining piece to divide it into three.

2 Snip a piece from the top of the rolled marzipan and lift it gently to form the tail. Cut through the sausage from beneath the tail to the end to form the back legs. The front legs are formed in the same way.

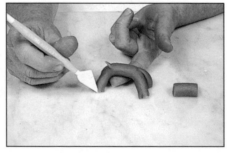

3 Twist the legs apart gently and arch the marzipan to form the dog's body. Adjust the legs so that the dog stands firmly. Mark its paws.

4 Take the head and pinch up two ears with your thumb and forefinger. Indent the ears with the dog bone tool.

5 Pull out the dog's whiskers by stroking with the thumb and forefinger, and snip it into a fringe with the scissors.

6 Press a small ball of pink marzipan between the whiskers with the 'U' tool to form the mouth, and add a red tongue. Make the nose of black marzipan.

7 Make eyes with white royal icing. Paint on black dots to complete the eyes.

8 Position the head on the body at an angle and fix it in place. The Tam'o' shanter cap is made with red and green marzipan. Complete the model by giving the dog a bone.

DUCK

1 Roll four balls of white marzipan, one 5 cm/2 in across, one 4 cm/1½ in across, and two 1 cm/½ in across. Roll two balls of orange, one 4 cm/1½ in across for the feet and one 5 mm/¼ in across for the beak. Form the large white ball into the body. Squeeze the medium white ball gently.

2 Flatten the two smallest white balls into teardrop shapes for the wings. Mark in feathers from the shoulder to the tip with shell tool no 2. Feather-mark the tail in the same way. Elongate the larger orange ball for the feet by forming a depression across the centre.

3 Press out the ends of the dumbell with your thumbs to make the feet. Mark the webs with shell tool no 2. Roll the other orange ball into a cigar shape and fold in half to form the beak. Pinch the beak up in the middle so that it forms an open 'V' shape.

4 Assemble the duck. Fix the body on the feet with egg white or melted chocolate. Position the beak on the body of the duck and press the head on top, sandwiching the beak between the head and body. Attach the wings with egg white and pipe in the eyes with white royal icing. Mark the eyeballs and eyebrows. Add character with a little hat and by making a simple umbrella from a cone of marzipan and slipping it between a wing and the body.

FROG

1 Form a ball of green marzipan 5 cm/2 in across into a pear shape, and flatten and bend it over slightly at the top. Slice through the narrowest part with a sharp knife to form the mouth. Taking about half as much marzipan again, roll a dumbell shape with one end larger than the other (as with the rabbit left). Roll two smaller balls for the protruding eye sockets.

2 Cut the dumbell shape in half along its length to make the frog's legs. Twist the smaller end outwards to form the foot and mark the webbed feet with tool no 4.

3 Attach the legs and eye sockets to the body and make indentations for the eyeballs. Pipe in the eyeballs with white royal icing and complete the eyes with dots of black. Add three small balls of green marzipan to each foot for the toes. Make a few small holes in the frog's back and fill with orange marzipan to make spots. Give the frog a red tongue, and fix a tiny marzipan butterfly on the end of it.

PIG

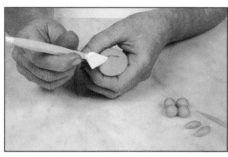

1 Take a fat cone of pink marzipan and drag the pointed end across the work surface to form an uptilted snout. With the blunt knife blade, tool no 2, make a deep 'V' on the snout for the mouth and then make two indentations above the 'V' with the dog bone or ball tool for the nostrils. Make two more indentations for the eyes and ears to fit into, and one more indentation at the back for the tail. Have ready four small pink balls for the legs, two cigar shapes for the ears, and a long thin sausage for the tail.

2 Push the slightly fatter end of the marzipan sausage into the pig and twist it round to form a curly tail.

3 Fill in the eyes with royal icing and dot them black. Flatten the ears between finger and thumb, fix them in the indentations and flop them forward to give the pig character.

4 Sit the body on top of the legs. For a finishing touch, add a bowler hat or a bonnet cut from a flower shape.

MARZIPAN FRUITS

Marzipan fruits can be made from different coloured marzipan, or from uncoloured marzipan which is painted afterwards. A combination of both techniques gives delicate shading and a greater degree of realism.

For most of these fruits, start with a ball of marzipan about the size of a walnut. You will need a variety of modelling tools, or improvise with kitchen equipment.

LEMON

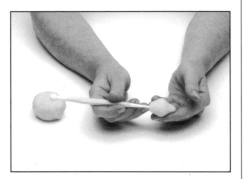

1 Roll a ball of yellow marzipan, squeezing to give it two slightly pointed ends. Using a ball tool, indent the stalk end.

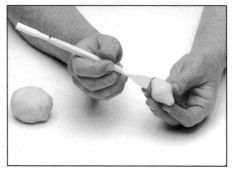

2 Using the serrated end of modelling tool no 4, work it over the fruit to give the appearance of lemon peel. Alternatively roll the marzipan lemon around on a nutmeg grater.

PEAR

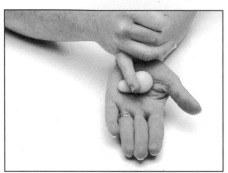

1 Roll out a ball of yellow or green paste. Elongate the ball by rolling one side of it with your finger to form the neck of the pear. Roll your little finger around the base of the neck to form the 'waist' of the pear.

2 Use the star tool to form the little indentations at the base and stalk of the pear. You can speckle it with brown marzipan to make it look more authentic.

BANANA

Roll a piece of yellow marzipan into a sausage shape. Curve it with your fingers and flatten the sides to give it a banana shape. Paint or dust on strands of brown food colour to give it a ripe appearance.

ORANGE

Roll a ball of orange marzipan. Either use the serrated end of modelling tool no 4 or a nutmeg grater to give the effect of peel. Use star tool no 5 to make an indentation for the stem.

APPLE, PLUM, GREENGAGE, APRICOT, CHERRY

For an apple, take red or green marzipan and roll it into a ball. Indent the top and tail with tool no 5. Make the other fruits in the same way as apples, using appropriate colours. Use tool no 2 to give an authentic crease to the fruit. Attach stamens to the cherries to represent stalks.

STRAWBERRY

1 Roll a red ball into a cone shape. Take a 10 cm/4 in square of fine tulle. Place the strawberry in the centre of the tulle.

2 Draw the tulle up tightly around the marzipan and the fabric pattern will give a strawberry effect. Add a green paste leaf, or a plastic culotte if available.

GRAPES

For a bunch of grapes, roll a cone of purple or green paste, and make several tiny balls to represent the grapes. Arrange the grapes all over the cone to form a bunch, pressing each one gently into position.

FINISHING TOUCHES

1 To finish your fruits, you can dust them with various colours for shading, give them a shine with gum arabic or coat them in sugar.

2 To coat them in sugar, brush a little egg white onto the palm of your hand and roll the fruit in it. This is quicker than painting the fruit, and you will get a lighter coat. Roll the fruit in caster sugar to create a very pretty effect.

3 Finally you can use chocolate non-pareils as miniature stems for the fruit. Alternatively, use cloves, but they may be too large. For the orange and the lemon, tiny star-shaped soup pasta can be soaked for a second or two in a weak solution of green food colouring. If you allow them to soak longer they will swell.

A variety of fruits grouped together makes an attractive decoration for a plain cake.

MARZIPAN CHRISTMAS DECORATIONS

These brightly coloured and festive decorations are great fun to make. When you are working with marzipan, keep two cloths handy, one damp and one dry, for cleaning your hands and tools. They get very sticky because of the almond oil. These decorations can also be made from fondant icing or moulding icing.

CHRISTMAS TREE

1 Form a cone of green marzipan. Take a very sharp pair of embroidery scissors and starting at the top of the cone, snip small 'V' shapes into the marzipan to form branches.

2 Lift each 'V' slightly as you withdraw the scissors to make the branches stand out. Continue snipping all round the tree until it is full of branches. (You can use the same technique to make marzipan hedgehogs.)

3 Let the tree dry out thoroughly, then give it a seasonal touch of snow by sifting a little icing sugar over the branches

HOLLY

1 Roll out a sheet of green marzipan on a smooth work surface lightly dusted with icing sugar. Use a holly cutter if you have one, or make a template and cut round it with a fine sharp knife.

2 Alternatively, use a small circular cutter, such as the end of a piping nozzle, and cut a series of circles in an oval shape, the sides of each circle touching the next to form the indentations of the leaf.

3 As you cut the leaves, lay them on a piece of foam rubber and score the centre of each leaf with a cocktail stick to form a vein. At the same time this will make the leaves curl up at the sides. Make clusters of berries from small balls of red marzipan.

SNOWMAN

1 Make a cone of marzipan, or for a true white snowman, fondant or moulding icing. With tool no 2, the blunt knife, make two upward cuts for arms and lever them out slightly to stand away from the body.

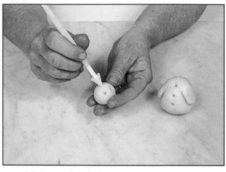

2 Make a ball for the head and make indentations with star tool no 5 where the eyes, nose and buttons are to be positioned.

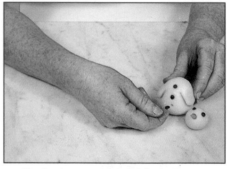

3 Push tiny cones of black marzipan into the holes for the eyes and buttons. A very small carrot cone shape makes the nose. A marzipan curl forms the mouth.

4 The scarf is made from a long sausage of marzipan with the ends flattened and snipped to make a fringe. Make the hat by rolling a sausage of marzipan. Cut the ends flat. Make the hat brim by flattening out a little marzipan at the base of the hat between finger and thumb. Make some snowballs and set them beside the finished snowman.

FATHER CHRISTMAS

1 The Father Christmas is rather more complicated and needs overnight drying before assembly. First roll a 10 cm/ 4 in sausage about 1 cm/½ in thick of red marzipan under the palm of your hand. Do not use your fingers because they will leave indentations on the sausage.

2 Flatten the ends of the sausage and turn them up to form feet. Bow the sausage for the legs. Stand the legs up and leave them to dry.

3 Make a cone for the body, indenting the base of the cone where the legs will be filled in.

4 Make the arms from a 10 cm/4 in sausage about 5 mm/¼ in thick and at both ends cut the thumbs with tool no 2. Smooth them off. Indent the palms with tool no 2.

5 Roll two equal-sized balls of marzipan for the head, one flesh coloured and one red. Cut each of them in half and sandwich a red one for the hat on to a pink one for the face. You will not need the spare halves.

6 Make a groove for the brow with tool no 2. Make two indentations for the eye sockets. Use two tiny flattened balls of black marzipan for the eyes.

7 Cut out the trimmings — the belt, beard, eyebrows and fur – with a knife. Stick the trimmings to the head, body, arms and legs with egg white. Leave all the pieces to dry overnight.

8 The next day, assemble the body by threading the legs, body and head on to a cocktail stick or piece of uncooked spaghetti. Make a sackful of presents for the finishing touch.

MOULDED ROSES

Making a moulded rose requires patience and a steady hand. The rose shown below is made with fondant icing. You can also use marzipan, though its slightly grainier texture means that the petals are less fine.

Moulding fine shapes like petals with fondant icing or marzipan can be a problem if your hands and fingers get hot, because the fondant or marzipan will stick to them. There are two ways of preventing this. Either dust your fingers very lightly with cornflour, or mould the petals inside a polythene bag. If you use the cornflour method, make sure you use only a very little, or it will spoil the look of the petals.

1 Roll a ball of fondant icing the size of an egg in your hands. Rub it in the heels of your hands until it forms a cone about 5 cm/2 in high, and put it point upwards on your work surface.

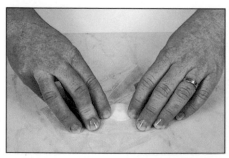

2 To make each petal, follow the same technique. Roll a ball of fondant about the size of a large pea.

Put it in a polythene bag or under a sheet of polythene.

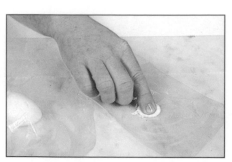

3 Squash it with your index finger. Using your two index fingers, flatten the paste at the top edge to form the edge of the petal. The base of the petal should remain thick so that it can be attached to the flower. Another way to mould the petals if you have cool hands, is to stroke and pull the edge of the petal between your fingers, or to lay the petal on your palm and flatten and thin it with a ball tool.

4 Wrap the first petal right around the cone with the top of the petal 5 mm/¼ in above the top of the cone. You should not need water to fix the petals on to the cone.

5 Gently squeeze it in with your fingers to form a 'waist' at the bottom of the petal. The first petal should be completely closed around the cone.

6 Place the centre edge of the second petal opposite the join line of the first petal and 5 mm/¼ in above it. Fix one side of the petal firmly to the cone and leave the other side free. Curl the tips of the petal back – do not wait too long to do this or the fondant will dry and crack.

7 Place the centre of the third petal over the closed side of the second petal. Fix it on both sides of the cone and curl the tip back.

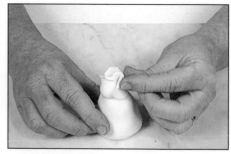

8 Place the centre of the fourth petal over the edge of the third and under the open side of the second. Close the edge of the second petal down. Curl the edge of the fourth petal back.

9 With four petals pinched in neatly at the base, the three outer ones curled back at the tips, you have formed a rosebud. If you wish to stop at this stage, look at the flower from all angles, decide which is the best, and cut the bud from the cone at a slant, so that it will rest on the cake with the best side up.

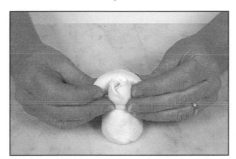

10 To make a bigger rose, continue to build up the flower with slightly larger petals. It does not matter where you start attaching the outer petals. Stretch the base of each petal round as you secure it to the cone. Apply each petal so that it overlaps the previous one about halfway, and curl the tips outwards.

11 Continue adding petals until the rose is fairly even and you have an attractive flower.

12 Turn the rose, gently pressing down each of the petals to ensure they are secured firmly at the base.

13 Cut the base of the rose so that it will stand upright on the cake. Angle the base of each rose carefully according to its position in the final arrangement.

14 To make a very small bud, roll a tiny cone shape on your palm into rosebud shape.

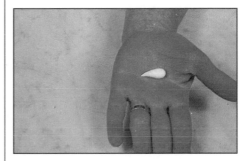

15 Make one petal, wrap it round the cone and pinch it at the base to form a bud.

These very attractive moulded roses can be grouped in small, neat arrangements or in generous cascades to create an elaborate cake.

PASTILLAGE

Pastillage work can be done with modelling paste, petal paste or gelatine icing in addition to the recipe given here. All three are equally suitable for moulding flowers, figures and other decorations, and the one you choose depends on the time and ingredients available.

MODELLING PASTE

This home-made recipe for pastillage includes icing sugar, edible gums and other edible materials which impart flexibility and elasticity to the paste. Gum tragacanth is available from specialist cake decorating sources.

> 2 tsp gelatine
> 5 tsp cold water
> 450g/1lb icing sugar, sifted
> 3 tsp gum tragacanth
> 2 tsp liquid glucose
> 2 tsp white vegetable fat
> 1 egg white

1 Soak the gelatine in the cold water for about half an hour. Meanwhile, heat the icing sugar and gum tragacanth in a bowl over a saucepan of hot water.

2 Dissolve the liquid glucose, fat and softened gelatine over a very low heat.

3 Beat the sugar mixture in an electric mixer at a slow speed. Add the glucose mixture and the egg white. Turn the machine to maximum speed and beat for about 15 minutes. The longer and harder you beat the paste, the whiter it will be.

PETAL PASTE

Petal paste is made simply by adding water to a special gum powder available from specialist cake decorating sources.

> 4½tbsp water
> 300g/10oz petal paste powder
> ½tsp white vegetable fat
> (optional)

1 Put the water into a bowl. Sift in most of the petal paste powder. Always use water and powder in the ratio of 1:10.

2 Sift the remaining powder onto the work surface. Work the contents of the bowl into a thick paste, then leave the bowl, covered, for 5 minutes to allow the gum to activate. Scrape the contents of the bowl out onto the work surface.

3 Knead the paste until the rest of the powder is incorporated. This creates a smooth pliable paste. For greater elasticity, knead the white vegetable fat into the paste.

4 The paste may be used immediately, but it is best left for 24 hours. Store the paste in an airtight container.

MOULDED FLOWERS

This section shows you how to make a spray of tiny flowers, a larger single flower, a briar rose and an azalea. All these flowers can be made with fondant icing, moulding icing or marzipan, but as these tend to spoil in damp or humid conditions, it is better to use pastillage, following either of the recipes on the previous pages.

Remember when you are working with petals, not to let them dry out completely before you finish moulding and shaping, or they will break as you try to put the flower together.

Egg white and water can both be used to fix petals into position on the flower. Egg white forms a stronger bond, but in most cases, water should be sufficient. If the petals are left to dry, or should break off and need replacing, then they must be attached with royal icing. Be very careful not to paint any egg white onto any part of the flower that will show, because it will dry shiny. If you make any mistakes with water, they will not be visible.

SINGLE BLOOM

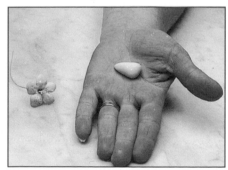

1 Form a cone of petal paste about 1.5 cm/¾ in long and 1 cm/½ in across the base.

2 Push the point of a wooden skewer up into the wide base of the cone. Using a fine sharp knife, cut five even petals around the base of the cone, turning the skewer as you work.

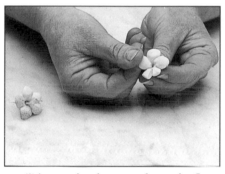

3 Take out the skewer and turn the flower out into your fingers, in order to pull out the petals. Flatten each petal between thumb and forefinger and pull from underneath with your finger against your thumb, flattening and broadening the petal at the same time.

4 For the stalk, make a small hook at the end of a piece of covered wire, dampen the hooked end in water or egg white and pull it through the centre of the flower, hooking into the side of the flower.

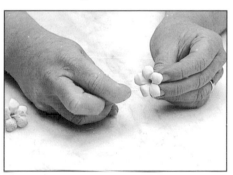

5 Cut the stamen in half, dampen the cut ends, and push them into the centre of the soft paste. As it hardens, it will hold them in position. Leave to dry in an upright position.

6 The result is a perfect flower that you can dust or paint to whatever shade you want.

BRIAR ROSE

1 To make a briar or Christmas rose, you will need a shallow curved container to set the flowers in. Bottle tops, a paint palette (as here) or polystyrene fruit trays from the greengrocer are all ideal.

To make the calyxes, colour a little petal paste green. Cut out the shapes with a calyx cutter – or you can make your own with a template. Put the template on the petal paste and cut round it with a fine sharp knife. Line the base of each container with a small square of waxed paper to prevent the petal paste sticking, and lay the calyxes on top. The calyx will curve to the shape of the container you put it in.

2 Cut five small circles for petals from pink petal paste using a plain round cutter 1.5 cm/¾ in. in diameter, and lay them on foam rubber. Curl the petals with a modelling tool, such as the dog bone, by running it gently along the edge of the petal, half on the petal and half on the foam. A delicately frilled edge will result. To curve the petal, indent the base with the ball tool or your little finger, by pushing down into the foam rubber. Pull the end of the petal out to elongate it slightly.

The end result is a very authentic-looking briar rose. Briar roses make very attractive decorations for royal-iced celebration cakes.

3 Paint inside the calyx with water or egg white and position the first petal carefully.

4 Brush one side of the petal lightly with egg white or water and leave the other side free (the fifth petal will be tucked underneath it). Lay the second petal in place overlapping the painted edge and continue until four petals are in position. Slip the fifth petal in under the edge of the first. Paint the underside of the first to secure them in place.

5 To make the centre of the flower, roll a very small ball of yellow paste and press it into a fine piece of tulle, so that the weave of the fabric is imprinted on the paste, giving the effect of stamens. This technique can also be used in making a daisy. Position it in the centre of the flower and fix it with egg white or water.

6 Cut a few stamens about 5 mm/¼ in long and insert them into the centre of the flower with a pair of tweezers.

AZALEA

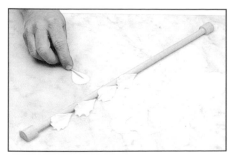

1 To make an azalea you need a piece of dowelling or a similar prop to fold the petals against. With a teardrop-shaped cutter, or with a template, cut out five petals from the paste. Cover the petals you are not working on with polythene. Gently mark the centre vein of the petal with a cocktail stick and mark two others on either side. Be careful not to press too heavily or you will slice through the petal. These marks will not really show until you come to colour the flower.

2 To create a frilled edge to the petal, roll the cocktail stick along the edge of the paste, thinning it to 5 mm/¼ in. Dust the work surface with icing sugar or cornflour. Roll the petal with the left index finger. Line up each petal as it is finished against the dowelling to curve it.

3 To set the petals into a flower shape you will need a small cone – a little funnel from the chemist is ideal. Line it with waxed paper or foil to stop the flower sticking in the funnel. Drop the first petal into the funnel, paint half the length of one side with egg white or water and put the next petal in position overlapping the painted edge.

4 To secure the petals in position press them gently together with the handle of the paint brush. Continue until you have four petals in position. The fifth petal will form the azalea's tongue. Nick off the point and drop it in over the first and fourth petals.

5 Pipe a tiny spot of royal icing from a bag into the throat of the flower and, with a pair of tweezers, insert seven stamens six of equal length and one longer for the pistil. Leave the flower to dry. Once the flower is completely dry, you can paint it with food colours or dust it with petal dust, which is a dry powder applied with a broad soft brush. Put a little cotton wool into the cup of the flower so that the petal dust touches only the edges. Brush from the outside inwards to get a graduated effect. Paint little spots on the tongue of the azalea by dampening a fine brush in water and then in the petal dust.

The petal dust gives the finished azaleas a sheen. These delicate flowers make a fine decoration for an otherwise plain cake.

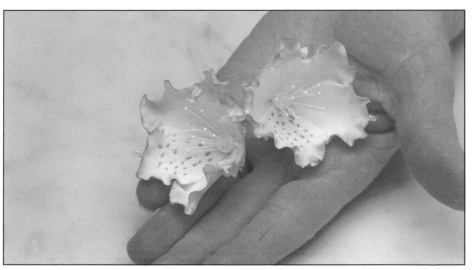

FLOWER SPRAYS

1 It is important to roll out the pastillage as thinly as possible. Put a piece of paste the size of a large pea on a smooth surface that you have lightly dusted with icing sugar or cornflour, or a mixture of both. Remember that cornflour is a drying agent, so use it very sparingly. Use either a stainless steel rolling pin or a short length of smooth wooden dowelling.

Each time the paste is rolled, lift the paste with a palette knife to ensure that it does not stick to the work surface. Roll the paste out so that it is thin enough to read through when you lay it on a printed page. The thinner the paste, the nicer the flower.

2 Plunger cutters are very useful gadgets for making petal paste flowers. Press the cutter into the paste and give it a gentle twist.

3 Lift the cutter together with the cut flower and, holding the cutter on a piece of foam rubber, depress the plunger As it is pushed into the foam, the paste will be cupped and will form the shape of a flower. You can use a cutter without a plunger, in which case push the flower out of the cutter with a paint brush.

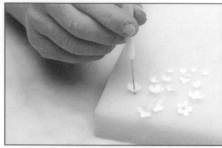

4 To wire the flowers into a spray, prick a hole in the centre of each one with a thick needle. Do this before they have dried or they will break.

5 Stamens come with a knob at each end so cut them in half and double the number. To insert a stamen, put it into the hole in the flower and pull it halfway through. Letting the flower rest on your fingertips, squeeze a little royal icing from a bag (you do not need a nozzle) into the base of the flower, and pull the stamen gently down into it. Turn the flowers upside down to dry.

6 To make a bud using a stamen as its base, take a tiny amount of paste, flatten it between finger and thumb and roll it up round the stamen. Dampen the tip of the stamen in egg white or water first so that the paste will stick.

7 To fix flowers and buds into a spray, use a white floristry tape called 'Parafilm'. Take a 10 cm/4 in strip and cut it in half widthways. Stretch it out until it is about four times its original length.

8 Lay the tape along your index finger and roll the wire stalk into the tape. Start arranging your spray. Put one or two buds at the top of the wire, catching the last 5 mm/¼ in of the stamen bases in the tape with the wire as you turn it.

9 Start adding the flowers one by one, and as you roll the tape around the stalk, catching the base of the stamens, the tape will travel down the wire so that each flower is slightly lower than the preceding one.

10 Use five to seven flowers to a spray. Finish by completely covering the wire with the tape, then cut the stalk off to a length of about 5 cm/2 in. Flower sprays can be used on a variety of cakes, in small numbers or grouped into elaborate displays.

RIBBON LOOPS

Ribbon loops are usually used in sprays of about 12 to 16 and each will take about ⅓–½ m/1–1½ ft of ribbon. They are a very useful decoration for celebration cakes and they can be used with silk flowers to make an impressive, yet simple decoration.

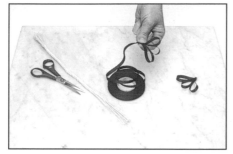

1 To make ribbon loops, you need 5 mm/¼ in ribbon, a sharp pair of scissors and some fine covered wire. Make three equal sized loops and cut off the remaining ribbon.

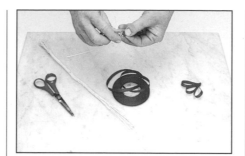

2 With the loops in your palm and the ends of the ribbon held between thumb and forefinger, place the covered wire under the ribbon ends. Turn the ends of the ribbon over the wire parallel to the sides of the ribbon. Twist the wire into the centre of the ribbon loop and wind it tightly together to cover all the ends. Cut the wire about 5 mm/¼ in from the ends of the ribbon.

3 To decorate a cake, place the ends of the wire into a ball of fondant which has been put in position on the cake.

4 Place the first loop into the centre of the ball of fondant with the ribbon ends facing out from the centre of the cake. Place another ribbon loop directly opposite, again with the ribbon ends pointing down and out from the centre. In order to form a cross, place two more loops at 90 degrees, and then fill in with more loops.

Ribbon loops are often used intertwined with flower sprays. The example below illustrates the way in which a cake can be beautifully decorated, involving little skill.

OTHER SIMPLE MOULDED FLOWERS

Simple Christmas Roses

Cut-out Pansies

 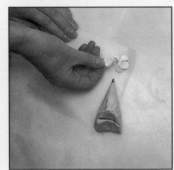 

These flowers illustrate simple ways in which fondant icings and moulding pastes can be used to create a wide variety of different flowers. Slight differences do not matter but it is important that complementary flowers are grouped together on a cake.

Once made, these decorations should be laid on non-stick paper on a baking sheet and left to dry, uncovered, in a warm place for 1–2 days.

SIMPLE CHRISTMAS ROSES

Roll out white icing on a surface lightly sprinkled with icing sugar or cornflour. Stamp out five plain rounds with a small cutter or the end of a plain nozzle. Pinch each round together at one side to form the petals. Arrange the petals against the side of a plate or patty tin so that they dry curved. When dry, attach the petals with royal icing. Leave to dry, then pipe dots of yellow.

MICHAELMAS DAISIES

Use purple icing. Stamp out a small fluted round, then, using a cocktail stick, press all round the edge to give a petal effect. Pipe dots of yellow royal icing in the centre. For buds, fold the round into an attractive shape.

CUT-OUT PANSIES

Use purple or yellow icing. For each flower stamp out four small circles and one larger one. Pinch each circle at one side and leave to dry. When firm stick the four smaller petals together in pairs, overlapping each other slightly. Attach the larger petal at the bottom. Leave to dry, then paint fine streaks of colouring in a contrasting colour.

DAFFODILS

Use yellow or orange icing. To make a trumpet, cut a small rectangle of icing. Press a cocktail stick along one long edge to flute it. Roll it into a cylinder, then squeeze one end together.

Cut out six petals for each flower. Carefully attach these round the base of each trumpet with a little unbeaten egg white. Shape the petals for a more realistic effect. If wished, paint the top of each trumpet with a little orange food colouring.

CUT-OUT ROSES

Use any suitable colour. Mould a small piece of icing into a cone shape. Press or stamp out small circles for the petals. Wrap each petal round the cone and secure with a little egg white. Curve or roll the tops of the petals outwards. For small roses, four or five petals will be sufficient; buds need only two or three petals.

Michaëlmas Daisies

Daffodils

Roses

SUGAR DECORATIONS

SUGAR BELLS

1 To make these attractive wedding decorations, you will need bell moulds of different sizes, caster sugar and egg white or water. Mix the sugar with the egg white or water until it has a coarse, thick consistency. Pack the mixture solidly into the moulds, which should be perfectly clean, and scrape the base with a knife to make it completely flat.

2 Hold the mould upside down over a sheet of greaseproof paper and gently tap out the bell. It should come out quite cleanly. Make sure the mould is completely clean and dry before using it again.

3 Leave the bells until they are dry to the touch. If they become too hard, they will break when you try to hollow out the centres.

4 Pick the bell up gently, or slip it back into the mould if you are afraid of breaking it, and carefully scrape out the centre with a sharp knife. Use the scrapings to make more bells or sugar mice. Either make a hollow just in the centre or scrape out the bell until it is a delicate 1.5 cm/¾ in thick.

SUGAR MICE

1 To make sugar mice, mix caster sugar with egg white or water as for the sugar bells. Leave half the mixture white and colour the other half pink, and pack solidly into the moulds. Turn the mice out onto greaseproof paper.

2 Make their tails with pieces of string, thin sausages of fondant icing, or pipe them with royal icing. Pipe pink eyes and noses for the white mice, and chocolate features for the pink mice. The same moulds can also be used for marzipan, chocolate or fondant mice.

MERINGUE MUSHROOMS

1 First make a meringue mix and, using nozzle no 3 or 4, pipe the stems of the mushrooms, bringing them up to a point. Make them flat at the bottom, so that they do not topple over when assembled. Pipe little beads or circles for the caps of the mushrooms. Pull the nozzle gently to the side to remove it, instead of pulling it up, or it will make a point. If you do get a point, however, push it down with a dampened finger and it will disappear.

2 Sprinkle the mushroom tops with sieved cocoa and bake on a baking sheet covered with greaseproof paper in a very slow oven (110°C/225°F/Gas ¼, with the oven door slightly ajar if possible) for an hour or two. To test if they arc done, tap them lightly with your finger. They should sound hollow and lift easily off the paper.

3 To assemble the mushrooms, make a tiny hollow under the cap with your little finger or a ball tool. Push the stem into the cap and stand them up.

LEAVES

1 Cut a paper pattern for the leaf shape you require. Pin it to a piece of green tulle, and cut round the tulle to the shape.

2 Place the tulle leaf on a strip of waxed paper and pipe round the edge with green royal icing. A delicate scalloped edge is shown, but you can pipe a shell border or a snail trail – as long as it hides the cut edge of the leaf.

3 Pipe the centre vein and the smaller veins at the side with pale green royal icing and a fine nozzle.

4 If you want to make the leaf curl, secure a rolling pin to the work surface by placing a small ball of icing under each end. Before the leaf dries, curl it on its waxed paper round the rolling pin. Stick the paper to the rolling pin with two dabs of icing.

CRYSTALLIZED FLOWERS

Crystallized flowers make spectacular decorations for a cake or gâteau.

Choose only the very best specimens for decoration. Paint the petals, the leaves or the whole flower with gum arabic, then dip them in caster sugar. Leave to dry overnight on a wire rack.

FROSTED FRUIT

Choose top quality soft fruit, such as strawberries, grapes or mandarin orange slices. Paint with egg white, dip in caster sugar and use as a centre decoration for the dinner table or serve after dinner with coffee. They can also be used to decorate very simple cakes; but they do not keep for longer than a day or so.

CHOCOLATE WORK

You can use cooking chocolate or dessert chocolate for many different kinds of decoration. The chocolate is first melted, then either poured out to make a sheet, from which the shapes are cut, or piped.

When melting chocolate it is important not to let it get too hot or it will thin out considerably and run everywhere. Break the chocolate into pieces and put it in a double saucepan over hot water. Do not allow the water to boil. The chocolate should never be above blood heat − if it gets too hot the oil will separate out of it and it will become unusable. A quick way to test for temperature without a thermometer is to dab your finger in the chocolate and touch it to your lip. It should feel neither hot nor cold. It may take up to half an hour to melt chocolate in this way, but the results will be well worth the extra time.

Remember that if you handle chocolate the warmth of your fingers will leave prints on it and dull the surface. Handle it as little as possible, preferably using a palette knife.

CHOCOLATE FOR CUTTING

1 When the chocolate has melted, pour it out onto a sheet of silicone paper. This is non-stick paper, so the finished shapes will come away easily.

2 Lift the edges of the paper and tilt the chocolate in different directions to ensure the surface is smooth and even after pouring. Leave it to stand until almost rubbery, but not hard, before you cut the shapes.

SQUARES AND DIAMONDS

With a sharp knife, cut parallel lines across the chocolate. Cut another set of parallel lines at 90 degrees to make squares. Cut the second set of parallel lines at 45 degrees for diamonds. Use a ruler, or cut freehand.

CIRCLES

Cut circles by pressing in and giving a slight twist with a round cutter. Make rings by cutting a smaller circle inside the first circle. You can leave the shapes in the sheet of chocolate or put them on one side to dry.

HORSESHOES, HEARTS AND STARS

Horseshoes, hearts and stars are all cut in the same way as circles. Cut small holes in your shapes with a tiny round cutter and thread ribbon through them when dry to hang on the Christmas tree or give as gifts. Hearts dressed with ribbon make attractive valentine gifts.

CURLS

Make long chocolate curls (or caraque) by pushing an icing smoother, or large cook's knife, down the length of the sheet of chocolate. This lifts a thin layer off the surface and the chocolate will curl up. Cut it into strips to decorate gâteaux or make bark for a forest scene.

LEAVES

One way to make chocolate leaves is to paint the back of a leaf with melted chocolate and peel off the leaf when it has dried. Alternatively, pipe a leaf shape using melted chocolate and draw on the veins with a cocktail stick after it has set slightly.

PIPING WITH CHOCOLATE

1 You can pipe an infinite number of attractive decorations to use on cakes with melted chocolate. Work quickly because the chocolate starts to set rapidly. With a fleur-de-lys shape, wait for the first section to dry slightly before attempting the second, and so on, otherwise the shapes will run into each other. Chocolate buttons are fun to make and can be coated with chocolate nonpareils or hundreds and thousands.

2 More intricate shapes, such as flowers or chandeliers, can be outline-piped to give a good contrast with the cake topping, which will show through underneath. These can be piped as a continuous line, provided the chocolate is the right consistency. If it is too hot, the lines will flow together. If it is too cold, it will not come out of the piping bag.

Squares

Diamonds

Circles

Hearts and Stars

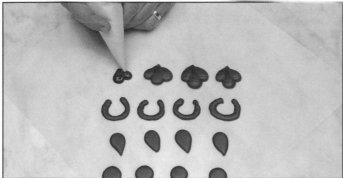

Fleur-de-lys and other piped shapes

Curls

Outline-piped shapes

Leaves

FAVOURITE CAKES

The cakes in this chapter can all be made fairly quickly and no doubt will be eaten with equal haste! Here you will find tempting gâteaux and cakes that are ideal for special teas. These recipes do not require years of experience or particular skills to ensure success but they are all just that extra bit special.

You may choose to make one of these special cakes as an alternative to dessert — also they make practical sweet courses for buffet-style meals. If you have not had time to plan ahead and create a complicated iced birthday cake, then one these recipes will be the perfect alternative.

Apricot and Almond Gâteau see recipe overleaf.

APRICOT AND ALMOND GÂTEAU

The combination of apricots with almonds is a classic one, particularly in French pastries.

> *3-egg quantity Genoese Sponge*
> *(page 19)*
> *2 × 425g/15 oz cans apricot*
> *halves, drained*
> *300ml/¹/₂pt double cream*
> *1 quantity Apricot Glaze*
> *(page 58)*
> *175g/6oz Almond Paste*
> *(page 28)*
> *a few flaked almonds, toasted*

1 Set the oven at 190°C/375°F/Gas 5. Grease and base line three 20 cm/8 in sandwich tins. Divide the sponge mixture between the prepared tins and bake for 10–15 minutes, until risen and firm to the touch. Remove from the tins and cool on a wire rack.

2 Use sufficient apricot halves to completely cover one layer of sponge. Chop the remaining apricots.

3 Whip the cream and reserve one-third, placing it in a piping bag fitted with a large star nozzle. Fold the chopped apricots into the remaining two-thirds and use to sandwich the cakes together finishing with the layer covered with the apricot halves. Brush the sides of the cake with apricot glaze.

4 On a surface lightly sifted with icing sugar, roll out the almond paste to a strip of the exact size to cover the sides of the cake. Trim the almond paste and press it gently into position.

5 Brush the apricot halves with apricot glaze and sprinkle with the flaked almonds. Gently 'dot' any remaining apricot glaze over the almonds using a pastry brush. Decorate with rosettes of the reserved whipped cream and chill until required.

VARIATIONS

Other fruits can be used to vary this gâteau recipe. Select tangy fruits to contrast with the sweet almond paste. Instead of using just one fruit, why not combine two or more types, selecting some fresh fruit with some canned varieties?

FRUIT-TOPPED RICH CHEESECAKE

This cheesecake can be served just as it is, or decorated with whatever fruit is in season.

Base
200g/7oz digestive biscuits, crushed
100g/4oz butter, melted
Filling
900g/2lb cream cheese or curd cheese
225g/8oz caster sugar
40g/1½oz plain flour
5 eggs
150ml/¼pt double cream
grated rind of 1 large lemon
Topping
about 225g/8oz fresh fruits in season
lemon juice
½ quantity Apricot Glaze (page 58)

1 Set the oven at 230°C/450°F/Gas Mark 8. Grease a 24 cm/9½ in spring-form tin. Mix together the digestive biscuits and butter and press on to the base of the prepared tin. Chill until firm.

2 Mix together all the ingredients for the filling until evenly combined. Pour over the base and bake for 15 minutes. Reduce the oven temperature to 110°C/225°F/Gas ¼ and continue to cook the cheesecake for a further 1 hour. Turn off the heat and leave the cake to cool in the oven.

3 When completely cold, remove the cheesecake from the tin. Prepare the fruits according to type and dip any that will discolour in lemon juice. Arrange the fruit attractively over the surface of the cheesecake. Brush with apricot glaze and serve as soon as possible after decorating, or chill until required.

COOK'S TIP

Instead of fresh summer fruits, the cheesecake can be topped with bottled fruit. A wide variety of commercially bottled fruits are available and they are usually packed in syrups flavoured with brandy or liqueurs. Drain the fruit before arranging it on top of the cheesecake, then thicken some of the syrup from the bottle with arrowroot. Allow the thickened syrup to cool before using it to glaze the fruit.

STRAWBERRY LAYER CAKE

The halved strawberries around the sides of this cake give a decorative finish, and adding the liqueur makes all the difference to the flavour.

3-egg quantity Genoese Sponge, baked in two 20cm/8in sandwich tins (page 19)
450g/1lb medium-sized strawberries
50g/2oz icing sugar, plus extra for dredging
225g/8oz cream cheese or curd cheese
15g/½oz gelatine
2 tbsp water
2 tbsp Kirsch, strawberry liqueur or other liqueur
300ml/½pt double cream

1 Line the sides of an 18 cm/7 in round cake tin with non-stick paper. Press one sponge cake into the base of the tin, trimming it if necessary.

2 Choose about 10 even-sized strawberries. Hull them and cut each one in half. Press the strawberries, cut side out, against the side of the tin, around the outside edge of the cake.

3 Hull 175 g/6 oz strawberries and purée them with the icing sugar and cream cheese until smooth. Dissolve the gelatine in the water in a basin over a saucepan of hot, not boiling, water. Stir until the gelatine has dissolved completely, then stir it into the strawberry mixture with the liqueur.

4 Whip half the cream until it holds its shape, then fold it into the strawberry mixture. Carefully pour the strawberry mixture into the tin taking care not to disturb the strawberry halves.

5 Chill until lightly set, then place the second sponge layer on top, trimming if necessary. Chill for several hours until firm.

6 Carefully remove cake from the tin and peel away the non-stick paper. Whip the remaining cream until it just holds its shape. Spoon it into a piping bag fitted with a star nozzle. Dredge the top of the cake with icing sugar, then decorate with piped cream and the remaining strawberries. Serve at once or chill until required.

LEMON CREAM HEART

A light whisked sponge, split, filled and covered with a delicious lemon cream, makes an ideal cake for a special celebration tea. If you don't own a heart-shaped tin, simply make a round one in two 20 cm/8 in sandwich tins and follow the chart on page 19 for cooking instructions.

3-egg quantity Whisked Sponge
mixture (page 18)
Filling
75g/3oz butter
100g/4oz granulated sugar
2 eggs, beaten
grated rind and juice of 2 small
lemons or 1 very large lemon
150ml/¼pt double cream
Decoration
fresh yellow flowers
sprigs of fern

1 Set the oven at 190°C/375°F/Gas 5. Grease and flour a 1.5 l/2½ pt heart-shaped tin.

2 Pour the sponge mixture into the prepared tin and bake for about 20 minutes until risen and firm to the touch. Allow to cool in the tin, then transfer to a wire rack and invert the tin over the cake. Leave until cold.

3 Melt the butter in a bowl over a saucepan of simmering water. Stir in the sugar, eggs, lemon rind and juice and stir well. Cook for about 20–25 minutes, stirring frequently, until the mixture is thick. Chill well. Whip the cream, then fold it into the lemon mixture.

4 Split the cake and sandwich together with about one-quarter of the lemon cream. Use the remaining cream to cover the surface of the cake, swirling it decoratively. Decorate with flowers and fern sprigs. Serve at once or chill until required. If the cake is to be chilled, then do not add the flowers until just before it is served.

RASPBERRY AND HAZELNUT GÂTEAU

The combination of raspberries with hazelnuts is a particularly good one. The cake may be made in advance, but do not fill it until the day it is required as the juice from the raspberries tends to seep into the cake layers and make them soggy.

6 eggs, separated
1 tsp vanilla essence
225g/8oz caster sugar
225g/8oz hazelnuts, toasted and
finely ground
6 tbsp dry white breadcrumbs
1 tsp baking powder
pinch of salt
Filling and decoration
450g/1lb fresh raspberries
450ml/¾pt double cream
½ quantity Redcurrant Glaze
(page 58)
tiny leaves or mint sprigs

1 Set the oven at 190°C/375°F/Gas 5. Grease and base line three 20 cm/8 in sandwich tins using non-stick paper.

2 Whisk the egg yolks with the vanilla essence and half the sugar until pale and thick. Stir in the hazelnuts, breadcrumbs and baking powder.

3 Whisk the egg whites with a pinch of salt until stiff. Add the remaining sugar a little at a time, whisking well between each addition.

4 Stir a little of the egg white mixture into the nut mixture to soften it slightly, then gently fold in the remaining egg whites. Take great care not to overmix the egg whites or all the air will be knocked out of them. Transfer to the prepared tins and level the surface of each. Bake for 25–30 minutes until risen and firm to the touch. Cool slightly in the tins, then trans-

fer to a wire rack and invert the cake tins over the cakes. Leave until completely cold.

5 Wash and pick over the raspberries. Whip the cream until it just holds its shape. Reserve a little to pipe, then use a very scant half to sandwich the cake layers using half the raspberries as well. Arrange the remaining raspberries on the top layer of sponge and brush them carefully with the redcurrant glaze. Chill until set.

6 Spread the remaining cream over the side of the cake. Pipe swirls on top of the cake and decorate with the tiny leaves.

COFFEE GALETTE

Thin layers of sponge cake may be sandwiched together with many different fillings to make a variety of delicious gâteaux; the side coating and decorations can be varied to suit the chosen flavour. For example, try lemon, orange or chocolate with praline.

4-egg quantity Whisked Sponge, baked in 6 × 20cm/8in sandwich tins (page 18)
1 quantity Coffee Marshmallow Buttercream (page 48)
½ quantity Coffee Glacé Icing (pages 42/72)
50g/2oz nibbed almonds, toasted, or chocolate, grated
chocolate coffee beans to decorate

1 Sandwich the sponge layers together using about half of the buttercream. Spread the glacé icing over the top layer of sponge and leave until set firm.

2 Use most of the remaining buttercream to cover the sides of the cake. Carefully press the nuts or grated chocolate onto the sides of the cake to coat it evenly.

3 Use the remaining buttercream to pipe rosettes round the top edge of the cake. Decorate with chocolate coffee beans.

VARIATION

BRANDY SNAP GALETTE

Instead of coating the sides of the cake with chopped nuts, press brandy snaps around the cake. Assemble the cake and complete the decoration on top before adding the brandy snaps. Press the biscuits vertically against the cream on the side of the cake, then tie a bow of ribbon round them to keep them in place.

CARROT CAKE

This is a deliciously moist cake made with finely grated carrot and lots of ground or finely chopped nuts. The strong, sweet flavour of passion fruit complements it particularly well.

7 eggs, separated
200g/7oz caster sugar
100g/4oz ground almonds
100g/4oz walnuts, ground or very finely chopped (alternatively use toasted hazelnuts)
50g/2oz desiccated coconut
300g/10oz carrots, peeled and finely grated
50g/2oz self-raising flour, sifted
grated rind of 1 lemon or orange
Icing and decoration
4 passion fruit
1½ quantity Crème au Beurre (page 43)
1 tsp lemon or orange juice
75g/3oz Almond Paste (page 28)
orange food colouring
12 small pieces angelica

1 Set the oven at 180°C/350°F/Gas 4. Grease and base line a 25 cm/10 in round cake tin.

2 Whisk the egg yolks with half the sugar until pale and thick. Stir in the ground almonds, walnuts, coconut, carrots, flour and lemon rind.

3 Whisk the egg whites until stiff, then whisk in the remaining sugar a little at a time until the mixture is really stiff and glossy. Stir a small spoonful of the egg whites into the carrot mixture to soften it, then very lightly fold in the remaining whites.

4 Transfer the mixture to the prepared tin, level the surface and bake for about 45 minutes until risen and firm to the touch.

5 Leave to cool in the tin, then transfer the cake to a wire rack. Invert the cake tin over the cake and leave until completely cold.

6 Split the passion fruit and put the pulp into a nylon sieve over a small bowl. Press out the juice with a wooden spoon. Mix the juice into the crème au beurre adding the lemon juice until the cream is smooth.

7 Split the cake in half horizontally and sandwich it together with a generous quarter of the icing. Use the remaining icing to swirl over the top and sides of the cake. Mark the cake into 12 portions.

8 Colour the almond paste with food colouring and shape it into 12 carrots. Mark lines across each one with a knife. Stick pieces of angelica into each carrot top and arrange the carrots round the top edge of the cake.

SACHERTORTE

A rich, firm, yet moist chocolate cake, covered with a shiny chocolate icing. Traditionally, the only decoration it has is the name 'Sacher' written in chocolate, but whirls of fresh whipped cream and small chocolate curls are a luscious addition to this recipe.

> 150g/5oz butter
> 150g/5oz caster sugar, plus extra for coating
> 6 egg yolks
> 1tsp vanilla essence
> 175g/6oz plain chocolate, melted
> 100g/4oz plain flour, plus extra for coating
> 25g/1oz ground almonds
> 2tbsp cocoa powder
> 1tsp ground cinnamon
> 8 egg whites
> Decoration
> 6tbsp Apricot Glaze (page 58)
> 1 quantity Mocha Icing made without the instant coffee (page 53)
> whipped cream
> chocolate curls (page 136)

1 Set the oven at 190°C/375°F/Gas 5. Grease and base line a 23 cm/9 in round cake tin. Mix together 1 tsp each of flour and sugar and use to coat the sides of the tin.

2 Cream the butter and sugar until light and fluffy. Beat in the egg yolks one at a time. Beat in the vanilla essence, Stir in the cooled chocolate.

3 Sift together the flour, ground almonds, cocoa powder and cinnamon and fold these dry ingredients into the mixture.

4 Whisk the egg whites until stiff. Stir a spoonful into the chocolate mixture, then carefully fold in the remaining whites.

5 Transfer the mixture to the prepared tin. Level the surface and bake for about 55 minutes until risen and firm to the touch. Leave to cool in the tin, then transfer to a wire rack and leave until cold.

6 Split the cake horizontally and sandwich it together with half the apricot glaze. Brush the remaining glaze over the top and sides of the cake.

7 Beat the mocha icing until smooth, then pour it over the cake, smoothing the sides with a palette knife.

8 Leave until the icing is completely set, then decorate with whipped cream and chocolate curls.

TRUFFLE LOG

This is a no-cook cake which takes minutes to prepare and it keeps your guests guessing for ages! It is also an ideal way to use up the off-cuts from rich fruit cakes.

450g/1lb rich fruit cake
50–75g/2–3oz apricot jam or marmalade
2tbsp rum or other spirit, or fruit juice
100g/4oz plain chocolate, melted
25g/1oz white or milk chocolate, melted

1 Crumble the fruit cake into a bowl, or process it in a food processor – but take care not to reduce it too fine or it will become a sticky mess. Add the jam, depending on how moist the cake is, and the rum and mix well.

2 On a piece of non-stick paper or clingfilm, form the mixture into a long, triangular shape; once you have the basic shape wrap the covering around it to continue moulding it. The cake may be stored in the refrigerator for two or three weeks at this stage if it is well wrapped.

3 Place the cake on a wire rack over a baking sheet or tray, and spread the sides and ends with the plain chocolate.

4 Fill a small paper piping bag with the white or milk chocolate. Snip off the end and drizzle the chocolate decoratively over the cake. Chill until firm, then transfer to a serving plate. Cut into thin slices to serve.

WALNUT ICEBOX CAKE

This is quick to make and delicious to eat. It uses broken biscuits to form the main part of the 'cake'.

> 225g/8oz plain sweet biscuits
> 100g/4oz butter
> juice of 1 orange
> 150g/5oz soft light brown sugar
> 50g/2oz walnuts, chopped
> 1tsp vanilla essence
> ½ quantity Buttercream or Crème au Beurre, flavoured with coffee or orange if liked (page 43)
> walnut halves

1 Grease an 18 cm/7 in sandwich tin. Break the biscuits into small pieces in a bowl.

2 Melt the butter, orange juice and sugar slowly stirring all the time. Pour over the biscuits, then add the chopped walnuts and vanilla essence. Mix well until the biscuit pieces are evenly coated. Press the mixture into the prepared tin and chill until firm, preferably overnight.

3 Turn the cake out onto a plate and spread with buttercream or crème au beurre. Pipe a decorative border, if liked and decorate with walnut halves.

COOK'S TIP

The Walnut icebox cake can be used as a base for a clever dessert. Prepare and set the mixture as above. Instead of adding buttercream or crème au beurre, combine some soft cheese with a little icing sugar and lemon rind to taste, then pipe it in large swirls round the top edge of the cake. Chill the cake until it is to be served. Fill the middle with scoops of ice cream, selecting one flavour or several different flavours as you wish. Decorate with pieces of fresh fruit and serve at once.

OLD-FASHIONED ALMOND CAKE

Ground almonds and ground rice make this cake wonderfully moist. It can be stored for weeks, if it lasts that long, and seems to improve in flavour. It is not essential to decorate it, but if you do, add the decorations on the day of serving.

225g/8oz butter, softened
225g/8oz caster sugar
3 eggs, beaten
½tsp almond essence
100g/4oz ground almonds
100g/4oz ground rice
50g/2oz self-raising flour, sifted
Decoration
1tbsp Apricot Glaze (page 58)
3tbsp flaked almonds, toasted
a little Glacé Icing (page 42)

1 Set the oven at 170°C/325°F/Gas 3. Grease and base-line a 20 cm/8 in round cake tin. Cream the butter and sugar until light and fluffy. Beat in the eggs, a little at a time, then beat in the almond essence.

2 Mix together the ground almonds, ground rice and flour and fold into the creamed mixture. Transfer the mixture to the prepared tin. Bake the cake for 1¼– 1½ hours until risen and firm to the touch. Cool in the tin, then turn out onto a wire rack. Invert the tin over the cake and leave until cold.

3 Brush the top of the cake with apricot glaze, sprinkle with almonds, then drizzle with a little glacé icing.

TROPICAL BANANA CAKE

Bananas, cream and toasted coconut are combined with maraschino cherries to make this tropically flavoured cake. For total authenticity try adding a dash of white rum to the fresh cream!

> 3 large ripe bananas, peeled
> 100g/4oz butter, softened
> 150g/5oz soft brown sugar
> 2 eggs, beaten
> 225g/8oz plain flour
> 1tbsp baking powder
> Decoration
> 300ml/½t double cream
> 50g/2oz desiccated coconut, toasted
> banana slices, dipped in lemon juice
> maraschino cherries

1 Set the oven at 180°C/350°F/Gas 4. Grease and base-line a 20 cm/8 in round cake tin. Mash the bananas well. Beat the butter and sugar until light and fluffy, then beat in the eggs until well mixed. Fold in the bananas. Sift the flour and baking powder together and fold into the mixture.

2 Transfer the mixture to the prepared tin. Level the surface, then make a slight dip in the centre. Bake for about 1 hour until a skewer inserted into the centre of the cake comes out clean. Cool on a wire rack, covered by the inverted tin. When cold, split the cake horizontally into three layers.

3 Whip the cream until it stands in soft peaks and use about three-quarters of it to fill and cover the whole surface of the cake. Press coconut all over the cream. Use the remaining cream to pipe swirls over the top of the cake and decorate with banana slices and cherries. Serve within a few hours of decorating.

MURRUMBIDGEE CAKE

This is an incredibly rich fruit and nut cake that originated in Australia; for good results fresh nuts are used and shelled just before they are added to the mixture. It needs no decoration whatsoever as the slices are so attractive.

> 175g/6oz whole brazil nuts, shelled
> 175g/6oz whole walnuts, shelled
> 225g/8oz stoned dates
> 100g/4oz mixed candied peel, chopped
> 50g/2oz each of red, green and yellow glacé cherries
> 50g/2oz raisins
> 75g/3oz plain flour
> pinch of salt
> ½tsp baking powder
> 100g/4oz soft light brown sugar
> 3 eggs, beaten
> 1tsp vanilla essence
> 2tbsp rum or other spirit
> 2tbsp Apricot Glaze (page 58)

1 Set the oven at 150°C/300°F/Gas 2. Grease and line an 18 cm/7 in round cake tin.

2 Mix all the nuts and fruits together. Sift the flour, salt and baking powder into a bowl. Stir in the sugar. Add the fruit to the dry ingredients and toss well to evenly coat all the pieces with the flour. Add the beaten eggs and vanilla essence and mix well.

3 Transfer the mixture to the prepared tin, pressing it down with the back of a spoon. Bake for 1½–1¾ hours until firm and golden. The cake is cooked when a skewer inserted into the middle comes out free of any sticky mixture. Cover the top of the cake loosely with foil if it begins to over-brown on the surface.

4 Cool the cake in the tin, then spoon the rum or other spirit over it. Leave to go cold, then wrap in clingfilm and foil, and store in a cool dry place.

5 Leave the cake to mature for at least one month, adding more rum as required. Before serving, brush the cake with apricot glaze.

DEVIL'S FOOD CAKE

This is a very dark chocolate cake with a light spongy texture. It is coated in chocolate fudge icing and for contrast it is filled with whipped cream.

225ml/8fl oz milk

1tbsp lemon juice or vinegar

225g/8oz plain flour

1tsp bicarbonate of soda

50g/2oz cocoa powder

100g/4oz butter or margarine

225g/8oz soft brown sugar

2 eggs, beaten

150ml/¹/₄pt double cream

1¹/₂ quantity Chocolate Fudge Icing (page 51)

1 Set the oven at 180°C/350°F/Gas 4. Grease and base line two 23 cm/9 in sandwich tins.

2 Mix the milk with the lemon juice and put to one side. Sift the flour, bicarbonate of soda and cocoa powder into a bowl.

3 Cream the butter and sugar together until light and fluffy, then slowly beat in the eggs a little at a time. Fold in the dry ingredients alternately with the milk mixture. Spoon the mixture into the prepared tins, level the surface and bake for about 25 minutes until risen and firm to the touch.

4 Leave to cool in the tin, then transfer to a wire rack and leave until completely cold. Whip the cream until stiff and use to sandwich the cake layers together. Place the cake on a plate and spread the fudge icing over the top and sides to cover it completely.

COOK'S TIP

Devil's food cake freezes very well. Unfilled it can be stored for several months, or with a cream filling and the fudge topping it can be frozen for a few weeks. To freeze the completed cake, open freeze it until the icing is firm, then pack it loosely in foil. Thaw the cake at room temperature if unfilled or in the refrigerator if decorated.

CHOCOLATE ORANGE CAKE

A good cake for family Sunday teas, this cake is quick to make and is full of flavour! As an alternative, buttercream can be used instead of the fresh cream; or try a combination of soft cheese sweetened with icing sugar and thinned to a piping consistency with a little natural yogurt.

1 quantity Chocolate Quick Cake Mix (page 15)
grated rind of 2 oranges
150ml/¼pt double cream
225g/8oz plain chocolate

1 Set the oven at 170°C/325°F/Gas 3. Line and grease a 23 cm/9 in round cake tin. Make the cake according to the instructions, adding the grated orange rind to the ingredients. Turn the mixture into the tin. Bake for 1¼ hours, until the cake is firm on top. Turn out and cool the cake on a wire rack.

2 Split the cake horizontally when cold. Whip the cream until it stands in soft peaks, then sandwich the cake together with a little of it. Set the remaining cream aside.

3 Melt the chocolate in a bowl over a saucepan of hot water. Use some of the chocolate to pipe shapes onto waxed paper (page 136) and set them aside. Top the cake with the remaining chocolate and mark it into an attractive pattern as shown. Leave the chocolate to set.

4 Put the reserved cream in a piping bag fitted with a medium star nozzle and pipe an edging of cream on the cake. Top the cream edging with the chocolate shapes. Keep the cake in a cool place until it is served.

CHOCOLATE TIPS

When working with chocolate, fine results are only achieved with practice. The more often you melt and use chocolate to cover or decorate cakes, then the more experienced you will become with the techniques and the better the results are likely to be. However, there are a few tips that help whether you are a beginner or experienced with chocolate work.

SUCCESSFUL MELTING

A simple mistake which is often made when melting chocolate is to overheat it. Always melt chocolate in a basin over hot water, not straight in a pan. Do not allow the water to boil or the chocolate may overheat. Do not allow any water to splash into the chocolate as this will cause it to separate and the texture will be ruined. Stir the chocolate occasionally during melting.

A GLOSSY FINISH

The sheen on the finished, set chocolate decoration depends to a great extent on the type of chocolate used. The better quality chocolate, then the better the finish. However, a useful tip is to stir a little delicate oil into the melted chocolate if it is used for covering cakes. This is not practical if you are making chocolate shapes but it is ideal for chocolate which is piped straight onto a cake or which is used as an icing. Grapeseed oil or sunflower oil can be used and it should be well mixed with the chocolate until smooth and glossy.

CHOCOLATE VARIATIONS

Take advantage of the different types of chocolate that are available to vary even the most simple decorations. For example, swirl melted dark and white chocolate evenly over a cake to make an unusual covering. Coat a cake in milk chocolate, then smooth random lines of dark chocolate through it for an unusual effect. A clever, simple combination is achieved by covering a cake with milk chocolate, then drizzling white chocolate over it before combing the surface with a serrated scraper.

CHOCOLATE BITS

Never discard small amounts of leftover chocolate. Leave it to set, then store it in an airtight polythene bag in the refrigerator. It can be melted again for decorating cakes or it can be used to make chocolate sauce, or to flavour a sweet, cornflour-thickened milk sauce.

GRATED CHOCOLATE

Small pieces of leftover chocolate can be grated in a rotary grater or food processor and kept in an airtight container in the refrigerator for coating cakes or sprinkling over desserts. Mix different types for a clever effect and interesting contrast in flavour.

SHABBY CHOCOLATE DECORATIONS

Piped chocolate decorations do not keep well and they are easily damaged. They loose their splendid appearance after a few days but they should not be discarded as the chocolate can be melted down and used again.

VARIATIONS

Chocolate cakes are a real family treat. The basic mixture can be varied by adding different flavours, and the fillings can also be adjusted.

CHOCOLATE NUT CAKE

Add some finely chopped nuts to the prepared mixture. Mixed nuts, walnuts, hazelnuts or almonds are all suitable. Sandwich the cake with chocolate nut spread and just sift a little icing sugar over the top if you want to keep the decoration very plain.

CHOCOLATE CREAM CHEESE CAKE

Instead of cream, make a filling from cream cheese, or low-fat soft cheese, beaten with a little icing sugar and milk or fruit juice to taste. The filling can be left plain or it can be flavoured with grated chocolate for a mottled effect, with honey or fruit syrup instead of icing sugar.

Combed chocolate. This is done directly on the cake. Spread the surface of the cake with melted chocolate and when beginning to firm, use an icing comb or fork to produce a pattern. Draw the comb across the chocolate in straight or wavy lines.

Easy chocolate curls. Use a vegetable peeler to scrape curls from a chocolate bar.

SPECIAL-OCCASION CAKES

The centrepiece of any special event is always the cake – whether it's Christmas, a wedding, coming of age or a retirement party. Yet, however spectacular the cakes in this section may look, they are all well within the grasp of the enthusiastic amateur cake decorator!

Icing a large area does take a little practice so before committing yourself to tackling a three-tier cake experiment on a polystyrene mould, a strong card box set on a cake board, or a 'practice' cake that the family will be happy to eat even if the decoration isn't perfect! Before you embark on the task of making and decorating any special cake, do read through the opening chapters of this book. Plan the type, size and shape of cake that you wish to make – use the ideas that follow exactly as they are presented if they suit your requirements. Alternatively, do not be afraid of using your imagination to add your own personal touches to the decoration.

Easy Wedding Cake see recipe overleaf.

EASY WEDDING CAKE

This simple but beautiful cake can be iced in hours! Choose your flowers – dried ones are lovely for an Autumn wedding – and colour co-ordinate them with the icing, lace and ribbon.

25cm/10in and 18cm/7in round
Rich Fruit Cake (page 22)
2 quantities Apricot Glaze
(page 58)
2 quantities Almond Paste (page
28)
30cm/12in and 23cm/9in round
silver cake boards
2 quantities Moulding Icing
(page 56)
colouring as required
cornflour for dusting
1.5m/5ft piece ribbon, about
0.5cm/¼in wide
1.5m/5ft gathered lace edging,
about 4cm/1½in wide
fresh or dried flowers
4 cake pillars
1 small round block of green foam
or similar, about 6.5cm/2½in. in
diameter, for securing flowers
(available from florists)

1 Brush the cakes with apricot glaze and cover them with almond paste. Place on boards.

2 Colour the moulding icing if liked. Dust a work surface with cornflour, roll out the icing and use it to cover the cakes and exposed surfaces of the boards. Leave it overnight to harden.

3 Secure the lace around the base of each cake. Moisten the green foam block if using fresh flowers and stand it in a small dish so it fits snugly. Alternatively, wrap the lower half of the foam in foil. Arrange the flowers and position them on the cake. Position the pillars and assemble the cake at the last minute before the reception.

Wedding Cake

WEDDING CAKE

It is best to have this cake finished at least a week before the wedding, so aim to start icing several weeks in advance. Once the cakes are completed, and all the icing has dried, store them in special cake boxes which are available from specialist shops.

Green makes an unusual colour for decoration, but any other colour can be substituted to tie in with the general colour scheme of the wedding.

> *15cm/6in square Rich Fruit Cake*
> *(page 22)*
> *20cm/8in square Rich Fruit Cake*
> *(page 22)*
> *25cm/10in square Rich Fruit*
> *Cake (page 22)*
> *2 quantities Apricot Glaze*
> *(page 58)*
> *2¾ quantity Almond Paste*
> *(page 28)*
> *3 square silver cake boards,*
> *measuring 35.5cm/14in,*
> *25cm/10in and 20cm/8in*
> *Royal Icing for flat icing, made*
> *using 14 egg whites (page 32)*
> *Royal Icing for decorating, made*
> *using 4 egg whites (page 32)*
> *green and yellow colourings*
> *gypsophilla or orange blossom*
> *posy of flowers for top of cake*
> *8 cake pillars*

1 Brush the cakes with apricot glaze and cover them with the almond paste. Place them on the boards and cover them with royal icing. It is best to allow plenty of time to build up the thin layers of icing perfectly. Leave them to harden.

2 Make a template: fold a 30 cm/12 in square of non-stick baking paper in half, then fold it in half twice more, to form a triangle consisting of 8 thicknesses of paper. Make a pencil mark on one folded side 6.5 cm/2½ in from the tip and make another mark the same distance from the tip on the opposite side. Use a pair of compasses to draw a concave curve linking the two marks together. Cut the paper along the curve. Open out the folded paper and lay it over the smallest cake. Mark the outline of the paper on the cake with a pin. Refold the paper and mark it again on each folded side, this time 9 cm/3½ in from the tip. Join the marks with a concave curve, as before, and cut along the curve. Open out the paper, lay it on the 20 cm/8 in cake and mark the outline as before with a pin. Refold the paper and cut out a third curve, marking the sides of the triangle 11.5 cm/4½ in from the tip. Unfold the paper and mark the outline with a pin on the largest cake.

3 Place about 2 tablespoons of the royal icing for decorating in a piping bag fitted with a writer nozzle (no 1). Use it to pipe over the marked outlines. Pipe more lines on each side of the boards, 5 mm/¼ in away from the edge.

4 Thin more icing with water to run-out consistency (page 104) and use it to fill the areas between the base of the cake and the marked line on the boards. Place more icing in a piping bag fitted with a medium star nozzle and use it to pipe a scroll border around the top and lower edges of the cakes. Run-out the area between the marked outline on top of the cakes and the scroll edges. Leave to harden.

5 Colour about 6 tablespoons of royal icing with green colouring. (If the green colouring is bright, you can tone it down with a drop of black or brown colouring.) Use the green icing to pipe decorative borders around the sides of the cake as in the photograph.

6 Colour the remaining icing yellow, and place it in a piping bag fitted with a writer nozzle (no 1). Use it to pipe triangles of dots around all the runout work on the boards. Pipe dots along the run-out edges on the tops of the cake. Use the remainder to complete the decorative borders around the sides of the cakes.

7 Arrange the pillars on the cakes and decorate the cakes with the flowers. Assemble the cakes as late as possible before the reception.

AMERICAN WEDDING CAKE

Traditional American wedding cakes are made of sponge cake, as opposed to rich fruit cake, and they do not have pillars. American cakes are often decorated with buttercream or frosting, but moulding icing is easier to use.

The two top tiers in this recipe are placed on thin silver cake cards before mounting. This is not essential, but it makes cutting much easier.

25 cm/10 in ROUND

350g/12oz self-raising flour
½tsp baking powder
350g/12oz sugar
350g/12oz butter or margarine, softened
6 eggs

20 cm/8 in ROUND

225g/8oz self-raising flour
¼tsp baking powder
225g/8oz sugar
225g/8oz butter or margarine, softened
4 eggs

15 cm/6 in ROUND

100g/4oz self-raising flour
good pinch of baking powder
100g/4oz sugar
100g/4oz butter or margarine, softened
2 eggs

BRANDY BUTTER

575g/1¼lb unsalted butter, softened
176g/6oz icing sugar
4-5tbsp brandy

DECORATION

2 quantities Apricot Glaze (page 58)
3 quantities Moulding Icing (page 56)
cornflour for dusting
30cm/12in round silver cake board
23cm/9in and 18cm/7in round silver cake cards
1 quantity Royal Icing (page 32)
several pieces of plastic fern or asparagus fern
colouring as required
tulle butterflies (page 113)
small posy of flowers

1 Make one cake at a time. Grease and line the tin. Set oven at 180°C/350°F Gas 4. Place the cake ingredients in a bowl and beat well with an electric whisk or wooden spoon for 1 to 2 minutes until evenly blended. Turn them into the tin and level the surface. Bake the 25 cm/10 in cake for about 1 hour to 1 hour 10 minutes, the 20 cm/8 in cake for 50 minutes to 1 hour, and the 15 cm/6 in cake for 40 to 45 minutes. Transfer the cakes to a wire rack to cool.

2 To make the brandy butter, beat the softened butter in a bowl with the icing sugar. Add the brandy and beat well until smooth.

3 Split each cake horizontally and sandwich together with brandy butter. Place the largest cake on the board and brush it with apricot glaze. Dust a work surface with cornflour and roll out about a third of the moulding icing on it. Use the icing to cover the surface of the cake on the board. Press the lower edge into the corners of the cake and trim the edges 2.5 cm/½ in away from cake.

4 Place the 20 cm/8 in cake on the 23 cm/9 in cake card. Brush with apricot glaze and position it on the first cake.

5 Cover with moulding icing, pressing the icing into the lower edge, and trimming off the icing at the edge of the card. Position and ice the smallest cake in the same way, reserving the trimmings.

6 Place a little royal icing in a piping bag fitted with a medium star nozzle. Use it to pipe around the trimmed edges of icing on all three cakes.

7 Use moulding icing trimmings to make cut-out flowers (page 132). You will need about 24 large and 15 small flowers. Secure them to the cake with the icing in the bag. Start by positioning 3 small flowers at regular intervals around the top tier. Continue arranging the flowers, letting them trail attractively in an anticlockwise direction as you work down the cakes.

8 Colour the remaining royal icing if liked, and place it in a piping bag fitted with a writer nozzle (no 1). Use it to pipe trailing lines and leaves from flowers. Make tulle butterflies following directions on page 113 using icing in the bag to secure them to the cake and to pipe the outline. Secure small pieces of fern to the cake with the icing.

9 Position the flowers on top of cake just before the reception.

A SIMPLE PIPED WEDDING CAKE

Most designs on formally iced cakes are geometric, so the skill is in accurate measuring as well as in mastering the art of piping. Any unevenness will show up dramatically on the finished cake. The best way to ensure this is to draw the design first on greaseproof paper, then use this drawing or design as a guide to mark out the pattern on the cake. This design is known as a template.

Ideas for designs may come from lace or other materials, wallpaper or birthday and Christmas cards. Try a simple design at first, then progress to more elaborate ones as your piping expertise improves. The section at the end of the book offers plenty of scope for creativity, for all standards of ability.

25cm/10in and 18cm/7in
round Rich Fruit Cake (page 22)
2 quantities Apricot Glaze
(page 58)
2 quantities Almond Paste
(page 28)
30cm/12in and 23cm/9in round
silver cake boards
Royal Icing for flat icing, made
using 8 egg whites (page 32)
Royal Icing for decorating, made
using 2 egg whites (page 32)
yellow colouring
4 silver cake pillars
posy of yellow flowers

Make the cakes well in advance. Brush them with apricot glaze, cover with almond paste and apply several coats of royal icing for flat icing until the surface is perfectly smooth (pages 30 and 34).

Cut a piece of paper the exact size of the top of the large cake. Fold the paper into eight sections. Mark a large design on the top section as shown in the step-by-step pictures. Use a saucer to draw the smooth shape. Open out the paper to see the full effect of the design. Cut a second template for the smaller cake in exactly the same way.

It is a good idea to copy the design on to some thin card. The design can then be transferred to the cake by centreing the template on the top of the cake and using a fine skewer or pin to prick or score the outline of the template.

4 Templates for the sides of cakes can also be made in a similar way. Measure the circumference of the cake and cut a piece of greaseproof or waxed paper exactly the same length and depth of the cake. Fold into sections to correspond with the template for the top of the cake. Draw the required design, then cut away the appropriate pieces.

5 Open out the paper to see the full design. Secure the paper in position around the cake and mark out the design with a series of pin pricks or score it with a fine skewer.

6 Pipe along the lines of the pattern, ensuring the icing covers the pin pricks or score marks. Any further icing which is added to build up the design can be done freehand once the basic pattern is piped.

7 To pipe the loop, squeeze out a little icing and secure it in position at the start of the loop at the top edge of the cake. Squeeze out more icing so that it hangs in mid-air away from the cake. Once there is a sufficient length of icing, loop it up and attach it at the end of the first scallop marking.

8 Continue around the cake in the same way. Follow the original lines to add further icing. The icing does scrape off easily without leaving a mark, so don't worry too much about mistakes. It is a good idea to practise on the side of a tin before you start the actual decorating.

9 Fill in the scallop shapes with cornelli icing (page 100) and pipe a border of beading icing round each cake. Additional beading should be added as shown.

10 Lastly, colour some royal icing yellow and pipe 16 roses for the cake. These can be made well in advance and stored in an airtight container. A posy of fresh flowers completes the cake.

TO PIPE ROSES

1 Hold the icing nail in one hand and the piping bag with the thin part of the nozzle uppermost, in the other hand.

2 With the nozzle in the centre of the piece of paper, squeeze out a cone of icing. This will come automatically as the icing nail is slowly revolved in the thumb and forefinger. Twist the nozzle downwards to finish off the cone.

3 To form the petals, hold the nozzle horizontally with the thin part away from you and twist the nozzle through 180°, squeezing out a little icing as you do so.

4 Continue piping 3-5 petals in the same way starting each one a little way back from the finish of the previous petal.

5 Carefully lift the paper off the icing nail and leave to dry for 24 hours, then peel off the paper and store the rose in an airtight container until required.

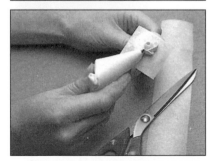

To make a template *Cut a piece of paper the exact size of the top of the cake. Fold the paper into sections, either four, six or eight. Mark a design on the top section, then cut along the line with scissors. Open out the paper to see the full effect of the design.*

It is a good idea to copy the design on to some thin card. The design can then be transferred to the cake by centreing the template on the top of the cake and using a fine skewer or pin to prick or score the outline of the template. Pipe along the lines of the pattern, ensuring the icing covers the pin pricks or score marks. Any further icing which is added to build up the design can be done freehand once the basic pattern is piped.

COMING-OF-AGE CAKE

This is a rather plain coming-of-age cake, but extra decorations and a brighter colour scheme would make it more elaborate.

> 25cm/10in round Rich Fruit
> Cake (page 22)
> 1 quantity Apricot Glaze
> (page 58)
> 3 quantities Almond Paste
> (page 28)
> 30cm/12in round silver cake
> board
> 4 quantities Royal Icing
> (page 32)
> black and yellow colourings

1 Brush the cake with the apricot glaze and cover it with almond paste. Place it on the board and cover with royal icing.

2 Using the key template (page 243) and the 18 or 21, transfer the outlines onto the cake. Using a ruler as a guide, mark diagonal lines across the cake (avoiding the surface inside the 'key') about 2.5 cm/1 in apart.

3 Place a little icing in a piping bag fitted with a writer nozzle (no 1) and pipe over the outline of the key, the numbers and diagonal lines. Pipe another line around cake board 5 mm/¼ in away from outer edge. Reserve the icing in the piping bag.

4 Place about 5 tablespoons icing in a bag fitted with a small star nozzle. Divide the remaining icing between two bowls. Colour one portion grey (using a little black food colouring) and one yellow. Use yellow icing to run-out the space between the base of the cake and the piping near edge of board (page 104). Use the icing in the bag fitted with star nozzle to pipe around top edge of cake. Use grey icing to run-out the number on the key, then run-out alternating bands of yellow and grey across the top of the cake. Leave overnight to harden.

5 Pipe a star border around the lower edge of cake. Using the icing in the piping bag fitted with the writer nozzle, pipe dots all round the edge of the key, around the run-out on base of board and where the colours meet on the diagonal bands of coloured icing. Finish with small loops of icing around the sides of the cake.

CHRISTENING CAKE

This simple decoration works well on any size cake, round or square.

20cm/8in square Rich Fruit Cake (page 22)

1 quantity Apricot Glaze (page 58)

2 quantities Almond Paste (page 28)

30cm/12in square silver cake board

1½ quantities Moulding Icing (page 56)

cornflour for dusting

yellow colouring

½ quantity Royal Icing (page 32)

a little yellow ribbon, 0.3cm/⅛in wide

1 Brush the cake with apricot glaze and cover it with almond paste. Place it on the board. Reserve a small piece of moulding icing about the size of an egg and colour the remainder pale yellow. Use a little to cover the surface of the board. Roll out the remainder to a 30 cm/12 in square. Lay it over the cake so the icing falls in soft folds around the sides. Smooth the icing on top of the cake, using hands dusted with cornflour and emphasize the folds by stretching sections of the icing around the sides of the cake with your fingers. Using a knitting needle, pierce a border of holes around the edge of the icing and make groups of holes on the sides and top of cake for a broderie anglaise effect.

2 To make the booties, reserve a quarter of the white icing and shape the remainder into two balls. Lengthen and flatten them slightly to make the base for the booties. Roll out the reserved icing and cut out two 2.5 x 7.5 cm/1 x 3 in rectangles. Make decorative holes with knitting needle. Brush one long edge of each strip with water and secure it to the bootie bases with joins at the front. Position on top of cake.

3 Colour a little of the royal icing yellow and place it in a piping bag fitted with a writer nozzle (no 0). Use it to pipe the edging on the booties. Using a slightly larger writer nozzle (nos 1 or 2) pipe all the features and dots that create the broderie anglaise effect. Use the remaining icing to run-out the child's name on top of cake (page 104). Tie a ribbon around the booties with a bow at the front.

ENGAGEMENT CAKE

The lace effect on this cake makes a good cover up for less than perfect flat icing! A posy of roses completes the simple design.

> 25cm/10in square Rich Fruit Cake (page 22)
> 1 quantity Apricot Glaze (page 58)
> 3 quantities Almond Paste (page 28)
> 30cm/12in square silver cake board
> 4 quantities Royal Icing (page 32)
> cream colouring
> 1.2m/4ft piece white ribbon, about 2cm/¾in wide
> fresh flowers to decorate

1 Brush the cake with apricot glaze and cover it with almond paste. Place it on the board. Reserve a quarter of the royal icing. Colour the remainder pale cream, and use it to flat ice the cake and the surface of the board. Leave it to dry completely.

2 Using a plate as a guide, mark a 23 cm/9 in circle on top of the cake. Using a ruler as a guide, mark 2 lines 2.5 cm/1 in apart around sides of cake. (The area between the lines will be left unpiped for ribbon.)

3 Place some of the reserved icing in a piping bag fitted with a medium star nozzle. Use it to pipe a scroll around the top and lower edges of the cake. Place the remaining icing in a piping bag fitted with a writer nozzle (no 1) and use it to pipe a cornelli design on the areas shown (page 100). Pipe small dots over the marked circle on top of the cake and along the lines marked for ribbon. Place the ribbon around cake securing the ends with icing. Using the same nozzle, pipe the outline of the couple's name in a semi-circle on top of cake. Thin down the icing left in the bag to run-out consistency (page 104) and colour it a darker shade of cream. Use it to run-out the lettering.

4 Arrange a posy of flowers on the cake just before it is presented.

FIFTIETH WEDDING ANNIVERSARY CAKE

This special cake can easily be adapted for a silver anniversary by using silver colouring, or a ruby anniversary using red colouring. The flower centres have been dusted with 'gold lustre', available from cake decorating specialists but cream food colouring could be used instead.

> 25cm/10in square Rich Fruit
> Cake (page 22)
> 1 quantity Apricot Glaze
> (page 58)
> 3 quantities Almond Paste
> (page 28)
> 33cm/13in square silver
> cake board
> 2 quantities Moulding Icing
> (page 56)
> cream and gold colouring
> cornflour for dusting
> 1.2m/4ft gold ribbon, about
> 5mm/¼in wide
> ½ quantity Royal Icing
> (page 32)
> cocktail stick
> gold lustre
> white stamen heads

1 Brush the cake with apricot glaze and cover it with almond paste. Place it on the board. Colour a small piece of moulding icing, about the size of an apple, with cream colouring and reserve. Reserve a quarter of white icing and use the remainder to cover the top and sides of cake.

2 Reserve a little of the cream icing for the top of the cake and use the remainder to cover the surface of the board. Roll out some reserved white icing to a 30 x 6.5 cm/12 x 2½ in strip. Brush the underside of the rolled icing with a little water and secure it to one side of the cake, allowing the lower edge to fall away from the cake and trimming excess. Repeat on all sides of cake using the remaining icing and folding it neatly at the corners.

3 Roll out the reserved cream icing to a 10 cm/4 in square. Secure it to the centre of cake. Cut the ribbon into 2 cm/¾ in lengths. Beginning at one corner of the cake, and using a thin-bladed knife, make a small cut into the top of the strip of icing. Press one end of the ribbon length into this, using a knife to ease it in. Make a second cut 2.5 cm/½ in along the length of the strip and push the other end of the ribbon into it. Attach the remaining ribbon to the cake in the same way.

4 Using the small flower template (page 250) mark 4 designs along the lower edge of each side of cake. Use the larger template to mark designs on top of cake. Place the royal icing in a piping bag fitted with a writer nozzle (no 1). Use it to pipe over the outlines of the flowers on one side of the cake. Using a cocktail stick, drag the piped line into the centre of the flower to create the delicate edge. Repeat with the remaining flowers then pipe over the leaf outlines. Using more icing, pipe a small fluted border around the edge of the cake and around the cream icing on top of the cake. Use the remaining icing to pipe lines on either side of the ribbon. (Use the same technique with the cocktail stick to give fluted finish, as for flowers).

5 Colour the centres of the flowers with lustre powder and press stamen heads into them.

6 Using the template (page 245) to mark the numbers on the top of the cake. Paint the numbers, leaves and piped edging with gold colouring to finish.

SEASONAL CAKES

The Christmas season is never complete without a pretty cake to accompany the celebrations. Throughout the book you will pick up clever ideas for decorating Christmas cakes – fun-to-make marzipan shapes, festive run-outs and so on. Here you will find a few ideas for completed cakes for Easter as well as Christmas, including last-minute specials that will delight all the family.

The emphasis in this section is on the clever use of colour and design rather than on the intricate execution of long-practised skills. Use these cakes as a basis for developing your own ideas, and if you are planning on preparing a special cake later in the year, then why not take the opportunity to experiment with small areas of piping, trying out edgings or writing festive messages.

Christmas Wreath Cake see recipe overleaf.

CHRISTMAS WREATH CAKE

Semi-rich, chocolatey, and above all, easy to ice, this cake is ideal for last minute bakers – or those who prefer a lighter Christmas cake.

150g/5oz soft margarine
150g/5oz light brown sugar
2 eggs
150g/5oz self-raising flour
¼tsp baking powder
25g/1oz cocoa powder
½tsp ground cinnamon
½tsp ground mixed spice
350g/12oz mixed dried fruit,
chopped

DECORATIONS

28cm/11in round silver cake
board
1 quantity American Frosting
(page 46)
2 leaves rice paper
100g/4oz icing sugar
green and red colourings
1 egg white
red candles and holders

1 Set the oven at 170°C/325°F/Gas 3. Grease a 1.1 L/2 pt ring tin. Place the margarine, brown sugar, and eggs in a bowl. Sift together the flour, baking powder, cocoa, cinnamon and mixed spice and add this to the bowl. Beat well with an electric whisk for 1 to 2 minutes until evenly blended. Stir in the dried fruit. Turn the mixture into the prepared tin and bake for about 35 to 40 minutes, or until firm to the touch. Leave the cake in the tin for 10 minutes then turn it out onto a wire rack to cool.

2 Place the cake on the board and coat it with the frosting, raising it into peaks. Leave it to dry, preferably overnight.

3 Cut out the holly leaves from the rice paper, using the template (page 243). Spoon 2 tablespoons of the icing sugar into a bowl. Add a little green food colouring and mix it until the icing sugar turns green but remains powdery. (This is easiest done with your hands although they may turn a little green!)

4 Place the remaining icing sugar in a separate bowl and mix it to piping consistency with a little of the egg white. Colour the icing red and place it in a piping bag fitted with a writer nozzle (no 1 or 2). Wrap in clingfilm and set aside.

5 Place the green icing sugar in a sieve, and sprinkle it over the surface of the cake. Press the candles and holders into the cake. Secure the holly leaves to the cake by pressing one end into the surface of the icing. Using the icing in the piping bag pipe around the edges of the leaves to finish.

VARIATIONS

The idea for this wreath cake can be adapted to make splendid cakes for other seasonal celebrations.

CELEBRATION RUM RING

Make the cake as in the main recipe, then soak it with rum while it is still warm. Cover with whipped cream instead of frosting and decorate with rum truffles all round the top, alternating them with candles or loops of ribbon.

CHAMPAGNE SPECIAL

Make the cake as in the main recipe, covering it with frosting. Tiny champagne bottles, filled with sparkling wine, can be purchased from cake decorating suppliers. Tie bows of narrow ribbon round the necks of the bottles and position them at intervals around the outside of the cake. Seasonal marzipan holly leaves and berries can be added for Christmas, or fruits and flowers can be added if the cake is intended to celebrate a birthday.

EASTER RING

Omit the cocoa, replacing the quantity with extra flour, and flavour the mixture with grated lemon rind. Beat the lemon rind into the mixture. Make the cake as in the main recipe and cover it with frosting. Instead of the holly leaves and candles, decorate the cake with moulded flowers and sprigs of fresh fern. Small loops or bows of fine yellow ribbon can be added to complete the spring-like decoration.

SUMMER FRUIT RING

The ring can be used as the base for a beautiful, summery cake, ideal for celebrating a July or August birthday. Omit the cocoa from the cake mixture, making up the weight with flour. Add grated orange or lemon rind to the mixture. Instead of the frosting, cover the cake with whipped cream. If you like, flavour the cream with a little fresh strawberry purée and icing sugar to taste. For decoration add frosted fresh fruits – strawberries, redcurrants or blackcurrants, green grapes and cherries. Add a few tiny sprigs of mint between the fruit and position birthday candles between the decoration of you like.

BONFIRE NIGHT RING

Make the chocolate cake and cover it with a fudge icing instead of the frosting. Add mini chocolate flakes, criss-crossed over each other round the top of the cake and stick cocktail sparklers in between them. Light the sparklers just before you take the cake to the table.

CHRISTMAS CAKE

If you want to spend a little more time on decorating the Christmas cake this year – try this pretty window scene.

> 20cm/8in square Rich Fruit Cake
> (page 22)
> 1 quantity Apricot Glaze
> (page 58)
> 2 quantities Almond Paste
> (page 28)
> 25cm/10in square silver cake
> board
> 1½ quantities Moulding Icing
> (page 56)
> blue, red and silver colourings
> cornflour for dusting
> 100g/4oz icing sugar
> a little egg white
> about 1.5m/5ft red ribbon,
> 5mm/¼in wide

1 Brush the cake with apricot glaze and cover it with almond paste. Place it on a board. Colour a quarter of the moulding icing pale blue. Roll it out on a surface dusted with cornflour and use it to cover the top of the cake. Trim the edges and use the trimmings to cover the surface of the board. Dust the top of cake liberally with cornflour.

2 Roll out the remaining icing and use it to cover the top and sides of the cake. Trim the edges. Working fairly quickly, cut out a 19 × 12.5 cm/7½ × 5 in rectangle from the top of the white icing and lift it out to expose blue icing underneath. Roll out the trimmings and cut out half a Christmas tree. Secure it to the lower left-hand side of the 'window'. Mark the other half of the tree on the white icing with a pin.

3 To make the window panels, cut out long, thin strips of icing about 0.3 cm/⅛ in wide. Dampen the undersides with water and position them as in the photograph. Use the rest to shape 'parcels'. Secure to the cake.

4 Beat the icing sugar with egg white until it forms stiff peaks. Spread the mixture into the Christmas tree area, and roughen the surface to form peaks. Place the remaining icing in a piping bag fitted with a writer nozzle (no 1). Use it to pipe an outline around the Christmas tree, a 'MERRY CHRISTMAS' message and ribbon on the parcels. Use food colourings to paint the frame on the window, parcels and the writing on the tree. Tie a ribbon around the cake, securing the ends with icing.

SNOWMAN CAKE

A mint-flavoured frosting would suit this wintry birthday cake. As only a little almond paste is needed, it may be easier to buy a small quantity.

1 quantity Quick Cake Mix (page 15)
100g/4oz icing sugar
50g/2oz desiccated coconut
green, orange, brown and red colourings
25cm/10in round silver cake board
candles and holders
1 quantity American Frosting (page 46)
100g/4oz Almond Paste (page 28)
raisins

1 Set the oven at 170°C/325°F/Gas 3. Grease a 20cm/8in sandwich tin. Line and grease two large, empty fruit cans (the 780g/1lb 14oz size). Use a little of the cake mix to half fill the sandwich tin. Divide the remaining mixture between the cans. Bake the mixture in the tin for 25–30 minutes and the mixture in the cans for 45 to 55 minutes or until the surfaces feel firm to the touch.

2 Beat the icing sugar in a bowl with about 1 tablespoon water to make a thin glacé icing. Place the coconut in a separate bowl and beat in a little green food colouring. Spread two thirds of the glacé icing over the board and sprinkle it with the coloured coconut to make the grass. Make holes for the candle holders with a skewer or knitting needle and press the holders in the board about 1 cm/½ in from the edge.

3 Place the cake baked in the sandwich tin in the centre of the board. Trim the top of one remaining cake level and centre it on the first cake. Place the untrimmed cake on top, securing the cakes in place with the remaining glacé icing.

4 Cover the cake completely with frosting, spreading it onto the grass around the candle holders. Leave the icing to set firmly overnight.

5 Colour a little almond paste orange, and shape it into a carrot. Position it on the face as a nose. Use the raisins for the buttons and mouth. Roll out a little almond paste and cut out strips, about 1 cm/½ in wide. Use for the scarf, and paint it brightly. Colour remaining almond paste brown and position two small pieces to make eyes. Shape the remainder into a hat. Position all these items on the cake. Insert the candles into the holders.

CHRISTMAS CRACKER

A Swiss roll covered with brightly coloured almond paste makes this cake a pretty centrepiece for the Christmas teatable.

> *1 Swiss roll filled with jam or*
> *Buttercream (page 18)*
> *½ quantity Almond Paste*
> *(page 28)*
> *red and green colourings*
> *3–4tbsp Apricot Glaze (page 58)*

1 Prepare the Swiss roll and allow it to cool. Colour three-quarters of the almond paste with red colouring. Reserve a tiny amount of natural almond paste, then colour the remaining paste with green colouring.

2 Measure the length and circumference of the Swiss roll with two pieces of string. Roll out the red paste on a surface lightly sprinkled with icing sugar, to a rectangle 2.5 cm/1 in larger than the length and circumference of the cake. Trim the edges neatly.

3 Cut 1 cm/½ in slashes along both short edges of the paste, at regular intervals. Use most of the trimmings to make 2 rounds large enough to cover the ends of the roll. Brush with apricot glaze and press in place.

4 Brush the red paste with apricot glaze and carefully roll it round the Swiss roll to cover it completely. Squeeze the cake at both ends about 4 cm/1½ in from each end to make a more realistic cracker.

5 Roll out the green paste to make two ribbons and trim to size. Arrange these around the cake on the 'squeezed' sections and secure with apricot glaze.

6 Use any green almond paste trimmings to make holly and mistletoe leaves, and red and natural paste for holly and mistletoe berries. Arrange a garland in the centre of the cracker and secure with apricot glaze.

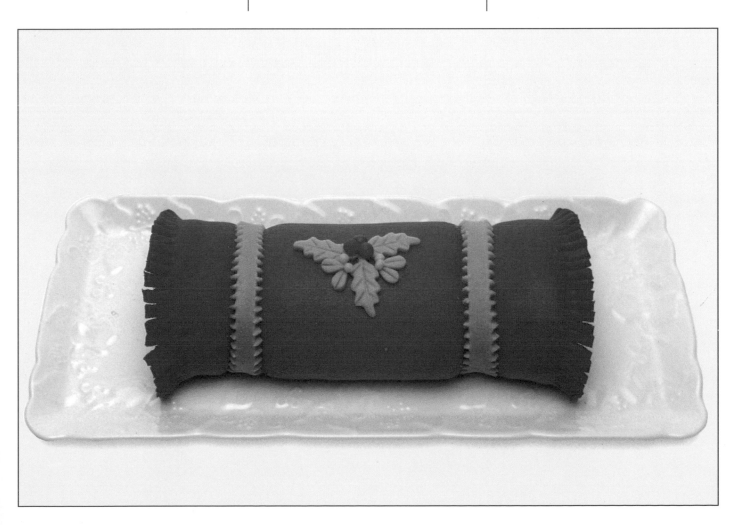

ROUGH-ICED CHRISTMAS CAKE

This cake can be decorated in minutes rather than hours. The rough icing can be used on a rich fruit cake which is covered with almond paste. Alternatively, you could make a base of light fruit cake, or even madeira cake. The following chart gives the quantity of icing sugar needed to make the royal icing, using the instructions on page 32.

Quantities of royal icing required to give two coats to top and sides of a fruit cake
The g/lb quantity refers to the weight of icing sugar required.

Size of cake	Quantity of royal icing
15cm/6in square 18cm/7in round	550g/1¼lb
18cm/7in square 20cm/8in round	675g/1½lb
20cm/8in square 23cm/9in round	900g/2lb
23cm/9in square 25cm/10in round	1kg/2¼lb
25cm/10in square 28cm/11in round	1.2kg/2½lb
28cm/11in square 30cm/12in round	1.4kg/3lb
30cm/12in square	1.6kg/3½lb

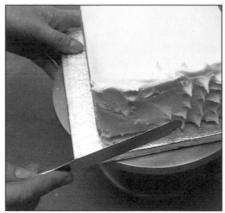

1 Add sufficient icing sugar so that the icing will stand in stiff peaks if pulled up with the back of a wooden spoon.

2 Spread icing evenly over the top and sides of the cake (already covered with almond paste). Using the tip of a round-ended knife, or a palette knife, pull up the icing at regular intervals to form peaks. Leave to set for about 8 hours.

3 Extra decorations, such as almond paste shapes or bought decorations should be placed in position before the icing dries.

DECORATION IDEAS

The secret to success when rough icing a cake is to decide in advance on the type of decoration which is to be added and to have all the items ready at hand to put in position as soon as you have finished peaking the icing.

A wide variety of decorations can be purchased, from miniature models to decorations created from icing. Often the most impressive decorations are the ones that are just a little bit different. For example, bright red and green candles can be used as part of a decoration on a Christmas cake, combining them with holly leaves and berries made from marzipan.

Look out for silk flowers that can be added to the Christmas cake. Christmas roses or poinsettia flowers made of silk can be used to great effect with a bow of bright red ribbon round the side of the cake. Flowers of this type can be placed on the icing once it has dried. If candles are to be used, then the holders must be placed in position while the icing is wet.

Gold and silver dragees can be used to create sparkling designs. They can be arranged in the shape of a small star on the top of the cake, topping each peak of icing within the shape. Alternatively they can be used to create a simple edging, with pieces of angelica and cherry in a festive pattern.

More elaborate designs can be created by colouring the icing and applying it to different parts of the cake. For example, mark the shape of a Christmas tree in the middle of the cake and apply green rough icing within the shape. Do not apply white icing at this stage. Add silver and gold dragees to the green icing to represent decorations on the tree. Add tiny parcels shaped from marzipan or little sweets. Leave the green icing to dry completely before rough icing the remainder of the top of the cake with white icing. Use the point of a knife to nudge the white icing up to the green icing. Attach a star to the top of the tree to complete the decoration.

EASTER CAKE

This pretty cake design is made with a rice paper 'cut-out' which is edible so you needn't worry about removing it before eating. A little care is needed when cutting out the design so use a good craft knife rather than scissors, work on a wooden board.

15cm/6in square Rich Fruit Cake
(page 22)
1 quantity Apricot Glaze
(page 58)
1 quantity Almond Paste
(page 28)
20cm/8in square silver cake board
1 quantity Moulding Icing
(page 56)
yellow, green and violet
colourings
cornflour for dusting
16.5cm/6½in square of rice
paper
½ quantity Royal Icing
(page 32)

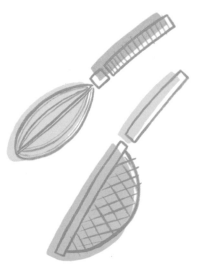

1 Brush the cake with apricot glaze and cover it with almond paste. Place it on a board.

2 Colour a small piece of moulding icing, about the size of an egg, with yellow food colouring. Colour a second piece pale green and a third pale violet. Divide each colour in half. Press the colours haphazardly together. Dust a surface with cornflour and roll out the mixture into a square large enough to cover top of cake. Once rolled, the colours should have blended slightly to create a marbled pastel effect. Lay the icing on the cake and trim the edges. Use the remaining moulding icing to cover the sides of the cake and the surface of the board.

3 Using the template (page 245), transfer the flower design onto the square of rice paper, and cut out flowers and leaves.

4 Place the royal icing in a piping bag fitted with a basket nozzle and pipe a line around the top edge of the cake. Lay the rice paper square over the piped border, so the edges of the paper are secured to the icing. Pipe a second line of icing over first to secure the paper. Pipe another line of icing around the base of the cake.

5 Place the remaining icing in a piping bag fitted with a writer nozzle (no 1). Use it to pipe an outline around the edges of the cut-out and to make the garlands around the sides of the cake.

VARIATIONS

The clever idea for the decoration on this cake can be adapted to make a stunning Christmas cake. The cake should be made as for the main recipe. The almond paste covering should be coloured according to the decoration. Try some of the following ideas, or experiment with shapes cut from Christmas cards.

STAR SHINE CAKE

The almond paste should be coloured yellow and gold petal dust should be lightly dusted over the surface. Cut out a pattern the same size as the cake and draw small or large stars all over it. Use this as a guide for cutting out the rice paper. Attach the paper as in the main recipe, piping the edges in a golden yellow icing.

CHRISTMAS BELL CAKE

The marzipan for the top of the cake can be marbled with gold and white. Gold and silver petal dust should be dusted over the areas of marbled colours. Draw a pattern to fit the top of the cake, with pairs of bells round the edge or all over. Cut these out of the rice paper and continue as in the main recipe. Pipe gold or silver icing round the bells.

HOLLY LEAF CAKE

Colour the almond paste green and cut holly leaves out of the rice paper. Pipe the edges in green icing and add red dots for the berries. The leaves can be cut out in a border pattern or all over the cake.

POINSETTIA CAKE

Colour the almond paste red. Draw a pattern for the top of the cake and cut out poinsettia flowers from the rice paper. Edge the flowers with red icing, then add tiny dots of yellow icing for the centre of each one.

ESPECIALLY FOR CHILDREN

There's nothing more rewarding than watching a child's face light up as you present them with a special cake – candles glowing – on that all-important birthday. And if you can make it in a novelty shape that depicts their favourite toy or latest craze, then so much the better. When time is at a premium there is no need to spend long hours baking; many of these cakes are based on quick-to-prepare one-stage mixtures.

The following recipes, from the very simple to the slightly more involved, are all fun to make and may inspire you to try out your own creation for the next big event!

Red Riding Hood see recipe overleaf.

RED RIDING HOOD

Don't be put off by the intricate looking detail – all you need is a little patience!

> 15cm/6in square Rich Fruit Cake
> (page 22)
> 1 quantity Apricot Glaze
> (page 58)
> 1 quantity Moulding Icing
> (page 56)
> cornflour for dusting
> 25cm/10in round silver cake
> board
> 100g/4oz plain chocolate
> green, red, cream, brown and
> blue colourings
> 10 chocolate finger biscuits
> 3tbsp icing sugar

1 Cut a 2.5 cm/1 in slice from one side of the cake. Secure the slice with apricot glaze to one short side to make a rectangle. Trim off the surplus. This is the bed.

2 Colour a little moulding icing beige and roll it out on a surface dusted with cornflour into a 20 cm/8 in round. Lay it on the board to make the rug. Position the cake on the board. Brush the cake with more apricot glaze.

3 To make the headboard and footboard of the bed, melt the chocolate and spread it thinly on a sheet of non-stick baking paper or wax paper. Leave to set. Cut out a 12.5 × 6.5 cm/5 × 2½ in rectangle. Cut out all but one long side of a second rectangle measuring 12.5 × 7.5 cm/5 × 3 in. Cut the remaining side in a curve to shape the headboard of the bed. Cool your hands under cold water and position chocolate cut-outs at short ends of cake. Secure a chocolate finger biscuit at each corner, with the remaining apricot glaze, to make the bedposts.

4 Roll out a wide strip of moulding icing and position it at the top end of the cake. Pile remaining chocolate fingers in centre of cake to make wolf's body. It will not be visible, just a lump under the covers.

5 Roll out more icing into a large rectangle to make the bedspread. Make diagonal markings with a knife (being careful not to cut right through the icing) and position the 'bedspread' on the cake. Shape more icing into two pillows and position them on the bed.

6 Divide the remaining icing into four. Colour one piece red, one cream, one brown and leave the remainder white. Shape a small piece of cream icing into a thin sausage and position between pillow and bedspread to make the wolf's shoulders. Form another piece into a ball for Red Riding Hood's head. Secure a small nose on the face with a little water. Shape two small pieces of icing into hands and reserve. Form the remaining icing into a round and secure it to the bedspread to make Red Riding Hood's body. Position her head on top. Shape a little red icing into a tongue and reserve it. Roll out the remaining red icing very thinly and wrap it around Red Riding Hood's body to form a cloak. Cut a slit on either side of cloak for armholes, and position her hands.

7 Shape a little brown icing into a basket. Mark lines on it with a sharp knife and secure it to the bed. Knead a little red food colouring into the remainder to make a richer colour. Shape this into the wolf's head and paws and secure it to his shoulders.

8 Roll out a thin strip of white icing and secure it to the wolf's head, gathering it up slightly to make mob cap frill. Shape more icing into a ball. Flatten it to 5 mm/¼ in thickness and place on top of head for the cap. Roll small pieces of icing very thinly between your fingers and shape them into glasses. Roll another piece of white icing into a square. Use it to cover the basket.

9 Place the icing sugar in a bowl. Thin it down with a little water to the consistency of thick cream and place in a piping bag fitted with a writer nozzle (no 1). Use it to pipe wolf's teeth, claws, trim on hat, Red Riding Hood's hair and the edging on the bedspread and carpet. Leave overnight to harden.

10 To finish, paint the carpet edging, flowers on bedspread, Red Riding Hood's hair, basket napkin, wolf's claws, glasses and cap in the appropriate colours.

GOLDFISH BOWL

Try to form a good bowl shape by neatly trimming and filling the gaps in the cake before starting to ice it. Don't go to the expense of buying a second mixing bowl if you only have one; bake half at a time.

1 quantity Quick Cake Mix
(page 15)
1 quantity Apricot Glaze
(page 58)
1 quantity Moulding Icing
(page 56)
cornflour for dusting
20cm/8in round silver cake board
blue, orange, brown, green and
red colourings
4tbsp demerara sugar

1 Set the oven at 170°C/325°F/Gas 3. Grease and line bases of two 2½ pt/ 1.1 L oven-proof glass mixing bowls. Divide the cake mixture between the bowls and level the surfaces. Bake for about 40 to 50 minutes or until the surfaces feel firm to the touch. Leave to cool in the dishes, then turn out onto a wire rack.

2 Slice the tops of the cakes level and discard the slices. Sandwich the cakes together with apricot glaze. Fill in gaps around the join with the moulding icing. Roll out a little icing very thinly on a surface dusted with cornflour and use to cover board. Mark the icing into 1 cm/½ in squares with the back of a knife. Reserve a quarter of the icing and colour the remainder blue. Roll out and drape it over cake. Smooth the icing down the sides of the cake, trimming the lower edge to fit.

Roll out the trimmings into a long thin sausage. Dampen the underside with water and position it around top of bowl for rim. Paint an uneven band of water around base for bowl and press the sugar against it to make the gravel.

3 Colour a little icing orange and shape the goldfish, using the template (page 250). Use trimmings to shape a goldfish head for the top of the cake. Secure the fish to the cake with a little water. Shape three bubbles in white icing and the small signpost in brown icing. Secure to cake. Place the remaining icing in a mixing bowl. Thin it down with water to piping consistency and colour it green. Place the icing in a piping bag fitted with a number 2 nozzle and pipe plants. Paint the birthday message, 'NO FISHING' sign and gingham on cloth.

'SQUEEZE ME' BEAR

This cake makes a rather appealing 'toy' too, as the central button on teddy's sweat-shirt is a small squeak cushion. A joke shop is the most likely place to see them.

1 quantity chocolate-flavoured Quick Cake Mix (page 15)
2 quantities chocolate-flavoured Buttercream (page 43)
covered board, measuring about 40 × 30 cm/16 × 12 in
½ quantity Moulding Icing (page 56)
cornflour for dusting
cream, red and brown or black colourings
2 brown chocolate buttons

1 Set the oven at 170°C/325°F/Gas 3. Grease 4 × 18 cm/7 in sandwich tins and divide the cake mixture between them. Bake for 25 to 30 minutes. When completely cool, cut two of the cakes following diagram.

2 Sandwich the two uncut cakes with a little buttercream and place on the board. This forms teddy's body. Sandwich the remaining pieces and secure to the body in the appropriate places. Scoop out a circle in the centre of the cake to allow for the 'SQUEEZE ME' button. Use the remaining buttercream to cover the cake completely, fluffing it up with a fork.

3 Shape two small buttons, about 2.5 cm/1 in diameter, and a 'T' from moulding icing. Colour a quarter of the icing cream colour and the remainder red. Roll out the red icing on a surface dusted with cornflour. Lay this over teddy's body and shape it for the sweat-shirt pressing into the cavity in the centre of cake. Reserve the trimmings. Use cream-coloured icing to shape paws, feet and snout. Secure to cake. Position chocolate buttons for eyes.

4 Shape the red icing trimmings for the mouth and nose. Secure the mouth, nose, buttons and 'T' with a little water. Press the squeak button into the cavity in the sweatshirt and write 'SQUEEZE ME' in brown or black food colouring.

CLOCK CAKE

Any child learning to tell the time will love this birthday clock with hands that actually move. Set the hands at the number denoting the child's age.

*1 quantity Quick Cake Mix
(page 15)
1 quantity Buttercream
(page 43)
green, yellow, red, brown and
blue colourings
225g/8oz white Almond Paste
(page 28)
20cm/8in round silver cake board
red candles
a little card
1 cocktail stick*

1 Set the oven at 170°C/325°F/Gas 3. Line and grease a 20 cm/8 in round cake tin and turn the prepared mixture into it. Bake for about 1 hour, until the surface feels firm.

2 Colour the buttercream green and spread it around the sides and outer edge of the top of cake. Draw a fork from the base of the cake over the top edge to make a decorative pattern. Repeat all around cake. Colour half the almond paste yellow and roll it out in a 16.5 cm/6½ in round. Press this onto the top of the cake. Use a wide metal spatula to turn the cake on one side and position on the cake board. Colour the remaining almond paste red. Shape a small piece into a round, about the size of a cherry, and reserve it for the nose. Shape another piece into a larger round, flatten it slightly and place it on top of the cake to support the candles. Press candles into the paste.

3 Divide the remaining almond paste into four and roll into balls. Arrange these to resemble the clock's feet. Use brown food colouring to paint clock numbers, eyes and eyebrows. Paint a large red mouth and colour eyes blue.

4 Using the template (page 243) cut out clock hands in card. Make a hole in each end with a pin and press the cocktail stick through holes and into centre of clock face leaving 1 cm/½ in of stick exposed. Press the reserved nose on to the cocktail stick to secure the hands in place.

TRAIN CAKE

If you're feeling really ambitious, this cake could be further enhanced with a butter-cream stream and grassy bank under the bridge.

*1 quantity Quick Cake Mix
(page 15)
1 quantity chocolate-flavoured
Buttercream (page 43)
30cm/12in round silver cake
board
½ quantity Almond Paste
(page 28)
red food colouring
½ quantity Apricot Glaze
(page 58)
450g/1lb liquorice allsorts or
round sweets (for making train
wheels, chimney, etc.)
candles and holders*

1 Set the oven at 170°C/325°F/Gas 3. Line and grease a 25 cm/10 in square cake tin. Turn the mixture into the pre-pared tin and bake it for about 1 hour or until the surface feels firm to the touch. Cool slightly in the tin, then transfer the cake to a wire rack.

2 When completely cooled, cut the cake following the diagram. Sandwich the two long strips of cake together with butter-cream and place this sandwich on the board. Cut out a small 'archway' from the lower cake. Cover the cake with butter-cream and make brickwork markings with a sharp knife.

3 To make the train, colour the almond paste red and roll it out thinly. Use to cover the sides of the two small pieces of cake for the trucks, securing them with apricot glaze. Cut out a 12.5 × 5 cm/5 × 2 in rectangle and reserve it for the base of the engine. Cover the cylindrical cake with almond paste and secure a slightly domed piece of paste at one end for the front of the train. Cover the remaining piece of cake with paste for the driver's cab, shaping the sides and roof as shown.

4 Slice a liquorice allsort or round candy into three for the wheels. Chop plain liquorice for coal and halve square liquo-rice or sweets to decorate the bridge walls. Position the rectangular engine base on the bridge, lifting it off the surface slightly with spare sweets. Secure the driver's cab and engine with apricot glaze and position the trucks behind the engine.

5 Lastly, press candles and holders into the trucks and surround them with chopped liquorice. Complete the cake with liquorice decorations.

BUILDING BLOCKS

This cake is specially designed for a toddler's birthday party. At the end of the day, each partygoer can take home a 'complete' cake in the shape of a building brick.

1 quantity Quick Cake Mix
(page 15)
1 quantity Moulding Icing
(page 56)
pink, blue and violet colourings
1 quantity Apricot Glaze
(page 58)
cornflour for dusting
20cm/8in square silver cake board
candles

1 Set the oven at 170°C/325°F/Gas 3. Line and grease an 18 cm/7 in square cake tin. Turn the prepared mixture into the tin and bake it for about 1 hour until the surface feels firm to the touch. Cool the cake slightly in the tin, then transfer it to a wire rack to cool completely. When completely cooled cut the cake into nine squares, trimming the top of cake level so squares are even sided.

2 Divide moulding icing into four. Colour one piece pink, one blue and one violet, leaving the remainder white. Brush the sides of the cakes with apricot glaze. Roll out the icing, one colour at a time, on a surface dusted with cornflour. Cut squares to cover each side (except the base) of the cakes, pinching the edges together to form neat cubes.

3 Stack the cakes attractively on the board and leave the icing to harden for a couple of hours. Using a fine paint brush and blue food colouring, paint the child's name and age on the blocks. Decorate any remaining blocks with simple shapes, and position candles on holders to finish.

COOK'S TIP

The cake for the building blocks can be made in advance, cut to shape and the blocks frozen. Open freeze the pieces of cake, then pack them when firm to avoid breaking them. Remove the blocks of cake from the freezer when required and apply the decoration while they are half frozen. It is easier to get a neat finish while the cake is firm.

SPACE SHUTTLE

Allow several days for the wings to dry before positioning them on the cake. The horizontal candles may be inclined to drip so be prepared!

> 1 quantity Moulding Icing
> (page 56)
> cornflour for dusting
> 18cm/7in square quantity Rich
> Fruit Cake mixture (page 22)
> 38 × 25cm/15 × 10in board,
> covered with shiny blue paper
> 1 quantity Apricot Glaze
> (page 58)
> cocktail sticks
> black, red and blue colourings
> 4tbsp icing sugar
> 3 red candles and holders

1 Roll out a little moulding icing on a surface dusted with cornflour to 5 mm/¼ in thickness. Cut out two triangular wings, each measuring 19 cm/7½ in at the longest side, and 9 cm/3½ in at the shortest side. Curve the third side to shape the outer edge of the wings. Shape a third triangle for a tail. Press 2 cocktail sticks into one side of the tail for securing it to the cake once it has hardened. Leave these icing shapes on non-stick baking paper, wax paper or foil for at least 2 days, for the wings to dry.

2 Set the oven at 170°C/325°F/Gas 3. Line and grease 3 × 400 g/14 oz cans (from fruit or similar foods). Divide the cake mixture been the cans and bake it for about 1½ hours or until a skewer inserted into the centre comes out clean. Cool the cakes on a wire rack.

3 Shape the cakes : slice one in half and trim one piece for the nose of the plane. Place on the board, sandwiching with apricot glaze. Brush the sides with the remaining glaze.

4 Roll out the remaining icing and use to cover all the sides of the cake. Using a knife mark a line all around the cake 2.5 cm/1 in up from base. The area beneath this line will be painted black. Mark the window in the same way.

5 Press four cocktail sticks, horizontally into each side of cake along the marked line. These will support the wings. Leave the cake to dry.

6 Using appropriate food colourings paint the space shuttle, writing the name and age of the child along the sides. Mix the icing sugar with a little water to make a glacé icing. Use it to secure the wings and tail to the cake. Press the candles and holders into the cake.

RAINBOW'S END

A simple design that can be made using bought almond paste.

> *1 quantity Quick Cake Mix*
> *(page 15)*
> *1 quantity Buttercream (page 43)*
> *25cm/10in square silver cake*
> *board*
> *red, yellow, green and blue*
> *colourings*
> *100g/4oz Almond Paste*
> *(page 28)*
> *candles and holders*

1 Set the oven at 170°C/325°F/Gas 3. Line and grease a 20 cm/8 in round cake tin and turn the mixture into it. Bake for about 1 hour or until the surface feels firm to the touch. Cool the cake on a wire rack. When completely cooled, slice the cake into two semi-circles. Cut out a small semi-circle from the base of each cake to form rainbow arcs. Sandwich the cakes side-by-side with a little buttercream, and arrange them on the board.

2 Divide the buttercream between four bowls, varying the quantities in each bowl, as only a small amount of red is needed, compared to the blue. Colour each portion red, yellow, green and blue. Spread the red buttercream under the arc of the rainbow and add a band around the front. Spread a second band of yellow above the red one. Continue with the green, then the blue buttercream, spreading blue buttercream on the top of the cake. Run the tines of a fork along the bands to make a decorative pattern.

3 Colour half of the almond paste yellow. Reserve a little paste for the umbrella and shape the remainder into a sun. Position the sun at one end of rainbow. Shape the remaining almond paste into a cloud, umbrella and raindrops and paint in the appropriate colours. Position the cloud, umbrella and raindrops at the other end of the rainbow. Press the candles and holders into the top of the cake.

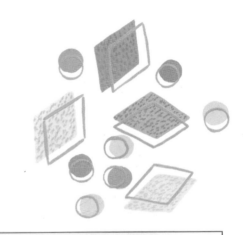

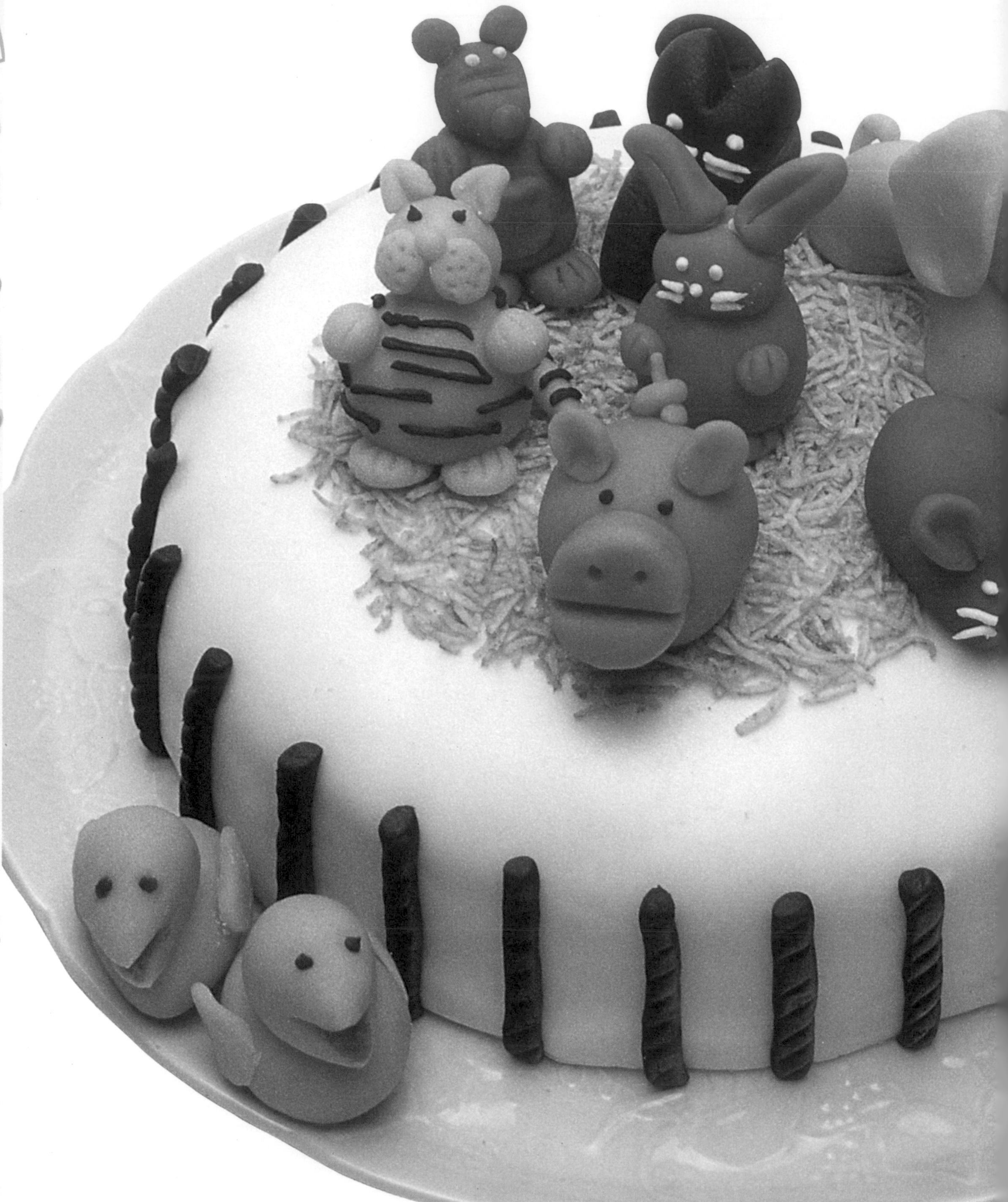

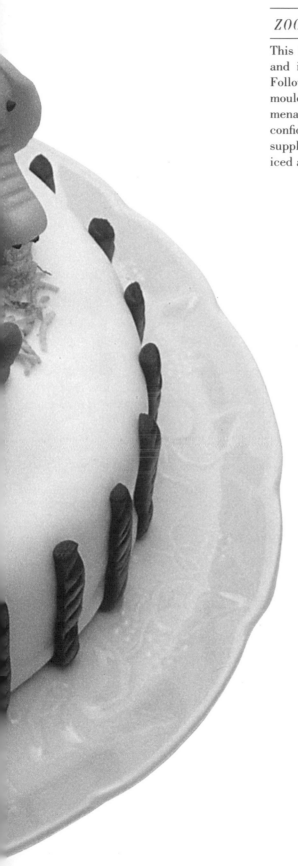

ZOO CAKE

This is a cake on which to exercise skill and imagination with moulded animals. Following the techniques described for moulding animals you can create a whole menagerie of exciting beings! For the less confident, many good cake decorating suppliers sell a selection of moulded or iced animal shapes!

225g/8oz butter, softened
225g/8oz caster sugar
4 eggs, beaten
2tbsp golden syrup
grated rind of 1 orange and 1 lemon
300g/10oz plain flour
350g/12oz sultanas
100g/4oz crystallized pineapple, chopped
100g/4oz crystallized ginger, chopped
100g/4oz glacé cherries, halved
100g/4oz blanched almonds, roughly chopped
Decoration
6tbsp Apricot Glaze (page 58)
1½ quantities Moulding Icing (page 56) or Fondant Icing (pages 36/37)
50g/2oz long-thread or desiccated coconut
black and green colourings
selection of almond paste animals (page 118)

1 Set the oven at 150°C/300°F/Gas 2. Grease and line a 23 cm/9 in round cake tin. Cream the butter and sugar until light and fluffy. Beat in the eggs, a little at a time, then beat in the golden syrup, orange and lemon rinds.

2 Sift the flour, stir in the fruits and nuts and fold into the creamed mixture until evenly mixed. Add a little milk, if necessary, to give a dropping consistency.

3 Transfer the mixture to the prepared tin. Level the surface, then make a slight dip in the centre. Bake for 2–2¼ hours until a skewer inserted in the centre of the cake comes out clean. Leave to cool in the tin, then transfer to a wire rack. Invert the tin over the cake and leave to go cold.

4 Brush the cake all over with apricot glaze. Reserve a small piece of icing to make the bars. Then roll out the remaining icing on a surface lightly sprinkled with icing sugar. Use to cover the cake. Neaten the edges and reserve the trimmings.

5 Colour the reserved fondant with black colouring and roll into short lengths to make the bars of the cage, attaching each one as you roll it.

6 Rub the coconut with a few drops of green colouring, in a small bowl, until evenly coloured. Sprinkle over the centre of the cake and top with the almond paste animals.

FLOPPY-EARED BUNNY

This charming novelty cake is simple to make and it will delight any small child on a birthday or other occasion.

2 × 20cm/8in Victoria Sandwich Cakes (page 16)
1 quantity Buttercream (page 43)
pink and brown colourings
100g/4oz desiccated coconut
1 glacé cherry
about 45cm/18in ribbon

1 Each cake should have two layers. Sandwich them together with a little buttercream. Cut a 13 cm/5½ in square from the centre of one cake. Cut a 13 cm/5½ in circle from the second cake. Cut 4 small sections from the remaining ring of cake: these will form the paws. Cut two oval ears from the remains of the cake with the square cut from it. Set aside all the trimmings for another use.

2 Reserve 2 tablespoons buttercream and colour it with brown food colouring or coffee essence. Colour the remaining buttercream pale pink. Cover the ears with a thin layer of pink buttercream. Cover the round and square sections and the paws with pink buttercream. Arrange all the sections in position on a tray or board (preferably covered).

3 Gently press the desiccated coconut all over the surface of the cake until evenly coated. Using a piping bag filled with brown buttercream and fitted with a no 2 writer nozzle, pipe the face and paw markings. Cut the glacé cherry in half: use one half for the nose and two quarters for the eyes.

4 Tie the ribbon in a bow and arrange it in position. Candleholders with birthday candles can be used as buttons down the front of the bunny.

PARTY TIP

It is a good idea to think up a simple theme for a children's party and the cake can be the centrepiece for the idea. For example, this jolly bunny cake would make an ideal centrepiece for a bunny party.

Cut out party invitations in the shape of bunnies and ask all the young guests to dress up. The simplest form of fancy dress need only include a head band with some large bunny ears sewn in place.

Keep the theme going in some of the other food. For example, bake a carrot cake in a large roasting tin, then cut out neat squares of cake. Top each with a little icing and a marzipan carrot.

Make simple cup cakes and top them with marzipan rabbits, carrots or tiny marzipan lettuces. Use a bunny-shaped biscuit cutter to cut out biscuits. Make simple sandwiches and use the same cutter to cut these into bunny shapes too.

Look out for napkins, paper table cloths and other stationery which has bunnies as part of the decoration. Make place tags by cutting out cardboard bunny shapes, then writing the names of the children on them.

Make sure that you have a competition for the best dressed bunny and include items like chocolate bunnies as prizes.

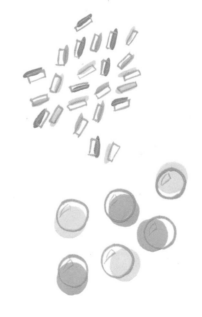

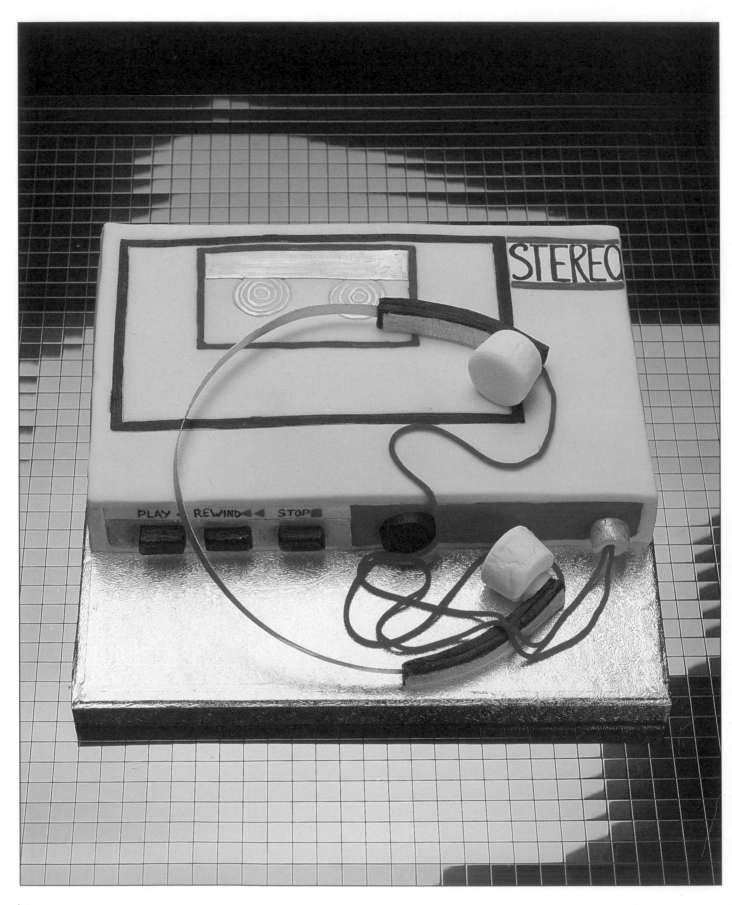

NOVELTY CAKES

Here is a section that will prove that many adults are still children at heart! As you look through the pages you will, no doubt, find cakes to inspire you to surprise someone, with cakes for all ages and all sorts of occasions.

A novelty cake can be the ideal solution for a difficult or unusual occasion, and will be a delightful, surprise gift for birthdays, retirement occasions, examination passes or the move to a new home. In addition to the ideas here, use your imagination to adapt the cakes to suit particular individuals – remember, plan the cake thoroughly to ensure success.

Stereo Cassette Player see recipe overleaf.

STEREO CASSETTE PLAYER

This is a very easy cake to decorate, but looks so effective. For a speedy version follow the recipe for Quick Cake Mix on page 15 instead of making fruit cake.

1 quantity Rich Fruit Cake for 18cm/7in square tin (page 22)
28cm/11in square silver cake board
1 quantity Apricot Glaze (page 58)
¾ quantity Moulding Icing (page 56)
cornflour for dusting
thin strip of card 35.5cm × 5mm/14 × ¼in painted with silver colouring or covered with foil
red, black and silver colourings
2 red or black liquorice 'bootlaces'
2 white marshmallows

1 Set the oven at 150°C/300°F/Gas 2. Line and grease a 28 × 19 cm/11 × 17½ in rectangular shallow tin. Turn the mixture into it, spreading it out evenly, and bake for about 2 hours 30 minutes or until a skewer inserted into the centre comes out clean. Allow to cool in the tin. When completely cooled trim the sides of the cake to form a straight-sided rectangle.

2 Place it on a board and brush it with apricot glaze. Roll out the moulding icing on a surface dusted with cornflour. Cut it to fit the sides of the cake, brushing with water and sealing where the corners meet. Roll out the remaining icing and use it to cover the top of the cake, reserving the trimmings.

3 Make shallow cuts in the icing to mark the controls and cassette areas. Shape three small rectangles of icing and position them on the control panel. Shape a round piece of icing for the volume control and plug socket. Roll out the trimmings and cut out four strips, each measuring 7.5 × 1 cm/3 × ½ in. These are the holders for the marshmallow 'earphones'.

4 Sandwich each end of the silver, or foil-covered, card between 2 strips of icing securing with water. Position the card on the cake bending it to make headphones. Secure a marshmallow to each end of headphones with a little icing. Position the liquorice 'bootlaces', pressing ends into headphones and plug socket. Use red, black and silver food colourings to paint appropriate parts of cake.

SPORTS BAG

If you enjoy moulding fiddly shapes, here's the cake for you. The wide liquorice 'handles' look particularly effective, but if liquorice is not available, then use strips of icing and paint them black instead.

20cm/8in round quantity Rich Fruit Cake mixture (page 22)
20cm/8in square silver cake board
1 quantity Moulding Icing (page 56)
brown, violet, silver, red and blue colourings
cornflour for dusting
1 breadstick, about 15cm/6in long
1 quantity Apricot Glaze (page 58)
4tbsp icing sugar
several wide strips of liquorice (totalling about 81cm/32in. in length)

1 Set the oven at 150°C/300°F/Gas 2. Line and grease two 780 g/1 lb 14 oz empty cans – the large size fruit cans are ideal. Divide the cake mixture between the cans, smooth the top and bake for 2 hours or until a skewer inserted into the centre of the cakes comes out clean of mixture. Allow the cakes to cool in the tins, then trim their tops level.

2 To cover the board with 'wood effect' flooring, dot a quarter of the moulding icing with a little brown food colouring. Roll it out to a long thin rope on a surface dusted with cornflour and fold in half. Keep rolling and folding until the icing is streaked with colouring. Roll out the icing thinly and use it to cover the board, securing it with water.

3 Knead the trimmings together and wrap them around the breadstick. Wrap a piece of white icing around one end of the stick. Press the white icing over a fine cheese grater to create a towelling effect. Leave the racket to harden.

4 Sandwich the two cakes together, end to end, with a little apricot glaze, then coat all the cake with apricot glaze. Colour three-quarters of the remaining icing violet. Use it to cover all sides of the cake. Arrange the cake on the board with the icing join facing upwards. Pull the join apart slightly to represent the opening in the bag. Roll out two thin strips of icing, about 18 cm/7 in long and 5 mm/¼ in wide. Make small cuts in the strips and secure the strips to the edges of the bag opening to represent the zipper. Paint this silver. Mix the icing sugar with a little water to make a glacé icing and use this to secure the liquorice to the bag for handles.

5 Use the remaining moulding icing to shape items in the bag. Wedge the breadstick in the top to serve as the racket handle. Roughen towelling surface with a cheese grater and paint items in appropriate colours. Pipe laces onto the shoes.

DEEP-PAN PIZZA

Silver food colouring is inedible so discard the 'pan' before eating. For an edible alternative use silver lustre (available from cake decorating specialists) or colour the icing brown or grey.

> *1 quantity Rich Fruit Cake for*
> *15cm/6in round cake (page 22)*
> *25cm/10in round silver cake*
> *board, covered with shiny black*
> *paper*
> *1 quantity Apricot Glaze*
> *(page 58)*
> *1 quantity Moulding Icing*
> *(page 56)*
> *brown, red, yellow, green and*
> *silver colourings*
> *cornflour for dusting*
> *2 cocktail sticks*

1 Set the oven at 150°C/300°F/Gas 2. Line and grease an 18 cm/7 in cake tin. Spoon the mixture into the tin, pressing it flat. Bake for about 2½ hours, or until a skewer inserted into centre comes out clean. When completely cooled, trim the sides of cake with a sharp knife to give it a pan shape. Place the cake on a board and brush the top and sides with apricot glaze.

2 Colour a quarter of the moulding icing pale brown and use it to cover the top of cake. Smooth the surface with hands dusted with cornflour. Roll out two-thirds of the remaining icing into a strip 5 cm/ 2 in wide and long enough to wrap around the sides of the cake. (You may find it easier to do this in two separate pieces.) Place the strip in position.

3 Colour half the remaining icing red. Reserve a small piece for the centre of the olives. Divide the remainder in half. Break off small pieces from one half and scatter them over the top of the cake to resemble tomatoes or peppers. Thin down the second half to a thick paste with water, and brush it over the top of the cake leaving a little of the brown base exposed around the edges.

4 Colour a little more icing yellow and grate it over cake, using a metal cheese grater.

5 Colour more icing brown, roll it out and shape into 'anchovy fillets'. Position them on the cake. Roll the reserved red icing into a thin sausage. Colour a little icing green and wrap it around the red icing. Cut it widthways into slices and position it on the cake to resemble stuffed olives.

6 To make handles for the pan, roll out some white icing into two thin pencil-shapes about 9 cm/3½ in long and form them into handles. Halve the cocktail sticks and press a half into each end of the handles. Set these aside on foil overnight to set.

7 Gently press the exposed ends of the cocktail sticks into the icing around the sides of the cake so that handles sit on the edges of the pan. Paint the pan silver and lightly paint the edges of the 'bread base' a darker shade of brown.

COMPUTER GAME

This novelty design can be made equally well using moulding icing. If you are feeling artistic, paint the current favourite game on the screen.

1 quantity Quick Cake Mix
(page 15)
25cm/10in square silver cake
board
1 quantity Apricot Glaze
(page 58)
2 quantities Almond Paste
(page 28)
yellow, blue, black and red
colourings
mint or spearmint sweets
1 cocktail stick

1 Set the oven at 170°C/325°F/Gas 3. Line and grease a 900 g/2 lb loaf tin and a 20 cm/8 in square cake tin. Put enough of the cake mixture into the loaf tin to half fill it. Turn the remainder into the second prepared tin. Bake the loaf tin for 50–60 minutes. The mixture in the cake tin needs 35–40 minutes. When you put the second tin in open the oven door for the minimum amount of time to avoid disturbing the first cake. Cool the cakes on a wire rack.

2 Place the square cake on the board and brush it with apricot glaze. Cover the top, then each side of cake with almond paste. Brush the second cake with apricot glaze and cover it with almond paste, trimming off the excess at the base and corners. Brush one side of loaf cake with apricot glaze and position it on the square cake. Roll out more almond paste and cut out a rectangular computer screen. Round off the corners and secure it to cake with apricot glaze. Using a knife, mark a line around the sides of the loaf cake, 1 cm/½ in away from front edge.

3 Paint behind the marked line and around the side of the square cake with yellow food colouring. Paint the computer screen pale blue, paint the remaining almond paste black, leaving a panel unpainted for the controls.

4 Position the sweets on the cake, securing them with a little glaze. Cut the remaining controls out of almond paste and position them on the cake, securing the joystick to the cake with a cocktail stick. Paint the controls and symbols on the screen in the appropriate colours. Use black colouring to write a message on the screen and keys.

CAR CAKE

A driving test pass is always worthy of a celebration cake. The model used could be the new driver's own car, or the car he or she dreams of owning. Add suitable licence plates, such as 'UR 16', and this could become a birthday cake.

> *1 quantity Quick Cake Mix*
> *(page 15)*
> *a few chocolate biscuits or*
> *chocolate chip cookies*
> *board measuring 40 × 20cm/16*
> *× 8in*
> *1 quantity Apricot Glaze*
> *(page 58)*
> *1 quantity Moulding Icing*
> *(page 56)*
> *cornflour for dusting*
> *blue, black, red and silver*
> *colourings*
> *2 square clear boiled sweets*
> *100g/4oz sugar*
> *a little beaten egg white*

1 Set the oven at 170°C/325°F/Gas 3. Line and grease a 900 g/2 lb loaf tin and a 28 × 19 cm/11 × 7½ in rectangular, shallow tin. Spoon a 1 cm/½ in depth of cake mixture into the loaf tin and spoon the remainder into the second tin. Bake the mixture in loaf tin for about 30 minutes and the mixture in cake tin for about 50 minutes or until firm to the touch.

2 Place a row of biscuits on the board and cover them with the large cake. (This raises the car body up off the board.) Brush the cake with the apricot glaze. Trim the top of the smaller cake level and slope its sides to form the top of the car. Position the car on the base. Cut out small wheel arches in appropriate parts of cake base.

3 Reserve a quarter of the moulding icing. Colour the remainder blue. Roll out the icing to a 30 × 25 cm/12 × 10 in rectangle and lay it over the cake. Dust your hands with cornflour and use them to smooth the cake, working in a smooth circular motion. Press the icing under the cake and into the wheel arches, trimming it to fit where necessary.

4 Using a sharp knife, make lines over the icing to indicate the boot, bonnet, doors and radiator. Press the boiled sweets into the icing for headlights.

5 Roll out a little white icing to 5 mm/¼ in thickness. Cut out four circles, 3 cm/1¼ in. in diameter, and fit them into the wheel cavities, securing with a little water. Roll and cut out two long strips of icing 1 cm/½ in wide and 25 cm/10 in long. Secure one strip to the front of car and one to the back for bumpers. Shape two more pieces for licence plates and secure them to the bumpers.

6 Shape two small squares of icing for 'L' plates, if used. Colour a little icing cream colour and shape into an arm. Secure the 'L' plates to the arm. Press a cocktail stick into the arm and leave to thoroughly dry on non-stick baking or wax paper. Shape 2 small 'matchsticks' of icing and reserve them for the windscreen wipers.

7 Colour the remaining icing grey (using black colouring). Roll it out and shape it for windows. Secure them to the cake. Shape a small triangle of icing and position to represent an emblem on the bonnet.

8 Beat a little black food colouring into the sugar to make it gravel colour. Brush the exposed board with egg white and sprinkle with the sugar. Leave the cake to dry overnight. Paint the outer edges of wheels black. Paint the appropriate parts of the car with silver food colouring. Paint red 'L's' on the plates and a message on the licence plate. Secure the windscreen wipers to the windshield. Press the arm on to a cocktail stick and into the window to finish.

ICE CREAM SODA CAKE

Small round sweets form the bubbles on this cake, or you could use small balls of coloured moulding icing instead.

> *20cm/8in round quantity Rich*
> *Fruit Cake mixture (page 22)*
> *1 quantity Moulding Icing*
> *(page 56)*
> *cornflour for dusting*
> *3 cocktail sticks*
> *pink, green and yellow colouring*
> *1 quantity Apricot Glaze*
> *(page 58)*
> *15cm/6in round silver cake board*
> *6tbsp icing sugar*
> *about 100g/4oz small round*
> *sweets*
> *a few clear mint sweets*

1 Set the oven at 150°C/300°F/Gas 2. Line and grease two 780 g/1 lb 14 oz empty fruit cans. Divide the mixture between the cans and bake them for about 2 hours. Cool the cakes in the cans. Level the surface of one cake.

2 Using an ice cream scoop, scoop out 2 balls of moulding icing to form ice cream. To make the straws, dust the work surface with cornflour and roll out more moulding icing into 2 thin rolls, about 10 cm/4 in long. Trim the ends. Make several bands of cuts into the straws, about 5 cm/ 2 in from one end, to form the bendy parts of the straws. Bend the straws slightly, and press a cocktail stick into their other ends for securing them to cake, once hardened. Shape a swizzle stick out of a little pink coloured icing. Press a cocktail stick into its end in the same way. Transfer the shaped moulding icing to non-stick baking paper, wax paper or foil and leave to harden.

3 Sandwich the cakes together with apricot glaze to form the glass shape, placing the trimmed cake underneath. Brush the surfaces with glaze.

4 Colour the remaining icing pale green and use it to cover the sides of the cakes. Place them on the board. Blend the icing sugar with a little water to make a glacé icing. Press the straws and swizzle stick into the cake and secure the ice cream with a little icing. Secure bubbles and mints to the cakes with more icing. Paint straws, a band of colour around the cake and a message on the swizzle stick, if liked.

MAKING A WISH

This unusual design makes for an interesting 18th birthday cake or it can be adapted to many occasions.

> *20cm/8in Rich Fruit Cake*
> *(page 22)*
> *1 quantity Apricot Glaze*
> *(page 58)*
> *2 quantities Almond Paste*
> *(page 28) (optional)*
> *25cm/10in square silver cake*
> *board*
> *1 quantity Moulding Icing*
> *(page 56)*
> *cornflour for dusting*
> *1 quantity Royal Icing (page 32)*
> *red and black colourings*
> *91cm/3ft red ribbon, about*
> *3cm/1¼in wide*

1 Brush the cake with apricot glaze and cover it with almond paste, if liked. Place it on the board and cover it with the moulding icing, smoothing down the sides of the cake with hands dusted with cornflour. Use the trimmings to cover the edges of the board.

2 Trace the template for the design on the top of the cake (page 244). Place a little royal icing in a piping bag fitted with a writer nozzle (no 3). Use it to pipe the outline of the collar, the lower outline of the hat and the piping on the cake in picture. Place more icing in a piping bag fitted with a writer nozzle (no 1) and pipe the remaining outlines. Use more royal icing in a bag fitted with a medium star nozzle to pipe a scroll around the top and lower edges of cake.

3 Use the remaining icing to make run-outs for the hat, hair, ear-ring, mouth and collar areas (page 104). Leave to set.

4 Paint the cake in the appropriate colours and secure the ribbon with a little icing.

GET KNITTING

A fun cake for the knitting enthusiast!

> *2 quantities Almond Paste*
> *(page 28)*
> *cornflour or icing sugar for*
> *dusting*
> *20cm/8in round Rich Fruit Cake*
> *(page 22)*
> *1 quantity Apricot Glaze*
> *(page 58)*
> *25cm/10in round silver cake*
> *board*
> *2 quantities Royal Icing*
> *(page 32)*
> *yellow, brown, peach and gold*
> *colourings*

1 To make the needles: roll out a little almond paste on a surface dusted with cornflour or icing sugar until it is 18 cm/ 7 in long and about 5 mm/¼ in. in diameter. Pinch each end to a point and secure two small flattened rounds to other ends.

2 Shape three small pieces of almond paste, each about the size of a plum, into balls, and flatten them slightly. Transfer them to non-stick baking paper, wax paper or foil with the needles and reserve.

3 Brush the cake with apricot glaze and cover it with the remaining almond paste. Place it on the board.

4 Spoon about 4 tablespoons royal icing into a bowl and colour it pale yellow. Colour a second quantity pale brown, and a third peach. Cover and reserve. Colour the remaining icing cream (using just a dash of brown colouring) and use it to flat ice the cake and board.

5 Position the needles on the cake as in the photograph and paint them gold. Position the three balls behind the needles. Place the yellow icing in a piping bag fitted with a writer nozzle (no 2). Pipe lines to completely cover one ball. Use the remainder to pipe three to four fluted lines around the top edge of the cake.

6 Place the brown icing in the piping bag and use it to cover the second ball. Add more fluted lines around cake. Place the peach icing in the bag and use it to cover the third ball and the last section around the side of the cake. Use the remaining icing in the bag to outline 'HAPPY BIRTHDAY' below the needles. Fill in the outlines with wavy lines and pipe stitches at the point where wording joins needles.

COOK'S TIP

Adapt the colours used to ice the cake to suit the person for whom it is intended. Do not mix lots of different bright colours as they will look rather crude; however, pastel colours and muted shades work very well.

The idea can be used for a round, square or oblong cake; alternatively, the decoration can be applied to a cake which is baked in the shape of a numeral or number.

If you are feeling particularly adventurous, then why not adapt the idea for the sports bag on page 194 to make a cake that resembles a knitting bag? Instead of the sports gear, shape knitting needles and lots of colourful balls of wool to fill the bag.

The message on the cake can be varied; for example a new grandmother may be delighted to receive a cake in honour of the occasion. Select delicate pink, blue or yellow for the icing and 'hang' baby booties on the knitting needles. Write 'Congratulations Grandma' on the cake and tie a large bow of pastel ribbon round the side of the cake.

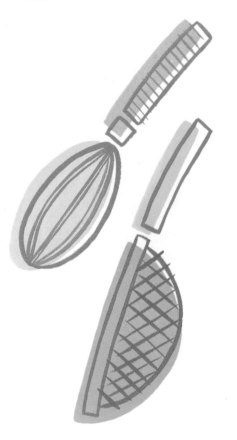

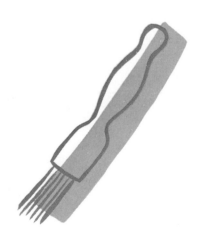

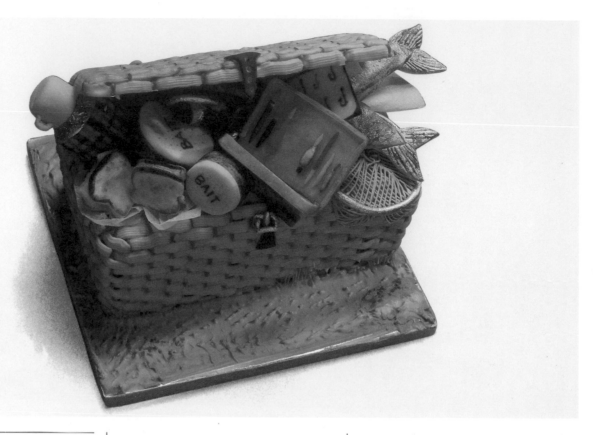

FISHING BASKET

Basket work is one of the most effective piped decorations, but is a very simple technique. The lid is made from almond paste and needs to be made several days in advance to allow time to dry out.

> 18cm/7in square quantity Rich
> Fruit Cake (page 22)
> 20cm/8in square silver cake
> board
> 1 quantity Apricot Glaze
> (page 58)
> 2 quantities Almond Paste
> (page 28)
> Royal Icing (page 32), made
> using 3 egg whites
> brown, red, blue, green, yellow
> and silver colourings
> few leaves of rice paper

1 Set the oven at 150°C/300°F/Gas 2. Line and grease a 900 g/2 lb loaf tin. Turn the mixture into the tin and bake the cake for about 3 hours or until a skewer inserted into centre comes out clean. Cool the cake in the tin.

2 Place the cake on a board and brush it with apricot glaze. Roll out a little almond paste to 5 mm/¼ in thickness and cut out a 16.5 × 9 cm/6½ × 3½ in rectangle. Transfer the rectangle to a sheet of non-stick baking paper, wax paper or foil and leave to harden.

3 Reserve 350 g/12 oz of the almond paste and use the remainder to thinly cover the top and sides of the cake. Reserve 6 tablespoons royal icing and use the remainder to pipe basket work on the lid and sides of the cake (page 98). Colour the reserved royal icing green. Place a little icing in a piping bag fitted with a writer nozzle (no 1 or 2) and reserve. Spread the remainder onto the board around the cake and fluff it up with a fork, to make the grass.

4 Use the reserved Almond Paste to shape the contents of the fishing basket. To make a landing net, shape a thin roll of paste about 23 cm/9 in long. Bend it into a circle and lay it to one side of cake. Pipe criss-cross lines of reserved green icing for netting. Pipe long grass around the basket with a little more icing.

5 Shape the other items in basket using the remaining paste (all are painted after shaping) and arrange them in the basket. Arrange the items towards the front of the basket so that the lid can sit securely at an angle of 45 degrees. Use the royal icing left in the piping bag to secure the almond paste where necessary. Paint the contents in appropriate colours and tuck the rice paper around the sandwiches and fish.

DOWNHILL SKIER

This simple design is one which sporty friends might appreciate. Make the skier in advance, but don't position it until the last minute, in case the colours run.

1 quantity Quick Cake Mix
(page 15)
225g/8oz Moulding Icing
(page 56)
cornflour for dusting
red, blue and yellow colourings
35.5 × 28cm/14 × 11in board,
covered with shiny blue paper
1 quantity American Frosting
(page 46)
1 small pasta wheel
1 piece uncooked spaghetti, about
5cm/2in long
1 red lollipop
several pieces of plastic fern

1 Set the oven at 170°C/325°F/Gas 3. Line and grease a 20 cm/8 in cake tin. Turn the mixture into the tin and bake it for about 1 hour or until the surface feels just firm to the touch.

2 Use a little moulding icing to shape the sun. Roll more moulding icing into a thin roll about 10 cm/4 in long and bend it to form the crouched skier. Use more icing to shape the hat, scarf, arms, boots and skis. Make two sets of skis, in case one breaks. Paint the sun and skier in appropriate colours and transfer them to non-stick baking paper, wax paper or foil to harden slightly.

3 Cut the cake into pieces and arrange it on a board following the diagram below. Cover the cake completely in frosting. Arrange the sun and skier on the cake, positioning the pasta wheels and spaghetti to make the ski sticks. Finish the cake with the lollipop post and trees made from plastic fern.

GREENHOUSE CAKE

An ideal cake for a keen gardener's retirement party or special birthday, in which case rows of candles could be pressed into the 'vegetable plot'.

18cm/7in square Rich Fruit Cake mixture (page 22)
25cm/10in square silver cake board
1 quantity Apricot Glaze (page 58)
1 quantity Almond Paste (page 28)
1½ quantity Royal Icing (page 32)
½ quantity Moulding Icing (page 56)
cornflour for dusting
100g/4oz raisins
matchsticks
green, red, yellow, blue and brown colourings
1tsp black poppyseeds

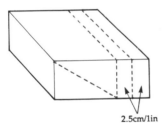

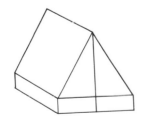

2.5cm/1in

1 Set the oven at 150°C/300°F/Gas 2. Line and grease a 15 cm/6 in square cake tin. Turn the mixture into the tin and bake the cake for 2½ hours or until a skewer inserted into centre comes out clean. When completely cooled, cut the cake into pieces following the diagram.

2 Arrange the two 2.5 cm/1 in strips of cake, side by side on the board, sandwiching the join with apricot glaze. Position the two remaining pieces on top as shown, sandwiching with more glaze. Cover the cake with almond paste. Cover all sides of the greenhouse with a thin layer of royal icing. Roll out the moulding icing to 5 mm/¼ in thickness on a surface dusted with cornflour. Cut out a 6.5 × 4 cm/2½ × 1½ in rectangle for the door, removing two panels for the windows. Transfer the rectangle to non-stick baking paper, wax paper or foil to dry out overnight.

3 Cut more moulding icing to make the framework over the greenhouse. Use a little water to secure it to the sides of the cake if the royal icing has dried out. Roughly chop the raisins. Spread a thin layer of royal icing on the surface of the board to make the vegetable plot and flower bed alongside the greenhouse. Press raisins into the icing for earth.

4 Press a row of matchsticks into the raisins alongside the greenhouse. Reserve 3 tablespoons royal icing and colour the remainder green. Spread it over the rest of the board and fluff it up slightly for grass. Shape four small pieces of moulding icing for the path. Sprinkle with the poppyseeds and position over the grass. Use the remaining moulding icing to shape the cabbages and spade, using a matchstick for the handle.

5 Place a little green royal icing in a piping bag fitted with a plain nozzle (no 2 or 3). Use it to pipe tomato plants on to matchstick supports and the plants in the plot. Use a little reserved icing, coloured red, to pipe the tomatoes. Spread one edge of the door with the icing (frosting) and secure to front of greenhouse. Paint the plants inside the greenhouse with watered-down colourings.

PINEAPPLE GÂTEAU

Drizzle a little kirsch, rum or brandy over this huge gâteau before icing to give it an extra special flavour. The chopping board provides an ideal surface – as long as it's not one you've used for crushing garlic!

1 quantity cherry-and-coconut-flavoured Quick Cake Mix (page 15)
board measuring about 35.5 × 28cm/14 × 11in
780-g/1lb 12-oz can pineapple rings
1 quantity Almond Paste (page 28)
green, yellow and brown colouring
1 quantity American Frosting (page 46)

1 Set the oven at 170°C/325°F/Gas 3. Line and grease a 28 × 19cm/11 × 7½in shallow tin and turn the mixture into it. Bake for about 1 hour or until the surface feels firm to the touch. Cool the cake on a wire rack. When completely cold cut off corners of cake to form an oval shape. Place the cake on the board. Crumble the cake trimmings into a bowl. Drain the can of pineapple rings, reserving the juice. Roughly chop the fruit and mix it with the cake trimmings, adding enough of the juice to bind the cake together. Mound the trimmings over the cake on the board to make a pineapple shape.

2 Colour the almond paste green and roll it out to 5 mm/¼ in thickness. Cut out the leaves to about 9 cm/3½ in long and 3 cm/¼ in at the widest point. Place 1 leaf base downward at the top of the pineapple and gradually build up the other leaves over the first, securing them, if necessary, with water to shape the top.

3 Whisk about 1 teaspoon yellow food colouring into the frosting. Place it in a piping bag fitted with a large star nozzle and pipe small blobs all over the cake. Reserve a little frosting. Leave the piped frosting to set.

4 Colour the reserved frosting brown and thin it down with a little water. Paint it between the blobs of frosting to highlight them.

CHOCOLATE LIQUEUR CAKE

Foil-wrapped chocolate liqueur bottles make this very simple cake look attractive.

1 quantity chocolate-flavoured
Quick Cake Mix (page 15)
25cm/10in round silver cake
board
3tbsp rum, Cointreau or other
liqueur
1 quantity chocolate-flavoured
Buttercream (page 43)
1 quantity Almond Paste
(page 28)
pink colouring
cornflour or icing sugar for
dusting
about 16 liqueur chocolates
candles and holders

1 Set the oven at 170°C/325°F/Gas 3. Line and grease a 20 cm/8 in round cake tin. Turn the mixture into the tin and bake for about 1 hour until the surface feels firm to the touch. Cool the cake on a wire rack.

2 When completely cooled, place the cake on a board and sprinkle it with the rum, Cointreau or chosen liqueur. Spread the cake with buttercream and decorate the surface, using a fluted cake scraper or a fork.

3 Colour the almond paste pink and roll it out on a surface dusted with cornflour or icing sugar. Cut out the shapes for the glasses and press them around the sides of the cake, and in a circle on the top. Position a liqueur chocolate in between each glass. Press the candles and holders into the cake.

A BOUQUET OF FLOWERS

Write the message on this cake to suit the occasion, whether it's for Mother's Day, a birthday or a retirement celebration.

*1 quantity Quick Cake Mix
(page 15)
board 35.5 × 25cm/14 × 10in
1 quantity Apricot Glaze
(page 58)
1 quantity Moulding Icing
(page 56)
cornflour for dusting
red, green, pink and yellow
colourings
½ quantity Royal Icing
(page 32)
30cm/12in length of ribbon,
about 1cm/½in wide*

1 Set the oven at 170°C/325°F/Gas 3. Line and grease a 28 × 19 cm/11 × 7½ in shallow cake tin. Turn the cake mixture into the tin and bake it for about 1 hour or until the surface feels firm to the touch. Cool the cake on a wire rack.

2 When completely cooled, cut one end of the cake to a point. Trim off the top edges of the cake to give it gently sloping sides. Transfer the cake to a board and brush it with apricot glaze.

3 Colour a small piece of moulding icing, about the size of an egg, with red food colouring. Colour a second piece green, and another smaller piece pink. Reserve them for decoration. Reserve a piece of white icing for decoration. Roll out the remainder into a rectangle 7.5 cm/ 3 in larger than cake. Lay it over the cake, smoothing down the sides using hands dusted with cornflour. Trim the edges. Roll out the trimmings into a rectangle measuring about 12.5 × 5 cm/5 × 2 in. Gather up one side and secure it to the pointed end of the cake.

4 Colour the royal icing green and place half of it in a piping bag fitted with a writer nozzle (no 3). Use it to pipe the flower stalks, starting at the pointed end of the cake and finishing where a flower will be positioned. Place the remaining royal icing in a piping bag fitted with a plain nozzle (no 1) and use it to pipe small ferns at irregular intervals towards the edges of the cake.

5 Use red moulding icing to make rosebuds and fully-opened roses. Use pink and reserved white icing to make carnations. Secure the flowers to the tops of the stalks with icing. Roll out the green icing and use it to make the leaves. Arrange them amongst the flowers. Tie the ribbon in a bow and secure it around the base of the cake.

VARYING THE BASIC CAKE

This stunning cake is the perfect gift for any special occasion. The dramatic arrangement of bold, moulded flowers makes the cake very special. However, underneath the cake itself is a very plain one as this is often preferred to very rich cakes. If you do not want to make either the very plain cake used or a rich fruit cake, then the basic mixture can be made more interesting by adding flavouring ingredients to it. For example, you may like to try the suggestions that follow.

RUM AND ALMOND CAKE

Add 100 g/4 oz of ground almonds, combining them with the flour. If you like, make the almond flavour more pronounced by adding a few drops of almond essence but do not add too much. Omit the milk from the basic recipe and add 4 tablespoons of rum instead. The combination of ground almonds and rum results in a moist, close textured cake that is absolutely delicious.

CHERRY AND BRANDY CAKE

This is a festive combination that creates a memorable cake. Chop 100 g/4 oz of glacé cherries fairly finely – they should not be mushy but the pieces must be quite small. Place them in a small basin and pour 4 tablespoons of brandy over them. Cover and leave to soak for at least 30 minutes. Stir occasionally. Drain the cherries in a sieve, collecting every last drop of brandy. Make up the cake mixture, adding the brandy instead of the milk. Dust the drained cherries with an extra 30 ml/2 tablespoons of self-raising flour, then fold them into the mixture last.

BOWL OF DAFFODILS

A cheerful cake that is ideal for birthdays but it is also a good candidate for an Easter cake.

> 18cm/7in round quantity Rich
> Fruit Cake mixture (page 22)
> 2 quantities Almond Paste (page
> 28) or 1 quantity Moulding Icing
> (page 56)
> 1 quantity Apricot Glaze
> (page 58)
> 20cm/8in round silver cake board
> brown, green and yellow
> colourings
> 50g/2oz raisins
> 6 wooden sticks, about 10cm/4in
> long

1 Set the oven at 170°C/325°F/Gas 3. Thoroughly grease two 1.1 L/2 pt ovenproof glass bowls. Divide the mixture between the bowls and bake for about 2 hours. Cool the cakes on a wire rack.

2 Roll out a little almond paste or icing very thinly and use to cover the board, securing it with a little water. Trim the edges and mark a pattern over the surface with a fluted biscuit cutter. Sandwich the cakes together with apricot glaze and fill the gaps around centre with paste or icing. Place the cake on the board and brush it with the remaining glaze.

3 Shape a small piece of paste or icing about 5 × 2.5 cm/2 × 1 in to make the label and reserve it. Colour half the remainder brown, a small piece green and the rest yellow. Use brown paste or icing to cover the cake. Roll the trimmings into a thin roll about 38 cm/15 in long and position it around the top of the cake to make a rim, securing it with water. Place raisins on top of cake to resemble soil. Roll out the green paste or icing and cut out several long thin leaves. Roll out the yellow paste or icing and, using a template cut out 12 daffodil shapes. Dampen the surface of half the yellow shapes with water and lay them on the end of each stick, across the cut-outs, so the ends meet in the centre. Press the remaining cut-outs over first so the ends of sticks are enclosed.

4 Roll out the trimmings and cut out six rectangles measuring 6.5 × 2 cm/2½ × ¾ in. Flute one long side of each with a pastry wheel. Roll each rectangle into a tube and secure it to the centres of flowers with water. Leave the flowers to dry for 24 hours.

5 Write a message on the label and secure it to the cake, using icing trimmings for string. Press the daffodils and leaves into the cake, first making holes in the cake with a skewer, so that the leaves are easier to press in.

CHOCOLATE BOX

This cake is ideal for many special occasions. If you like, moisten the cake with rum or an orange-flavoured liqueur before icing it.

> 1 quantity chocolate-flavoured
> Quick Cake Mix (page 15)
> 25cm/10in board, covered with
> shiny brown paper
> 1 quantity Buttercream
> (page 43)
> 25g/1oz cocoa powder
> 225g/8oz plain chocolate
> about 24 chocolates
> chocolate sweet cases
> 1.5m/5ft brown or cream ribbon,
> about 5mm/¼in wide

1 Set the oven at 170°C/325°F/Gas 3. Line and grease a 28 × 19 cm/11 × 7 in shallow cake tin and turn the prepared mixture into it. Bake for about 1 hour, then cool the cake on a wire rack. When cold, place the cake on the board.

2 Reserve a third of the buttercream and beat the cocoa powder into the remainder. Use it to cover the top and sides of the cake. Melt the chocolate and spread it thinly on a sheet of waxed paper into a rectangle measuring about 26.5 × 24 cm/10½ × 9½ in. Leave it to set, then cut out two 23 × 6.5 cm/9 × 2½ in rectangles, and two 16.5 × 6.5 cm/6½ × 2½ in rectangles. Secure one rectangle to each side of the cake. Cool your hands under cold water before handling the chocolate. Cut a small message tag from chocolate trimmings and reserve it.

3 Spread the reserved buttercream onto one side of the cake. Draw a serrated icing scraper over the side, so the chocolate shows through in lines. Coat the remaining sides in the same way. Arrange the chocolates in the cases and place them on top of the cake.

4 Place the remaining buttercream in a piping bag fitted with a writer nozzle (no 1). Use it to pipe a message on the tag and lay it over the chocolates. Use a little ribbon to make a bow and secure it to the tag. Tie the remaining ribbon around the cake, securing the ends with buttercream.

TEMPLATES AND THEIR USES

This section contains all the templates that you will need for making any of the cake designs within this book. In addition, there is a wide variety of templates that you can use to vary the cakes – different types of edgings, collars, run-outs and so on. This chapter provides a valuable source of ideas for styling your own cakes, so do put these drawings to full use.

TRACING TEMPLATES

Use greaseproof paper to trace the templates – they are all drawn to full size, so you do not have to worry about scaling them up or down. Once you have traced the outline, it is a good idea to go over it again with a soft pencil or pen to ensure that it is perfectly clear. The shape can be transferred to a piece of card, or the paper stuck to card, for durability. Remember to place the penciled, or inked, side away from the icing.

PRICKING SHAPES ON CAKES

Shapes can be transferred directly onto the surface of a cake. To do this, transfer the drawn outline onto a piece of grease-proof paper that is exactly the same size and shape as the cake. Position the outline in the exact position on the paper as required on the surface of the cake. Use a fine-pointed pin to lightly prick through the paper (keep the drawn side uppermost) and onto the cake. Take great care not to make large holes in the surface of the icing.

CREATING YOUR OWN TEMPLATES

If you cannot find exactly what you need in this section, then use pictures from cards, magazines or other sources to make your own, individual templates. This is particularly useful for decorating Christmas cakes. Trace the outline from the source, then transfer it to a card or clean paper, just as for the templates given here.

The template and run out designs on the following pages have been drawn to actual size. You may wish to use smaller or larger sizes depending on your cake design, or use the same motif in different sizes.

ASSEMBLING CAKES

The overall effect of an elaborately de-corated tiered cake can easily be spoiled by incorrectly positioned supporting pil-lars. Worse, an unstable cake not only creates enormous anxiety but can lead to disaster. The process of assembling the cake is the last, worrying, task that has to be completed. So, read through these in-structions and use the diagrams to ensure that all goes well.

The diagrams show you how to work out where to position pillars on different-shaped cakes. The principles involved for most of the shapes are the same.

Templates can be made from paper or thin card. To obtain a good shape in each case, either draw round the cake tin and cut the shape out just inside the line to allow for the thickness of the tin, or make a paper pattern following the instructions for each shape. You will need to make one template the size of the bottom tier for a two-tiered cake and two templates the size of the bottom and middle tiers for a three-tiered cake.

For some shapes you can use either three or four pillars. Either method holds the weight of the tier above, and it is a matter of deciding which you think looks better.

The diagram applies to all shapes of cake. The points indicate how far each pillar should be positioned from the centre of the cake for four sizes of cake, for example on a 20 cm/8 in cake, each pillar should be 6.5 cm/2½ in from the centre of the cake. This position will ensure maximum stability for the supported tier.

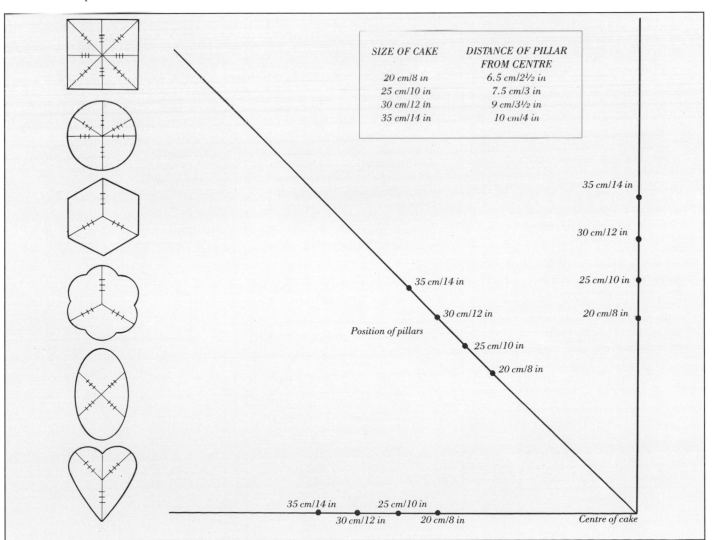

SIZE OF CAKE	DISTANCE OF PILLAR FROM CENTRE
20 cm/8 in	6.5 cm/2½ in
25 cm/10 in	7.5 cm/3 in
30 cm/12 in	9 cm/3½ in
35 cm/14 in	10 cm/4 in

SQUARE

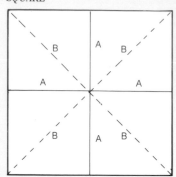

A square cake can have 4 pillars either on the cross (A) or on the diagonal (B). For the cross, fold the template into 4, open up and mark points (A) on the folds. For the diagonal, fold the square into 4 and then in half diagonally. Open up and mark points (B) on the diagonal folds.

ROUND

To obtain a round shape, fold a square into 4, draw a quarter-circle shape and cut out.

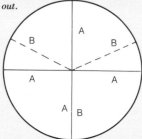

A round cake can either have 4 pillars on the cross (A) or 3 pillars on the triangle (B). For the cross, fold into 4, open and mark points (A) on the folds. For the triangle, fold as illustrated: fold in half and mark the first position (B) the correct distance from the centre of the cake according to the chart on p. 215; fold into 3 making an angle of 60°, and mark the second position (B) on the outside fold; open up and mark the third point (B) on the third fold.

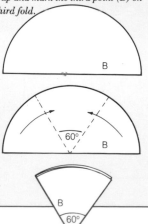

PETAL-SHAPED

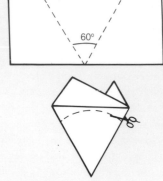

To obtain a petal shape, fold a square in half and then into 3 as illustrated. Draw a rounded shape as shown and cut out.

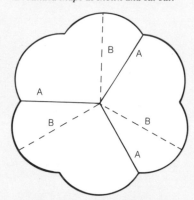

A petal-shaped cake can only have 3 pillars, positioned on a triangle as illustrated (A or B). For (A) use the folds made for obtaining the shape and mark the points on alternate folds. For (B) fold as for the round cake and mark as illustrated below.

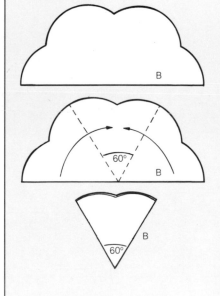

HEXAGONAL

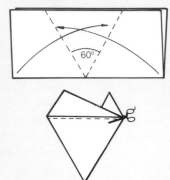

To obtain a hexagonal shape, proceed as for the petal shape but cut a straight edge rather than a rounded one.

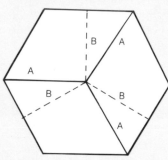

Mark the positions for the pillars (A or B) as for the petal-shaped cake and illustrated below.

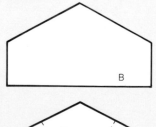

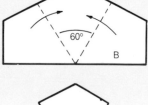

HEART-SHAPED

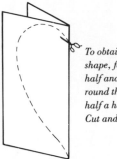

To obtain a heart shape, fold a square in half and either draw round the tin or draw half a heart freehand. Cut and open up.

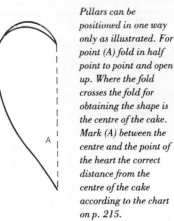

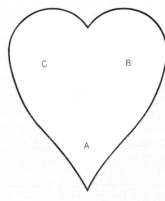

Pillars can be positioned in one way only as illustrated. For point (A) fold in half point to point and open up. Where the fold crosses the fold for obtaining the shape is the centre of the cake. Mark (A) between the centre and the point of the heart the correct distance from the centre of the cake according to the chart on p. 215.

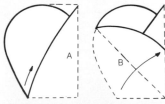

For (B), fold the heart in half, then in half again so that the point of the heart aligns with the top. Fold again diagonally as shown. Mark point (B) the correct distance from the centre of the cake. Open up the heart and mark point (C) in a position corresponding to point (B).

OVAL

To obtain the shape fold a square into 4. Use the tin to draw a quarter-oval shape or draw freehand. Cut out and open up.

The 4 pillars can be positioned either on the cross or on the diagonal (A or B) or 3 pillars can be positioned on the triangle as illustrated right.

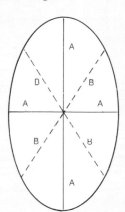

For the cross, fold into 4 and mark the points (A) on the folds.

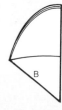

For the diagonal, fold into 4 and then in half again as shown. Open up and mark points (B) on the diagonal folds.

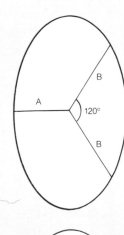

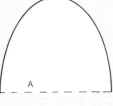

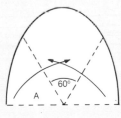

For 3 pillars, fold the oval in half and, taking the centre point used to obtain the shape, mark (A) the correct distance from the centre of the cake according to the chart on p. 215. Fold the 3 as shown and mark point (B) on the outside diagonal fold, again the correct distance from the centre of the cake. Open up and mark the second point (B) on the third fold. The angle between the folds should be 120°.

SIMPLE CHRISTMAS CAKE

ELABORATE CHRISTMAS CAKE

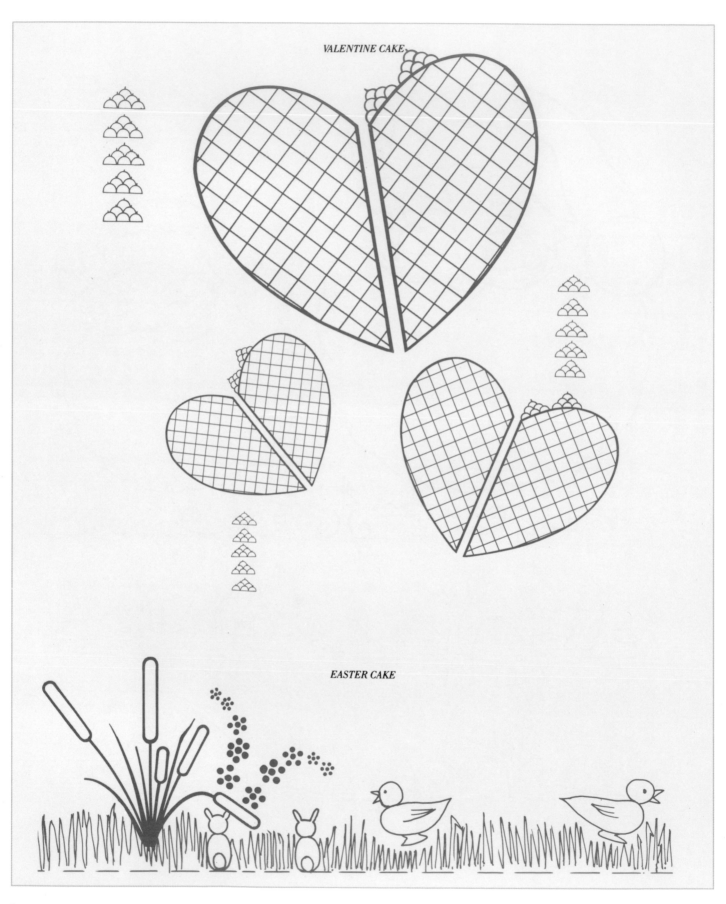

VALENTINE CAKE

EASTER CAKE

BOY'S CHRISTENING CAKE

GIRL'S CHRISTENING CAKE

21st BIRTHDAY CAKE

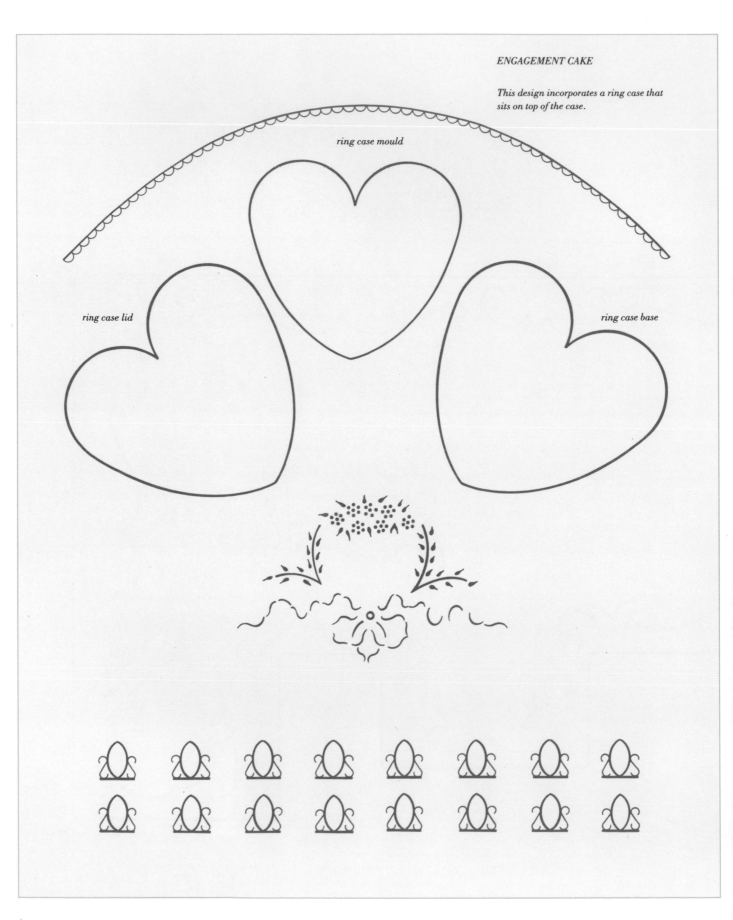

ENGAGEMENT CAKE

This design incorporates a ring case that sits on top of the case.

ring case mould

ring case lid

ring case base

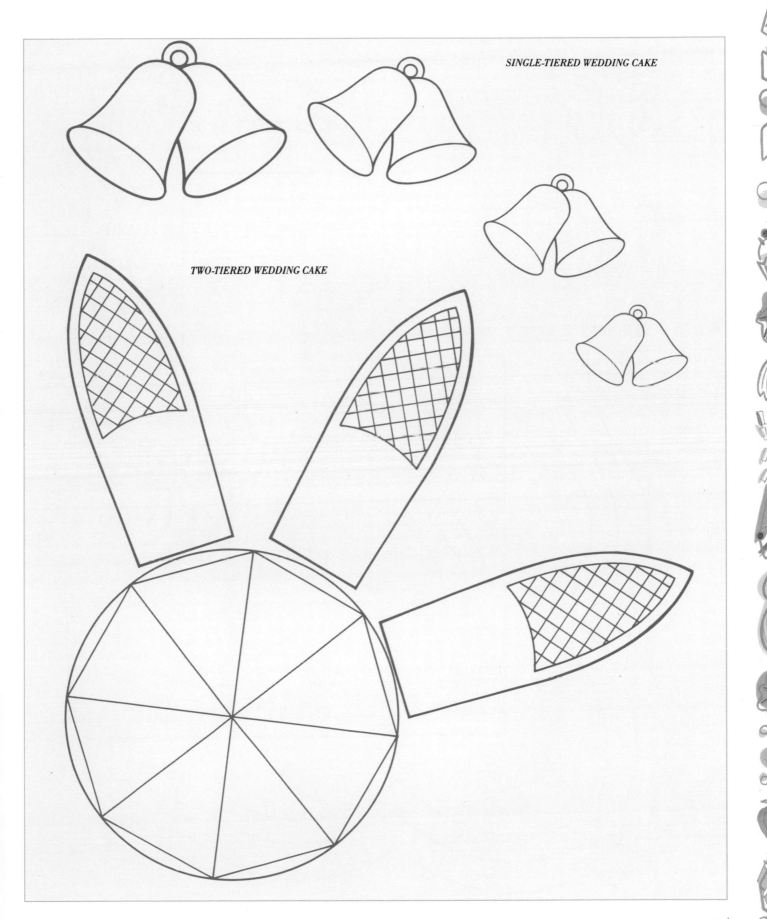

SINGLE-TIERED WEDDING CAKE

TWO-TIERED WEDDING CAKE

THREE-TIERED WEDDING CAKE

HEXAGONAL WEDDING CAKE

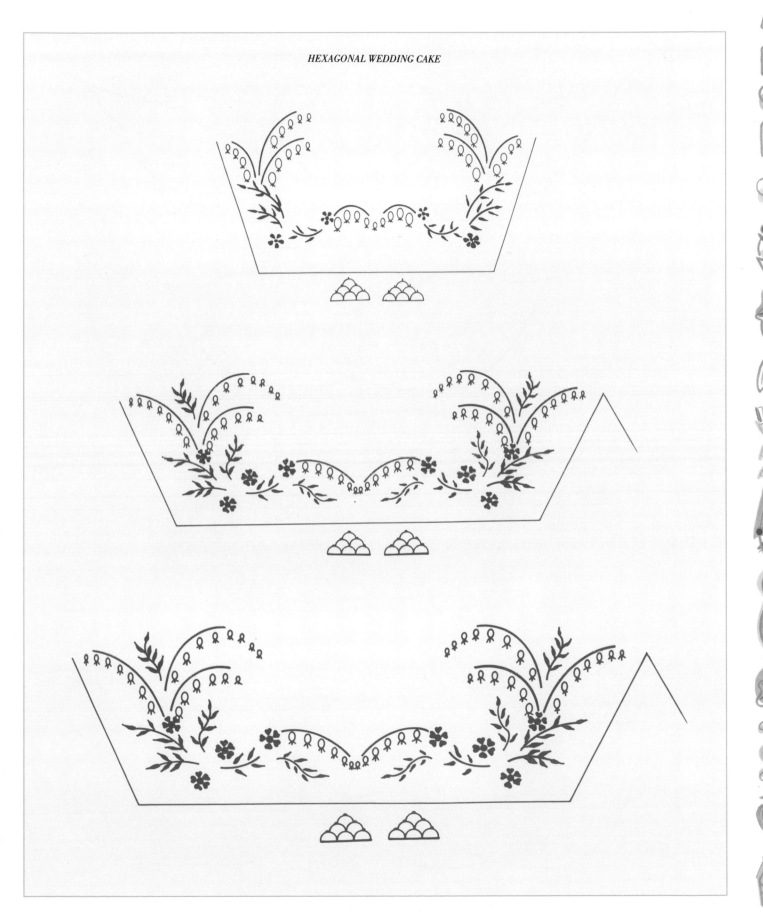

SWANS

base for swan

SILVER WEDDING CAKE

AMERICAN WEDDING CAKE

CELEBRATION CAKE

LARGE LEAF

RUN OUTS

EMBROIDERY PATTERNS

LACE PATTERNS

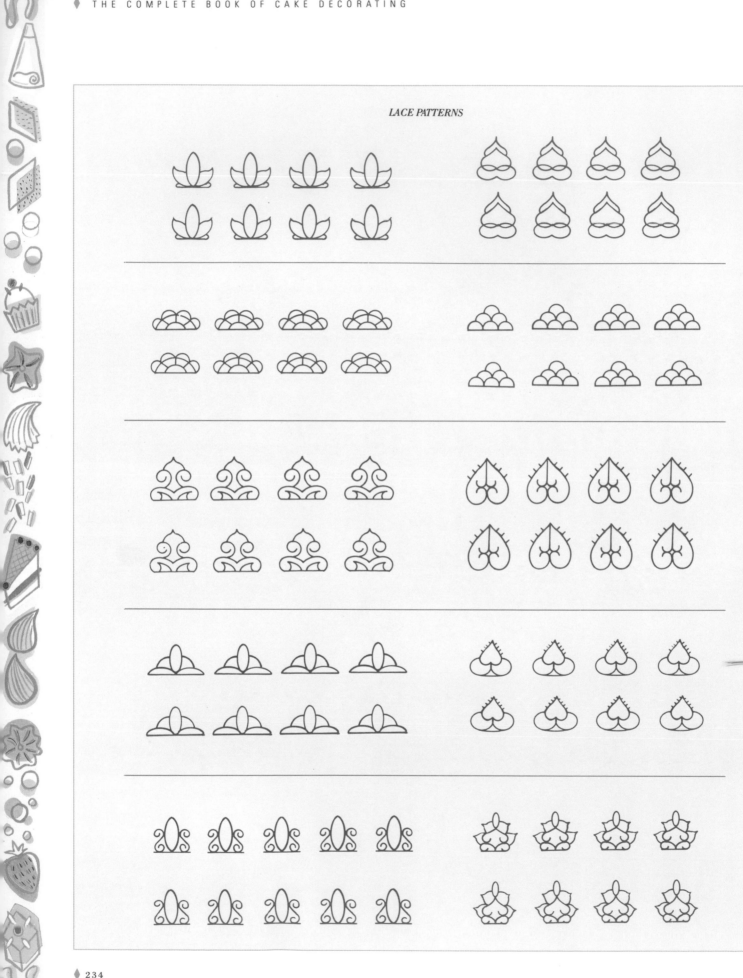

FIGURES

NUMERALS

ALPHABETS

A B C D E F G
H I J K L M N
O P Q R S T U
V W X Y Z

a b c d e f g h i j k l m
n o p q r s t u v w x y z

a b c d e f g h i j k l m
n o p q r s t u v w x y z

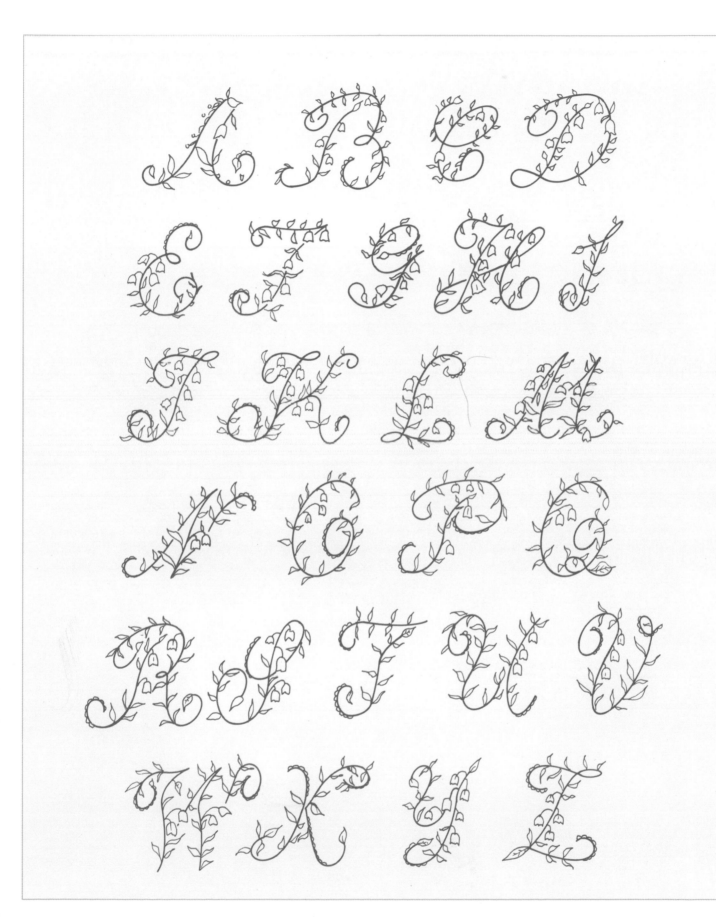

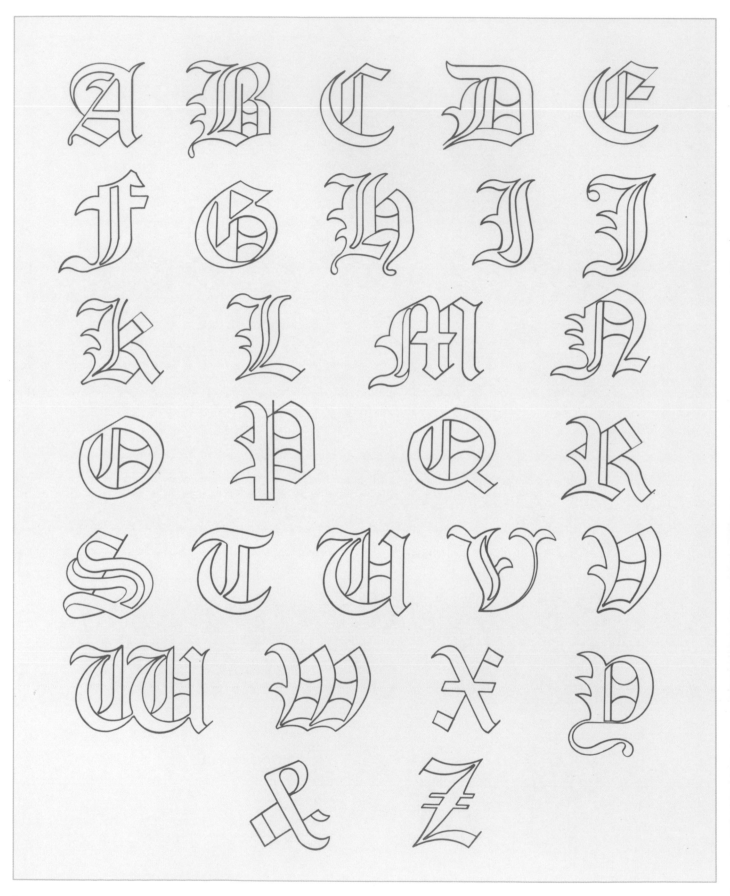

A A B C D E
F G H I J K
L M M N
N O P Q Q R S
T U V V W X
W X Y Y & Z

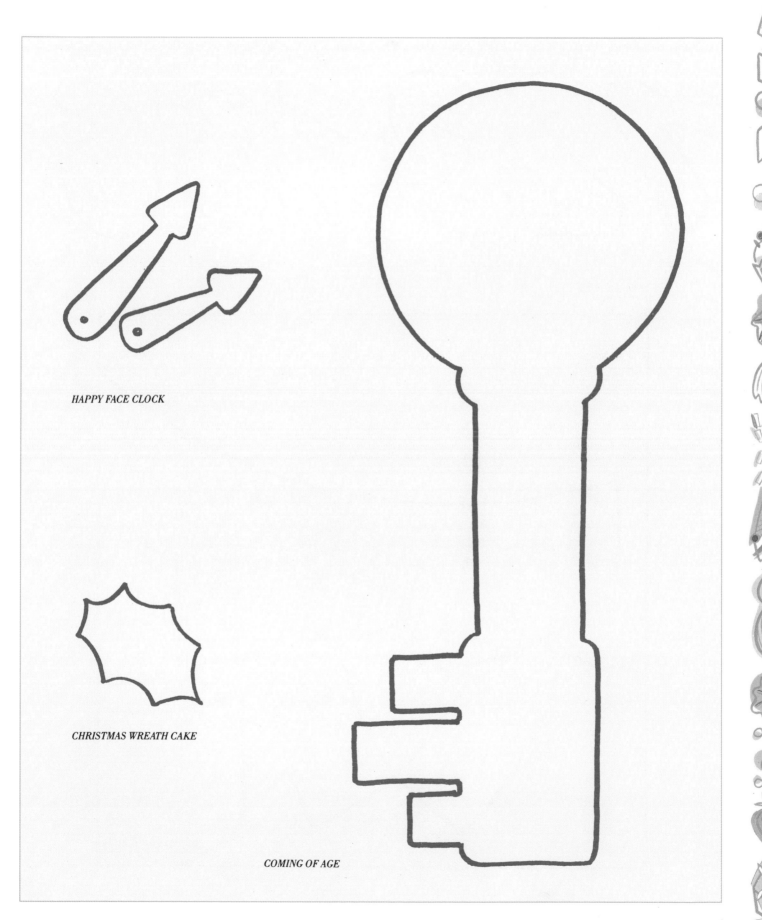

HAPPY FACE CLOCK

CHRISTMAS WREATH CAKE

COMING OF AGE

MAKING A WISH

EASTER CAKE

BUTTERFLY RUN OUT

VALENTINE HEART

Happy Birthday

21

EASTER CHICK

RAINBOW DESIGN

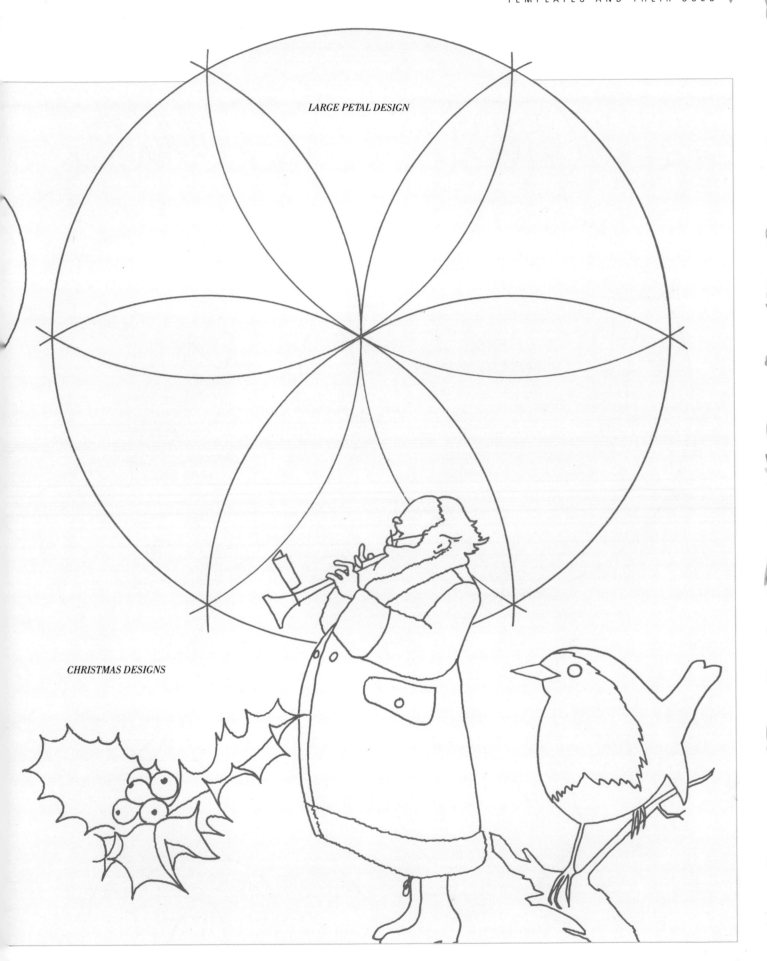

LARGE PETAL DESIGN

CHRISTMAS DESIGNS

ABCDEFGHIJKLM

SCALLOP OR HANGING LOOP DESIGN

TEDDY BEARS

18

STARS, MOON AND SUN DESIGNS

CIRCULAR DESIGN

CAT

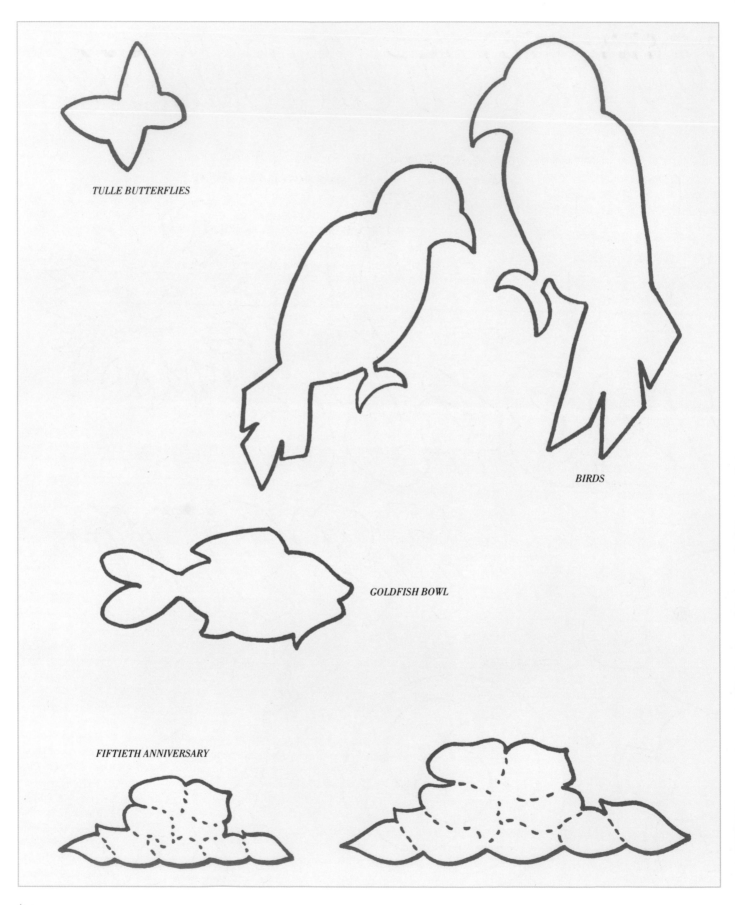

TULLE BUTTERFLIES

BIRDS

GOLDFISH BOWL

FIFTIETH ANNIVERSARY

USEFUL ADDRESSES

The following specialist shops have a mail order service and will supply catalogues on request. Some also have showrooms; enquire about times of opening so that you can pay them a visit.

COVENT GARDEN KITCHEN SUPPLIES
3, North Row, The Market, Covent Garden, London WC2.

GUY PAUL AND CO. LIMITED
Unit B4, A1, Industrial Park, Little End Road, Eaton Socon, Cambs PE19 3JH.

HOMEBAKERS SUPPLIES
157–159 High Street, Wolstanton, Newcastle, Staffs ST5 0EJ.

MARY FORD CAKE ARTISTRY CENTRE
28–30, Southbourne Grove, Southbourne, Bournemouth, Dorset BH6 3RA.

DAVID MELLOR
4, Sloane Square, London SW1W 8EE and
26, James Street, Covent Garden, London WC2.

B R MATHEWS AND SON
12, Gypsy Hill, Upper Norwood, London SE19 1NN.

SQUIRES KITCHEN
The Potteries, Pottery Lane, Wrecclesham, Farnham, Surrey GU10 4QT.

WOODNUTT'S LIMITED
97, Church Road, Hove, Sussex BN3 2BA.

ACKNOWLEDGEMENTS
Quintet Publishing would like to thank the following: G. T. Culpitt Limited, 74–78 Town Centre, Hatfield, Herts AL10 0AW; Guy Paul and Co Ltd, Unit B4, A1 Industrial Park, Little End Road, Eaton Socon, Cambs PE19 3JH; and the Mary Ford Cake Artistry Centre, 28–30 Southbourne Grove, Southbourne, Bournemouth, Dorset BH6 3RA.

INDEX